God bless yo dear One
Shalom
B. J. Cline
1 - 2018

A CACOPHONY OF
TREASURED FINDS

B.J. CLINE-WOODRUFF

Order this book online at www.trafford.com
or email orders@trafford.com

Most Trafford titles are also available at major online book retailers.

Printed in the United States of America.

ISBN: 978-1-4669-7873-7 (sc)
ISBN: 978-1-4669-7875-1 (hc)
ISBN: 978-1-4669-7874-4 (e)

Library of Congress Control Number: 2013901719

Trafford rev. 01/25/2013

Trafford
PUBLISHING®   www.trafford.com

North America & international
toll-free: 1 888 232 4444 (USA & Canada)
phone: 250 383 6864 ♦ fax: 812 355 4082

FOREWORD

Dear Friends,

A well-known author once said, "The Crafting of a good book has never eluded any professed scribe and yet there is one thing I've been totally naïve about and that is; a couple of phrases, one being, "Curling up with a good book," or the one; "Climb under the covers with a 'cup of hot chocolate,' or 'hot toddy.' Where did THAT come from? And what exactly does that really mean? I, myself, am not sure what to make of either statement. A cozy little enclave for one? Maybe, a destination or something more?" Author anonymous.

My words are these, concerning these two statements, *if* no book was involved and they were totally opposite "Honey? Meet me in 15 minutes in the kitchen. By the knife drawer!" Or, "Here! Let me help you open that can of worms!"

Reading a good book by an author you're familiar with is like a good marriage. It's to be enjoyed. As sexperts' tell us, "A mismatch, even though married, needn't mean the end of the relationship. Lots of married couples truly are a mismatch in everyway, just not in sex. Even the mere act of trying to; flirt with, and or arouse your mate as you did before you were married, tends to play out like, like being hungry for three meals a day and being handed a bowlful of chips, being expected to "Makedo" with that for the day, every day, or at the very least, every time you are wanting sex which may be once a month, or less for some." Prefers to be Anonymous.

Good books or a marriage should not have to be this way. Either you love the author or you don't, or you love your mate or you don't. I, for one, would hope you would want to read our Blessed Father's, Sons writings no matter the author, whether you know them or not—this book, case in point—it *is* His Word, nothing more, nothing less. Which brings me to my point. Sin.

What? Is sin?

Sin is rules. Lets say you're starting a new job with a new company. That company as well as any other company you worked for before, has rules an employee must abide by. Many are unspoken and yet you know them even though they're not written any where you can actually point your finger to, you know them because they are a given.

God's Word has rules too. His are written down, the ten Commandments and the beatitudes, hence, the sermon on the mount. If we turn our hearts toward Him, as in a born-again experience, we are His servants, and just as in being a new employee with a newer company and a larger paycheck, we are more than willing, in fact—happy—to obey that companies rules, spoken or unspoken.

Working for our Savior has a thousand to a zillion more everlasting amenities than *one* weekly paycheck *plus* a bad reputation if you intend to work for another company *after* you have broken a rule of the earthly company you just slandered and was fired from.

Our heavenly Father has something He calls Grace which He readily extends to us if we have broken one of His laws. Laws He so readily—again—wrote, all of them! Down for us, so we will instinctively know we have broken one of them. This word GRACE. What is it?

GRACE: "A manifestation of favor shown, especially by a superior, ie "it was shown through the Dean's grace that he or she was not expelled from school." MERCY. CLEMENCY. PARDON. "An act of God." Favor shown in granting a delay or temporary immunity. LAW. An allowance of time-delay to a

debtor before a suit can be brought against them after their debt has—by its terms—became payable, "he has given them 30 days of grace."
THEOLOGICALLY; "The freely given, unmerited favor and love of God.* The influence or spirit of God operating in people to regenerate or strengthen Him. The condition of being in God's favor, Moral strength."* JESUS: "Himself is the epitome of GRACE personified."

None of these attributes were shown to the afore mentioned employee of whom the employer of the large company the employee had just taken a job, *with* larger paycheck, was given. Instead, the employee was fired and given a bad reputation. Our Father, the God of Abraham, Isaac and Jacob would *never* do to His servants. When HE gives us a "job" to do . . . "Just as prince Harry when the Queen deployed him to Malta, he did it "as a favor to the Queen." *That* my dear friends, is how a monarchy works. When asked to do something we do it willingly KNOWING, in advance there will be *NO* pay for it, just as the angel told David before he became KING? Yes David was made King for his obedience. The angel said to David "Hello (paraphrase) Thou highly favored man of valor." David had always did what he was asked of the Lord, therefore he not only was favored in the earthly things that matter. Matter? For our working out a living while yet in the flesh. But in the hereafter as well, for the book of Psalms continues to explain to us David *will* reign as King in the hereafter.
Scripture, now has been brought to my mind that is very appropriate for this moment: That is, if we do not obey;
"Woe unto them that decree unrighteous decrees* that write grievousness which they have prescribed . . ."* I, personally, received such a letter! *". . . To turn aside the needy, to *take away* the *right to the poor* of my people, that widows may be their prey, and that they may rob the fatherless . . ." My father is dead! My husband is in a nursing home leaving me a "living widow," as the Air force wives call themselves when their husbands are

deployed. I know for my eldest brother was an Air Force pilot for 43 years, and my sister-in-law, who, also was my best friend for all her entire life, called herself when he was overseas.

". . . And what will you do in your day of visitation and in the desolation that shall! Shall? shall come from far. To whom will you flee for help? And where will you leave your glory?" Isaiah 10:1-3. Just wondering what will become of those people who sent ME that letter commiting *all* those sins written above. The 10 Commandments and the Beatitudes given to us by God the Father—respectively—and the Sermon on the Mount of Olives by our Savior Jesus, the Christ.

SIN: The laws of God and Man. When we commit sin, we have TRESPASSED. We have committed a sin that we knew was a sin to begin with, thereby crossing that linesay a landowner would post on his property "NO TRESPASSING" thereby causing our once innocent sin to become worse, and now trespassing making that once small sin a blatant, knowing trespass a now full-blown—iniquity. Wow!!

Reminds me of a true story of a brother and an older sister playing—happily—in their own yard, when another child came in to play as well. Only he was an enemy to the brother, who got up and left as soon as this other child entered into this quiet, serene picture. The sister knew they didn't like each other, neither did she. She could not place her finger on any one thing about this other kid, but whatever it was, it was not good and she was soon to find out how evil the kid really was.

For the sake of names we will just call them:

Brother,

Sister,

Evil kid.

The brother had left the scene, leaving his toy's behind. The sister kept playing, by herself, and the evil kid sat down across from her and began playing with the brother's toys, knowing full well the sister was becoming angrier by the minute. The evil kid, continued to taunt with his words, sneers and evil laugh; the sister

just put up with it without saying anything. Then the evil kid got up to leave putting her brothers toys in his pocket as he did so.
"Put them back!" The sister said in no uncertain terms.
"What! What did you just say?!"
"Put them back right now!" She said.
"Or what! If I don't! What will you do?!"

The sister stood up, took her foot and drew a line in the dirt they'd been playing in and said, "Put the toys back where you found them. Now! And don't even think of crossing this line! Now or ever!" The sister said.

Without even putting the toys back or even a hint he even would, he crossed the line and said, "Or what!"

Without even a hint she would do anything the sister turned—as if to leave—where upon the evil kid took a step further beyond the line, toward her. She turned back around, quickly with a strong shove to his chest, knocking him to the ground, she jumped on him and began raining blows with her little fists to his face, head, chest, while straddling him, and yelling all the while "put them back! Put the toys back! Have you had enough?!" She asked during the blows and his struggle to get up and trying all the while to catch her hands to stop his torment, he finally yelled "Uncle! Uncle!" The sister stood up.
The evil kid put the toys back, running as he did so, whimpering all the while.

END

What just happened here?
The evil kid came in. Trespassed.
Played with the baby brothers toys. Wrong! Sin.
Stole the baby brother's toys. Sinned again.
Crossed the sisters line in the dirt. Trespassed!
Again.

Refused to give back the toys and crossed the line KNOWINGLY. He knew both was wrong yet he did it any way. Turning all his wrong doing into INIQUITY. The worse sin of all.

"To sin and know it was sinning, to him it is doubly wrong." Jesus said.

1 – sin
2 – trespassing
3 – Now it has become iniquity. Double sin.

Two sins have now become iniquity. The worse sin of all.

Which brings us right back to our first story, all of which were true. The unjust employer who had no mercy on the employee's first offence. Offence is SIN. Usually an employee is caught, admonished, "don't do that again now that you know you did wrong." No. No mercy = grace = forgiveness was shown this employee at all. He was fired plus given a bad reputation against *any* job he might apply for in the future.

Our brother and sister showed—almost—everlasting favor to the evil kid. But the evil kid was having none of that. He sinned knowingly! Escalating his knowing sin into a trespassing sin. Now the evil kid aggravates his double sin, knowingly, into the worst sin of all, iniquity, of which our Savior says to him that sins knowingly, to him it is doubly wrong." Very hard to get forgiven of this sin. It's almost like one who commits this kind of sin must go through a series of things from our Lord to *prove* they're worthy of the forgiveness they're asking for.

Once again, all this brings us to our Father's *GRACE:* "The freely given, unmerited favor and love of God. The influence or Spirit of God operating in people to regenerate or strengthen Him. The condition of being in God's Favor, Moral strength:

—Belva—

P.S. The precious friend who wrote the dedication for this book, and myself, both, dedicate these writing's to the God of Abraham, Isaac and Jacob, who authorized them first: "For where a testament is, there must also, of necessity, be the death of the testator (Isaiah 53). For a testament is of force AFTER men are dead: Otherwise it is of no strength at all." Hebrews 9:16,17.

—Shalom—

CHAPTER 1

KNOWN UNKNOWNS

Here, we will be applying a few statistical, or should we have said; an analysis to the past in Scripture, preferably the happening's between Genesis 1:1 and 2.

Adonai God and His Word, Yeshua, built, RE-built
What is rightfully His to begin with, "Except the Lord build the house they labor in vain that build it . . ." Psalms 127:1

Ecclesiastes 3:3, ". . . A time to break down and a time to build up." And Genesis 1:1-2 needed to be rebuilt up, for then is when satan fell from heaven and all his fallen angels with him. Scientists tell us a few miles under our earth's mantel, the part where we live, is solid rock before it becomes molten rock," The wise man builds his house on rock . . ." Matt. 7:24, Lk. 6:48.

Our Savior said, "Which of you intending to build a tower does not sit down first and count the cost, whether he has sufficient funds to finish it, lest—unhappily—after he has laid the foundation he is not able to finish it and all that see it begin to mock him." Luke 14:28, 29.

This is what God and Yeshua did between verses one and two when Yeshua said "I beheld satan fall from heaven like lightening . . ." Luke 10:18.

Without the Word, Yeshua, the foundation of the second building of the world, after Genesis 1:2, same world, just had to be reshapened and everything rebuilt again, "For other foundation can no man lay then that is laid which is Christ Jesus." 1 Corinthians 3:11.

What? You were never taught all Scripture has more than one meaning? Scripture says, "It is the glory of God to conceal a thing the honor of Kings is to search out the matter." Proverbs 25:3. He said He would make *us* kings and priests in His—Yeshuas—Kingdom.

Our Father is the creator and just like any other Architect, others do the work for Him—them—. This is why each and every one of you reading God's work through these pages *must* understand each and every one of all-borrowed from the Greek word, ANTHROPO'S—with and English word attached. No one has ever taught you this before and we pray our heavenly Father to open your eyes to see—read and understand, all these anthropo's were created and finished on the sixth day of the creation of all the races of peoples on the face of this earth:

CREATION: "The act of creating. The act of producing or causing to exist. The fact of being created. The original bringing into existence of the universe by God. That which is or has been created. The world. The universe. Creatures Collectively. An original product of the mind especially an imaginative artists work."

"In the beginning was the Word and the Word was with God and the Word was God. The same was in the beginning with God. All things were made by Him and without Him there was not anything made that was made." John 1:1-3.

ARCHITECT: "A person." Person? Yes! God is a person, else He would not of said of Himself, "God is not a man that He should lie." Praise God He certainly is *NOT* a man.

"A person who engages in the profession of architecture, professionally engaged in the design of certain large constructions other than buildings and the like. The diviser, maker or creator of anything. To plan? Organize or structure as an architect."

Luke 14:28-32, "What man goes to build without sitting down to count the cost FIRST . . ."

Now that we have an Architect who designs things and has them put into existence, what will He—God—our Architect build? Or have built?

Genesis chapter one, the Words "And God said" occurs nine times. The Words "And God saw" occurs only once. Every time our heavenly Father speaks, things come into existence. How can anyone speak without WORDS. Yeshua is *the* Word of God "made flesh and lived among us." John 1:1,? Verse 3, "And without Him there was not anything made."

ARCHITECTURE: "The profession of designing buildings, open areas*, communities, usually with some regard to aesthetic effect. The professional services of an architect often include design or selection of furnishings and decorations, supervision of construction work, the examination, restoration or remodeling of existing buildings. The structure of ANYTHING."

*Open areas need landscaping. This is called "husbandry of vegetation in open spaces."

Genesis 2:5 ". . . Every, plant of the field before it was in the earth and every herb of the field before it grew for the Lord God had not caused it to rain upon the earth and there was not a MAN to (tend) till it." This speaks of the land area God intended to put the Garden of Eden. The land of Jerusalem where God said "Jerusalem is MY land. I have put My name." All herbs, plants of the field were in the earth and grew in the 1st chapter of Genesis. *This* is speaking of the garden in Gen. 2:

God is an archivest. He keeps records. And all you've just read and are about to read of the anthropo's are also His records:

ARCHIVES: "Documents or records relating to the activities, rights, claims, treaties, constitutions, etc. Any extensive record or collection of data are kept."

All my life I've heard preachers preach that Adam and Eve had son's and daughters, who copulated with one another, therefore populating the whole earth. This is one of satan's lies. A spawn of hell. At times, hearing this, makes me physically ill and I can no longer sit under these ministers preaching. I am 75 years old and was taught very differently, at the age of nine, that that, Adam and Eve were the first jews in the first Garden—Eden—that Almighty God ever created. Sure, He created trees, shrubs, flowers an herbs along with grass in Genesis chapter one, along with all the other races of the world, aside from the Israelites. Jewish Israelites were created on the eighth day AFTER Almighty God rested on the seventh day.

INCEST: "Sexual intercourse between closely related person's. The crime of sexual intercourse, cohabitation, or marriage between persons who are related."

All over the United States of America, it is a Crime to commit this atrocity. People are put in jail for this, and yet ministers still preach—to this day—Adam and Eve and their children committed this heinous crime. This is the secular world putting these people who commit this crime, in jail. Not the church.

Let me put it to you this way: *My* God did not create this, or think up this heinous atrocity of incest. *Your* God may have. Mine (again) didn't.

This, what follows, is the answer to Genesis 1:26-28, "And God said, 'Let us make man in our image, after our likeness: and let them have dominion over the fish of the sea, the fowl of the air, over the cattle, over all the earth, and over every creeping thing that creeps upon the earth . . ." Five times God said "let us give them dominion over . . ." Meaning all the five days BEFORE He—They—made man in their own image.

". . . So God created man in His image, in the image of God created He him male and female created He them . . ."

This verse, verse 27, alone, mentions "God created He them" three times. At the Seminary we are taught when God repeats Himself twice, its time for a "heads-up people!" God has something important He wants you to pay attention too. Two times "give me your attention. Three times? Your undivided attention is needed here. So, listen up people!

". . . And God blessed them and God said to them 'Be fruitful and multiply and replenish the earth and subdue it and have dominion over the (second time) the fish of the sea, the fowl of the air, every living thing that moves upon the earth."

A word or two, or three, about the word ANTHROPO: "It is a learned, borrowing from the Greek, meaning "HUMAN," used in the formation of compound words—Greek anthropo (s) meaning—man."

WEBSTERS
ANTHROPOCENTRIC: adjective. "1 – Regarding man as the central fact of the universe. 2 – Assuming man to be the final aim and end of the universe. 3 – Viewing and interpreting everything in terms of human experience and values."
ALMIGHTY GOD

On the 6th day of creation our Father YHWH said to His WORD—His One and Only Son—Yeshua, "Let us make man in our own image "Gen. 1:26, 27; ". . . In the image of God He made man." Gen. 9:6.
Genesis 2:7; YHWH "formed Adam out of the dust of the earth" outside the plot of land God had laid out for His garden He would call Eden. All the races of people on earth were made in the image of God and Yeshua on the 6th day. Gen. 2:1-6 "On the 7th day God rested from all his work. v-7 then on the 8th day "God formed Adam out of the dust of the earth."
Job 7:17, 15:14, Ps. 8:4, 144:3, Heb. 2:6, "Who or what is man that You (God) are so mindful of him?"

WEBSTERS
ANTHROPOGENESIS: "The genesis or development of the human race, especially as a subject of scientific study. Anthropogenetic."
ANTHROPOGEOGRAPHY: "A branch of anthropology dealing with the geographical distribution of mankind and the relationship between man and his environment." Gen. 1:26.

"And Cain went out from the presence of the Lord and went to live (dwell) in the land of Nod on the East side of the Garden of Eden, took a wife and knew her and she conceived and bare a son naming him ENOCH." Genesis 4:16, 17. Lets make this a little more clearer. Cain's son Enoch—by no means—is the righteous Enoch the father of Methuselah. This Enoch lived 365 years (same amt. of days in our calendar). This Enoch, "And Enoch walked with God: and then he was not for God caught him up to be with Him." Gen. 5:23, 24.
Cain, the first born's father was satan! "Not as Cain who was of that wicked one (the devil of Rev. 12:) who murdered his brother." 1 John 3:12.

WEBSTERS

ANTHROPOGRAPHY: "The branch of anthropology that describes the varieties of mankind and their geographical distribution."

ALMIGHTY GOD

Has been explained above from the word Anthropogeography. Nod is one place around the world where Cain took flight away from God, found a wife in Nod and married her.

There is no way—on this earth—from its beginning to end, or the world to come, did *MY* Father in heaven create, or even cause *incest*, as every preacher I've ever heard in all the days of my very long life; have preached, "Adam and Eve had more children than just Cain and Abel, they had girls too. How else did Cain get a wife!" My dear friends and loved ones, these preachers are preaching "incest is alright with God. After all Cain married his sister!" No! no! no! no! no!

This is the spirit of antichrist that Paul wrote about after our Lord had ascended back into heaven. Paul said the spirit of antichrist was in the world as he was writing his books. Way to go Paul! Our Father did not, or ever will, sanction incest! Not to mention how grossly—sick and utterly disgusting even the mere mention of the word makes me feel ugh—ugh—ugh! Again and again.

WEBSTERS

ANTHROPOLOGIST: "One who specializes in Anthropology."

ALMIGHTY GOD

Anthropoid means resembling man. Anthropoids in the shape of a man, we all know who is the master of that—satan. Read Revelation chapters 12 and 13 and you will see that it can be none other than satan. Especially since satan (antichrist) makes his false prophet create an image of himself, then causes all to take his mark and bow down to his engraved image."

WEBSTERS

ANTHROPOLOGY: "The science that deals with the origins, physical and cultural development, racial characteristics, and social customs and beliefs of mankind. The study of man's similarity to and divergence from other animals. The science of man and his works (also called philosophical anthropology). The study of the nature and essence of man."

WEBSTERS
ESSENCE: "The basic, real, and unvariable nature of a person or thing, or its significant individual feature or features."
ALMIGHTY GOD
A pot for our kitchen-stove is made to: hold things—to heat things in. It is made to withstand large amounts of heat temperatures, and yet it can hold cold things as well. Whether liquid or solid. Our bodies hold all things in as well.

Man is made of dirt and to survive must eat and drink things coming from the earth. Even the heat we use in winter time, some comes from the earth, some from the atmosphere—electricity.

Our spirit and soul which lives in our "hand-full of worms," a fisherman once said of our brain must be fed also or it too will die. Food for our spirit and soul is YHWH's only *WORD* He left with us to study on a daily basis. After all, where is our learning ability placed for us? In our frontal-lobe. The right side of our brain as well as our left side, are our creative areas. We can create any and everything we set our two sided brain to do, with our pre-frontal-lobe as well.

YHWH'S WISDOM BEYOND MEASURE

All of the above speaks only of our Father in heaven, His One Only Son Yeshua and the Holy Spirit that Jesus Himself said would come and live in our hearts. He said that when He went back to His rightful home in heaven He said "I will not leave you orphans. I will pray the Father and He will send you another comforter who will come *live in* your hearts until the end of the age."

John 14

Nothing breaks the heart of God like our rejection
of Jesus Christ!

Before we begin and you, the reader, become so irate at me you slam the book shut, perhaps the definition of a few choice words might ease your anger, somewhat.

Second, we'll review the word CREATURE again. You'd be surprised at the many, many people who think they know what the word means but really do not:

CREATURE: "Anything created, whether animate or inanimate. An animal, a person; human-being. A person who *owes* his or her position or fortune to someone or something under whose control or influence they continue to live, work or survive."

Scripture says we are all born in sin, from which we must be redeemed from. Thus, John 3:16, was born. Of which our Savior said "There is none righteous except our Father in heaven." Man cannot redeem man. Why? Because satan even told our Savior "All the world I will give to you if you will bow down and worship me." This after he'd shown our Savior the riches and "what—nots" of the world, Matthew 4:9. Luke 4:6, satan says to our Lord ". . . All this power I will give to you and the glory of them for they have been delivered to me and to who ever I will give it." satan is a spirit. God is a spirit, satan showed Yeshua worldly things. He is in charge of the world, dirt is of this world. We—Creatures—are made of dirt therefore we must be redeemed from dirt, is why Yeshua said "You must be born again, by water—your mothers womb—and of the spirit." We—this pile of dirt.—have a spirit and soul living within it. Our spirit and soul lives in our brain. Look it up! Don't just take my word for it. Our spirit needs redeemed from this "pile of dirt," and it took Yeshua—Gods Word "made flesh," and His God part of that

9

"... A body You have prepared for Me" Hebrews 10:5. As we've said before man cannot save man from a devil's hell. It took a sacrifice of part man (pile of dirt) part God "This is My beloved Son. Hear Him!" To redeem us from spirit, and earth that equals dirt. Which brings us to the word

MATTER: "The substance or substances of which any physical object consists of or is composed: The matter of which the earth is made, whether solid, liquid or gaseous, especially as distinguished from incorporeal substance as spirit or mind, or from qualities, actions and the like. That which OCCUPIES SPACE."

Which brings us to the word FLESH. Flesh is MATTER and matter is flesh. Both are substances.

FLESH: "The soft substance of an animal or a human body consisting of muscle and fat. The substance or tissue in animals viewed as an article of food, usually excluding fish and sometimes fowl; meat. The body. Physical body of man or animals nature distinguished from their moral or spiritual nature.
LIVING CREATURES: ie "in the flesh," before ones eyes. To overlay or cover a FRAME, skeletal, with flesh or fleshlike substance."

All of these, flesh, matter, or matter, flesh, are Adonai God's creation by the Hand of Yeshua; John 1:3, "All things were made by Him and without Him there was not anything made." Now, let us back up to verses 1 and 2, especially since Yeshua is the living, touchable WORD of Adonai God, "In the beginning was the Word and the Word was with God and the Word WAS God. The same was in the beginning with God." Genesis 1:1-26. "... Let *us* make man in *our* image."

On the sixth day—Genesis 1:26,—Were *all* the races of the earth created. PERIOD. Except for a Jewish man; Adam, created on the eighth day, and a Jewish lady soon after that. Don't believe it? Then why is Yeshua called "the second Adam" and *He* is a Jew!

What was Adonai, God, saying to the Jewish people in Lev. 20:26, "You shall be holy to Me for—I the Lord—Am holy and have separated you from the peoples That you should be Mine."

HOLY: Number one; "To be close to God." Number two; "To be separated from the world for God."

NOTE:
My God, THE God of Abraham, Isaac and Jacob, did not invent incest, satan did. These preachers who preach Adam was the first and only man on earth and Eve the only woman are preaching exactly what satan wants them to for that is HIS gospel.

Sure! Adam was the FIRST man. *In the Garden of Eden!* And sure! Eve was the FIRST Woman. *In the Garden of Eden:* They were the FIRST *Jews* in the whole world, that is true. *BUT* all the races were created on the (6) sixth day. Adam—the Jew—on the (8) eighth day. Pay attention to what you read! In Scripture as well as elsewhere.

I repeat. My God did not create incest! Yours may have!! But mine did NOT.

∽∾

First, we'll review the word CREATURE. You'd be surprised at the many many people who think they know what the word means but really do not:

CREATURE: "Anything created, whether animate or inanimate. An animal, a person; human-being. A person who *owes* his or her position or fortune to someone or something under whose central or influence they continue to live, work or survive."

Scripture says we are all born in sin, from which we must be redeemed from. Thus, John 3:16, was born. Of which our Savior said "There is none righteous except our Father in heaven. "Man cannot redeem man. Why? Because satan even told our Savior "All the world I will give to you if you will bow down and worship me." This after he'd shown our Savior the riches and "what—nots" of the world, Matthew 4:9. Luke 4:6, satan says to our Lord ". . . All this power I will give to you and the glory of them for they have been delivered to me and to who ever I will give it." satan is a spirit. God is a spirit. satan showed Yeshua worldly things. He is in charge of the world, dirt is of this world. We—Creatures—are made of dirt therefore we must be redeemed from dirt, is why Yeshua said "You must be born again, by water—your mother's womb—and of the spirit. We—this pile of dirt—have a spirit and soul living within it. Our spirit and soul lives in our brain. Look it up! Don't just take my word for it. Our spirit needs redeemed from this "pile of dirt," and it took Yeshua—Gods Word "made flesh," and His God part of that ". . . A body You have prepared for Me" Hebrews 10:5. As we've said before man cannot save man from a devil's hell. It took a sacrifice of part man (pile of dirt) part God "This is My beloved Son. Hear Him!" To redeem us from spirit, and earth that equals dirt. Which brings us to the word.

MATTER: "The substance or substances of which any physical object consists of or is composed. The matter of which the earth is made, whether solid, liquid or gaseous, especially as distinguished from incorporeal substance as spirit or mind, or from qualities, actions and the like. That which OCCUPIES SPACE."

Which brings us to the word FLESH. Flesh is MATTER and matter is flesh:

FLESH: "The soft substance of an animal or a human body consisting of muscle and fat. The substance or tissue in animals viewed as an article of food, usually excluding fish and sometimes fowl; meat. The body. Physical body of man or animals nature distinguished from their moral or spiritual nature.

LIVING CREATURES: ie "in the flesh," before ones eyes. To overlay or cover a FRAME, skeletal, with flesh or fleshlike substance."

All of these, flesh, matter, or matter, flesh, are Adonai God's Creation by the Hand of Yeshua; John 1:3, "All things were made by Him and without Him there was not anything made." Now, let us back up to verses 1 and 2, especially since Yeshua is the living, touchable WORD of Adonai God, "In the beginning was the Word and the Word was with God and the Word WAS God. The same was in the beginning with God." Genesis 1:1-26. ". . . Let *us* make man in *our* image."

On the sixth day—Genesis 1:26,—Were *all* the races of the earth created PERIOD. Except for a Jewish man; Adam, created on the eighth day, and a Jewish lady soon after that. Don't believe it? Then why is Yeshua called "the second Adam" and He is a Jew!

What was Adonai, God, saying to the Jewish people in Lev. 20:26, "You shall be holy to Me for—I the Lord—Am holy and have separated you from the peoples that you should be Mine."

HOLY: Number one; "To be close to God." Number two; "To be separated from the world for God."

NOTE:
My God, THE God of Abraham, Isaac and Jacob, did not invent incest, satan did. These preachers who preach Adam was the first and only man on earth and Eve the only woman are preaching exactly what satan wants them to for that is HIS gospel.

Sure! Adam was the FIRST man. *In the Garden of Eden!* And sure! Eve was the FIRST Woman. *In the Garden of Eden!* They were the FIRST *Jews* in the whole world, that is true. *BUT* all the races were created on the (6) sixth day. Adam—the Jew—on the (8) eighth day. Pay attention to what you read! In Scripture as well as elsewhere.

I repeat. My God did not create incest! Yours may have!! But mine did NOT.

CHAPTER 2

WE THE ANIMALS

"For the earnest expectation of the creature we all wait for the manifestation of the sons of God. For the creature was made subject* to vanity—not willingly—but because of the one who subjected it. But it—the creature—was given a reliable hope that it too would be set free from its bondage to decay and would enjoy the freedom accompanying the glory that God's children will have. We know that until now the whole of creation has been groaning as with the pains of childbirth. And not only it but we (creatures) ourselves—who have the first fruits of the Spirit—groan inwardly as we continue waiting eagerly to be made sons—that is—to have our whole bodies redeemed and set free, for it was in this hope we were saved. But if we see what we hope for it isn't hope—after all who hopes for what he already sees? But if we continue hoping for something we don't see, then we will still wait eagerly for it with perseverance."

Romans 8:19-25

* Subject: "Made slave to."

Yeshua said in Hebrews 10:5, "It has not been Your will (Father) to have an animal sacrifice and a meat offering: rather—instead—You have prepared for Me a body."

Yeshua could well have said "A Creature body You have prepared for Me." Which brings us to this, the book; "Think Again" and "Brain Bugs" by Dean Buonomano:
"The brain gets a lot of press these days, but not all the publicity has been good. Its reviews are reminiscent of Barack Obama's during the 2008 presidential campaign, when one side said he was a socialist Muslim foreigner and the other side thought he was a savior from on high. To its detractors, the brain is a kludge, a hacked-up device beset with bugs, biases and self deceptions that undermine our decision making and well-being at every turn." To the brains admirers it contains vast potential we can all unlock to improve our lives, thanks to "Neural plasticity" that enables the adult nervous system to change in mere dramatic ways than previously thought. Lately a growing army of Chicken Littles retorts that this very plasticity has been hijacked by the internet and other forms of technological crack that are rewiring our brains into a state of continual distraction and intellectual torpor.

The only difference between "animals" and "us" as creatures is, we have the ability to think, make decisions, and have free will.

At the expense of rendering myself hopelessly boring, nevertheless I must repeat myself yet again on the virtues of our brain:
Everything we hear, feel, see, think, even our sense of touch is controlled by our brain. It allows us to cope masterfully with our everyday environment, and is capable of producing breathtaking athletic feats, sublime works of art and profound scientific insights. But, our brain's most amazing achievement may be that it can understand its very own self. Amazing!

Which brings us right back to Hebrews 10:5, where Yeshua said to the Father "A BODY have you prepared for me." Meaning; "Thank you for the vehicle You've prepared for me to enable me to get to places You've sent me to during my time on earth."

When we ourselves become BORN AGAIN of the Spirit of God through the one and only DOOR—Jesus Christ, we have just accepted the very MIND of Christ Himself 1 Cor. 2:16, 2 Cor. 8:12, "If there be first a willing mind's able to accept this wonderful gift . . . "for without me you can do nothing." John 15:5.

We are the creatures! With the very mind of Yeshua. Our bodies are made of earth. What is "earth" but decomposed granite. The more decomposed the particles, the smaller they are, even beyond the sand of a beach somewhere, into dust "Dust we are and to dust we shall return," but not our brain where lives our spirit and soul, Genesis 3:19, Job 34:15, Eccl. 12:7, it is made to live forever (read section on "Anthropo's").

"Let the waters bring forth abundantly moving creatures that has life, then the fowl of the air. V-21, created whales and every living creature that lives in the waters, then He blessed them saying be fruitful and multiply."

Genesis 1:20, 21

On the sixth day—Genesis 1:26, 27,—"God and the Word Jesus, created man and woman in their image, blessed them and said for them to multiply and replenish the earth." These are the races of creatures on the earth yet today.
Genesis 2:1, 2, "On the seventh day God rested from all the work that He had created seeing it was all good." Then after He had rested on the 7th day,—"And the evening and the morning were the first, second, third, etc day."
On the eight day Almighty God created Adam BEFORE He created the Garden of Eden "and put the man in it." Gen. 2.
We are made of the earth. The things; vegetables and fruit grow in/ of the earth—we eat it. Water on/in the earth we drink it. Cow's, chickens, turkeys, hogs, other birds, fish in fresh and salt water, we also eat. To my knowledge, as of this moment, there is *NO* celestial food on earth or heavenly water for any of us to eat or drink here. Yet, our bodies (again) are made of earth. Who owns

the earth? Or is in charge of it? Here's a little, "for instance," of just who that is;

"The devil tempts our Savior after His 40 days of fasting and praying in the desert. satan said to Him, "All this power (of all the cities he just showed our Lord) I will give to you and the glory of them for the power has been delivered to me and I can give it to whomever I want to." What? I hear you loud and clear:

"Adonai, God said, "it isn't good for the man—Adam—that he should be alone. I will make for him a companion, suitable for helping him." So from the ground Adonai, God formed every wild animal and every bird that flies in the air and He brought them to the person to see what he would call them. Whatever the man would call each living creature, that was to be its name. So the man gave names to all the livestock, to the birds in the air and to every wild animal. But for the man there was not found a companion suitable for helping him. Then Adonai God caused a deep sleep to fall upon the man. While he was sleeping, He took one of his curves (a double-helix curve) (rib), closed up the place from which He had taken it, with flesh. The Curve (rib) which Adonai God had taken from the man He made a wo-man person and brought her to the man person. The man person said "At last! This is bone of my bone, flesh of my flesh. She is to be called woman—Hebrew: ishah, because she was taken out of the man—Hebrew: ish." Gen. 2:18-23. satan was cast out of heaven between Gen. 1:1 and 2, now in chapter three satan came into the garden tempted Eve, with all our five senses:

1 – Hearing
2 – Seeing
3 – Smell
4 – Taste
5 – Touch

1 – Eve heard him.
2 – Eve saw him.
3 – Eve smelled him
4 – Eve tasted his fruit
5 – Eve touched the evil fruit.

The tree was called "The Tree of knowledge of good and evil fruit. Hebrews feel without doubt the fruit was a Pomagranite. Very hard to eat for one cannot get past the 613 seeds this fruit has without scattering the pomagranite seeds everywhere just to get a taste of it, so one cannot eat it, without a container.

The Hebrew prayer shawl called the Tillit has a number of knots on both ends of the shawl that, when counted, number 613 and these tassles fly in the wind when one walks with it, while wearing it. Malachi says "The Savior will come with healing in His wings = tassles = wings = visa-versa.

When Adam ate of the same fruit Eve gave to him, his eyes were opened as was Eves, and from that moment on Adam was not in charge of the whole earth any more. Not just the Garden of Eden, but the whole earth = dirt = us!! That is the reason satan said to our Savior, who Redeems us from the earth's clutches = satans hold on us: ". . . For the power has been delivered to me to give it to whomever I please."
This too is the reason Michael, the archangel while disputing with satan over the body of Moses "did not bring an angry accusation against satan but said, the Lord God, Adonai, rebukes you satan."
Jude 9

Adonai, God has all authority and power. When our Savior walked the earth the four gospels explains what power and authority He had, "that even the demons believe—on Him—and tremble in His presence." Just before our Savior was led away for His own holocaust of hell on earth—the creation of the Gospel of Jesus Christ and Him crucified—He reminded all who were around

Him, "All power in heaven and earth has been given to Me," and at His resurrection all authority as well, praise the Lord, had been given to our Savior.

There are countless numbers of people who've described this verse—nine—in the little one chapter of Jude, that Michael the Archangel was afraid of satan. Not so! Satan has power over the earth. If it were not so then why did he tell our Savior Himself, "I have power to give the ownership to whomever I please." The reason Michael did not just scoop up Moses' body, carry it to paradise and be done with it. That reason why, is because that would be stealing and our Father, His angels or us, His servants, *know* it is wrong to steal. So Michael took a firmer hold on Moses' body and said to satan, "The Lord Almighty rebukes you satan," with great authority he evoked the Name of the One who has all authority, Adonai, God, who gave it to His Son, Jesus. AFTER Our Savior's resurrection.
Because of the ignorance of these people who think satan is stronger than Michael, Jude says this: "But these speak evil of those things they know nothing about, but what they know of the natural as brute beasts, in those things they corrupt themselves. Woe to them! For they have gone in the way of Cain and greedily ran after the error of Ba'laam for reward and perished in the gainsaying of Co're."

verses 10, 11

Adonai, God said to the races of people, He, with His Word, Yeshua, created on the sixth day, "Be fruitful, multiply and replenish the earth, have control over it, have dominion over it, the fish of the sea over all the fowl of the air and everything that lives and moves upon the earth." All this authority was just handed over to satan by Adam for one bite of fruit. But Christ returned that power back to man after His resurrection.

Yeshua said to His disciples and to all who follow Him, "You go into all the world and preach the gospel to every creature." Mark 16:15,

Col. 1:23. Paul said of the love of Adonai, God, "For I am persuaded that neither death nor life, angels or principalities nor powers, things present, things to come, nor height, depth; or any other creature will ever be able to separate us from the love of Adonai, God, which is in Christ, Yeshua, our Lord." Rom. 8:38, 39.

"If any person be in Christ they are a new creature old things are passed away and look! All things are become new." 2 Cor. 8:17.

In speaking of Yeshua, "Who is the image of the invisible Adonai, God, and the First born of every creature." Colossians 1:15;

"For every creature of Adonai, God, is good . . ."

1 Tim. 4:4

"Neither is there any creature that is not manifest in His sight, but all things are naked and open unto the Eyes of Him with whom we have to do."

Heb. 4:13

"And every creature that is in heaven and on the earth, even under the earth, such as are in the sea and all that are in them, I heard them saying, "Blessing and honor, glory and power be unto Him that sits upon the throne, and unto the Lamb for ever and ever." Rev. 5:13.

We know this Scripture does not apply to all of the above, but it goes with it. For this reason we can't help but put it in here, "This is the law of the beasts . . ." Lev. 11:46.

We have established that all sorts of flesh in the authoritive Word of Adonai, God, is considered "Creature," in His Eyes. And not a moment too soon, I might add.

"Adonai, God, said to Noah 'The end of all flesh in come before me for the earth is filled with violence through them, and look, I will destroy them with the earth." Genesis 6:13.

Is this some sort of coincidence? Man and woman created on the 6th day. The end of all flesh had come before the Great Creator and now this? Genesis chapter six? Could we then say, "the beginning and the end" in six chapters? The animals of the air, land and water were, created before man and woman. They, all, were created of the earth, Adam gave the deed to the earth to satan, "and look I will destroy them with the earth." Coincidence? I think not.

"And look I, even I, will bring a flood of waters on all the earth to destroy all flesh that has the breath of life from under the heaven and everything that lives in the earth shall die." 6:17.

But to Noah, Adonai, God, said, "But with you I will establish my covenant and you will come into the ark, you, your sons, your wife and their wives with you. And two of every sort of living thing of all flesh, you shall bring into the ark and keep them alive, along with yourselves, all of these, two by two's, shall be male and female. Of birds/fowl after their kind, of cattle after their kind, every creeping thing of their kind of the earth and two of every sort shall come—including human being creatures—to you and you are to keep them alive." 6:18-20.

Here we have it. Even the creatures—man—woman of every race created on the sixth day, also come to Noah, for him to "pick the prime of the stock," from all. Earlier we have already established the Word of God calls us—we who call ourselves, human—are creatures! Just the same as "all flesh of fowl of the air, cattle, creeping things on earth." We too are counted among, "the flesh of the earth."

Not only that but Noah had to bring, "And Noah built an alter to Adonai, God, took of every *clean* beast and every *clean* fowl and offered burnt offerings on the alter," 8:20.

Everyone whose familiar with Scripture knows there has to be seven animals for burnt offerings so Noah had to bring, of all those, in the ark as well. Everyone knows also, they had to be of the first year of their lives, never bred, were without spot or blemish of any kind. Pure in every way.

Scholars have long known the only reason Noah, his wife three sons and their wives—generation, was pure. Was not mixed as the whole world is today. Noah's DNA? Pure. His wife's DNA? Pure. Therefore their three sons blood, was pure, plus the DNA of their wives were with generational DNA, pure. For these reasons *ONLY* was Noah, "finding grace in the eyes of Adonai God." As a human creatore, Noah was not pure. He was full of faults as any and all of us. Gen. 6:8, speaks as though Noah was the beginning of a generation. Just as Adam and Eve were the beginning of a generation from the Garden of Eden, *NOT* of the others created in the world to occupy it, on the 6th day, along with all the animals of air, land and water before the 6th day. Adam and Eve were the first Jews!
Verse 9, explains, "These are the generation's of Noah . . ." Almost word for word as written about Adam, 5:1, "This is the book of generation's of Adam . . ."

The rest of that verse reads (Gen. 5:1, 2) as Genesis 1:26, 27,

Genesis 1:26, 27

Genesis 1:26, 27,

And Adonai, God, said, "Let us make man in our image after our likeness and let them have dominion over the fish of the sea, over the fowl of the air, over the cattle over all the earth, over every creeping thing that creeps on the earth. So Adonai, God created man in His own image, in the image of God He created him male and female. Adonai, God, blessed them and said to them to be fruitful and multiply and replenish the earth."

These are all the races of people, existing yet today.

Genesis 5:1, 2,

"This is the book of the generations of Adam. In the day that Adonai, God created man in the likeness of God, Adonai made him, male and female He created them, blessed them and called their name Adam in the day when *they* (they? more than 2??)."

Scholars, many many years ago, traced back through many book's, first and foremost the Bible, Josephus, the Egyptian book of the dead. Many many others have searched through *more* than these. These are the only one's I myself have studied. Every society has a historian, not just Egypt and Jerusalem as I have chosen to learn of. Italy has one. Rome has one for the world says "Rome is a country within itself." Turkey, Greece, all have historians. Even America.

Myself, personally, know a few people who've charted out the place of Adam. Even though all the races, even Adam were created outside of the Garden of Eden. *THEN* "Adonai, God, planted a Garden—Eastward in (a land called) Eden and put the man there whom He had formed." The very first Jew. Jesus? The second Adam. Gen. 2:7,8

While we're on this subject we must interject here that satan must have appeared to Eve as a form of one of the cattle? Or maybe the snake walked like a form of cattle? "And Adonai, God, said to the serpent; because you have done this you are cursed above all cattle . . ." Genesis 3:14. Just sayin!

∞

"Planted a Garden eastward of Eden."
Who named that town? It wasn't Adonai, God, for He said, "after He had made them in His image, "let *them* have dominion . . ."
Dominion means "I'm building my house over here!"
"Another says I'm building mine over there!" And so on until all the races had picked their plot, built on it, named it, and kept their families in their little named areas. One race called their plot, Eden. The Jews!
Another called theirs NOD.
All this we KNOW from Scripture itself. We also know NOD is where Cain decided to drift to; "Cain said to the Lord, my punishment is greater than I can bear. Look, You have driven me out this day from the face of the earth and from Your face I will also be hid. I will be a fugitive and a vagabond in the earth and it will come to pass that everyone . . ." Genesis 4:13, 14.

WHAT!?! "Everyone that finds me . . ." EVERYONE?
Who are these Everyone? If Adam and Eve and Abel and Cain were the only ones on earth—as churches teach—then who are these EVERYONE? Cain is talking about? Especially seeing as how God is driving Cain *away* from his mom and dad, not *to* them. Some people just do not have any common sense.

"And Cain went out from the presence of the Lord and lived in the land of NOD on the east of Eden. Cain knew his wife, she conceived and gave birth to Enoch."

Gen. 4:16, 17

Do *not* be confused with Cains firstborn son Enoch to the real—righteous Enoch of Genesis 5:22, "And Enoch walked with God after he begat Methuselah 300 years . . . And the days of Enoch were 365 years old. Enoch walked with God and then he was not." Gen. 5:23, 24.

GENERATIONS OF ADAM: lived 930 years.
begat
SETH   Eve said he was replacement for Abel. 912 years.

begat
ENOS   Who caused men to again call on Adonai, God. 905 years

begat
CAINAN   910 years then died.
begat
MAHALALEEL   895 years then died.
begat
JARED   962 years then died.
begat
ENOCH   365 years then died.
begat
METHUSELAH   969 years then died.

These are the generations of Adam. Genesis 5:1-24.

begat
METHUSELAH   lived 969 years then died.
begat
LAMECH   lived 777 years then died.
begat
NOAH   "And Noah was 500 years old and begat Shem, Ham, and Japheth." 5:25-32.

This is the reason Noah's genealogy was pure and clean. Unlike Cain's son Enoch whose blood—line (DNA) was tainted and unable to be used by Adonai, God, in the way pure Enoch's great great grandson Noah's was, used by Adonai, God."

All of the above had to be written so you would know just where the Garden of Eden was planted by Adonai, God. In the heart of Jerusalem where the threshing floor was of a man King David bought the land from him, made many sacrifices there. All this many thousands of years after Adam and Eve were cast out of it. After King David's death his son Solomon, built the tabernacle and temple there. This land was also the place Abraham, almost, sacrificed his one and only son Isaac, on the giant stone there. It is the place Muslim's say their god Allah, sitting on a white horse was taken up to heaven. Today, the whole world knows this place as, "the Dome of the Rock." In Jerusalem.

After Yeshua's resurrection and before His ascension He said to His disciples; "Now you go into all the world and preach the gospel to every creature."

In 2 Corinthians 5:17, we read where all of us are lumped—still—in the category of the unclean. The only difference between the four legged and the two legged creatures, Scripture says, is to "not copulate with them." And we have speech and the ability to think for ourselves. Our minds are not fixed on some program. When we become born again, the book of Galatians 6:15, 16, instructs us to, "Be a new creature in Messiah."

Leviticus 11:46, "Now this is the law of the beasts, fowl and creatures . . ." There were many animals on board Noah's Ark. Much more than anyone has ever thought of before, ". . . Every living substance * was destroyed which was on the face of the earth, man, cattle, creeping things, fowl of the heaven, all were destroyed which was on the face of the earth and only Noah remained alive, also they that were with him in the Ark. One hundred fifty days the water prevailed upon the earth." Genesis 7:23, 24.

SUBSTANCE:* "That of which a thing consists, matter, material, species."
MATTER: "The substance of which any physical object consists. That which occupies space."
FLESH: "Is matter created. Slowed down to earths time in space." Book of Science.

Matter at the speed of light is invisible—cannot be seen—yet it is there." Matter is flesh. Flesh is matter.

"God remembered Noah and every living substance. And the cattle that was with him in the Ark and God made a wind to pass over the earth and the waters subsided . . . God again spoke to Noah. "You, your wife, your sons and their wives can leave the Ark now and." This—"and"—seems to be so unimportant and yet it is not. ". . . AND let come forth with you every living thing you brought with you; of all flesh, of fowl, of cattle and every thing that creeps upon the earth that they may breed abundantly in the earth, be fruitful and multiply upon the earth." Genesis 8:15-17.

Humm. Where have I heard those words before? Now I remember! It was Genesis 1:20-23, 26, 27, 28. Days five and six. Verses 24, 25, God made the cattle, living things, and creeping thing and beast on the earth after their kind "And God saw that it was good." Not one mention of Adonai, God, saying "be fruitful and multiply. And God blessed them," to the animals. NO. Just goes right on into the 6th day; verses 26-28 where *They* created man in their own image. "In the image of God created He Him; male and female Created Hethem (twice) . . . and God blessed them and said to them Be fruitful and multiply and replenish the earth . . . And have dominion over the fish of the sea, over the fowl of the air, and over every thing that moves on the earth."

Other people; the races, created on the 6 day were brought forth of the ark. Remember Flesh? That is matter? And matter? That is substance? That is flesh? Except for Genesis 9:10, Adonai, God, established His covenant "With Noah and the other seven RIGHTEOUS soul creatures, and with every living creature that is with you and of the fowl, the cattle, every beast on the earth with you, from all that go out of the ark to every beast of the earth, will I establish my covenant with you; neither shall all flesh be cut off any more by the waters of a flood to destroy the earth."

Psalms 148:1-14 (complete chapter) Everything mentioned in this chapter, repeats Genesis chapter one, then commands them in verse 7 of Ps. 148, "To praise the Lord." Each and everything is under this command. Why? Because Scripture says, "For He commanded and they were all created." And as the old saying goes, "Rome wasn't built in a day," neither was the heavens and the earth and all that is therein. Even satan uses animals to get his point across. Jesus said, "Beware of false prophets which come to you in sheeps clothing . . ." Matt. 7:15, Mk. 14:27. It appears to me that the whole book of John is about sheep. We as sheep . . . Sheep as creatures. We the sheep are creatures. Then again, you don't have to take my word for it.

Solomon—I think. Although I've researched what I'm about to say, I cannot find it again, "It's the little foxes that spoil the vine." The Native Americans believe there is nothing slyer than a fox. He will outwit you every time. Sure, he's little, and yes, he's as cute as any small animal you've ever seen, and yet he has more wisdom than you, and is expert at using that knowledge.

The little foxes in our lives could be anything. Anything that creatures, such as we are, cannot live without. Me? Oh boy. Do I ever have a little fox eating at me. Chocolate. Oh yes that very wonderful tasting, chocolately sweet thing. Sometimes I can go for a month or two at a time then that little fellow causes me to have a creature, chocoholic, small fit. OK. A big one.

29

Well, I have "'fessed up" to you, what little fox is eating away at you? Some of us have more than one little fox eating away at us.

Scripture for you: Rev. 4:11, Eph. 4:24, Col. 3:10, 1:15-18, 1 Tim. 4:4, 5, Heb. 4:12, 13, Rev. 5:12, 13, 13:8, Mal. 2:10, 1 Cor. 11:8, 9, Eph. 3:9, 10,

CHAPTER 3

THE TESTIMONY OF PAUL

"I would not have you to be ignorant brothers and sisters concerning those who are asleep—in graves—, that you be not sorrowful even as others which have no hope. If we believe that Yeshua died and arose again even so they also who sleep in Yeshua will God bring with Him. For this we say to you by the Word of the Lord that we which are alive remaining unto the coming of the Lord Yeshua shall not prevent them which are asleep.
"For the Lord Yeshua Himself shall descend from heaven with a shout, with the voice of the archangel and with the trump of God and the dead in Christ shall rise first. Then we which are alive and remain shall be caught up together with them in the clouds to meet Yeshua the Lord in the air and so shall we ever be with the Lord."

1 Thess. 4:13-17

Regarding "The last trumpet," there are many theories. Is it the seventh and last trumpet of Revelation 11? Or, did Paul have something else in mind?
We've written Paul's account of 1 Thessalonians 4:16-18. Then, we have Paul's other account that is found in 1 Corinthians 15:51-53, "Behold! I have a mystery to show you; we shall not all sleep but we will all be changed, in a moment in the twinkling of an eye. At the last trump for the trumpet will sound and the dead shall be raised incorruptible and we shall be changed. Because

31

this corruptible body must put on incorruption, and this mortal body must put on immortality."

In case anyone has forgotten, Paul was in the military. He was a soldier with one thought on his mind, find, arrest Christians, take them to the Sanhedrian to be in a Kangaroo court and murdered. He was also a very learned man who sat at the feet of masters of Torah possibly knowing it from front to back and vice versa.

Paul wrote to Gentile Christian churches, which were strongly permeated by Romans and were influenced by Rome. The Roman culture as well as the Roman Military scene, was very familiar to them; it was part of their daily lives, so to speak. It is said of Corinth, that many retired Roman soldiers resided there;
"The Roman soldiers received citizenship after the end of their time of service and were given land in a newly-founded city so they could settle there. Such colonies existed in all the regions of the Roman world empire, and soldiers whose service was over, who had won citizenship through faithful service, formed the backbone of this city." Polybius History V1, 40.

The trumpet was an important signal instrument in the Roman army and was used daily to issue commands. Paul *wrote in his words* of the catching-away of a trumpet which would sound, without any further explanation. Why was the explanation lacking? Perhaps because it was not necessary? He knows of the Roman background that the inhabitants of Corinth and the Thessalonians were quite familiar with. They knew the customs of the Roman army full well, as many veterans lived among them, and they were continually surrounded by the Roman troops. The book of Revelation had not been written yet. The sound of the trumpet must have been something, therefore, that the Gentile Christians were quite familiar with.

When the Lord comes, the trumpet will sound. The trumpet was an important signal instrument in the Roman army, and was

used daily to issue commands. The Greek historian and writer; Polybius, describes among other things under the Roman military system;
"The following is their manner of breaking camp. Immediately upon the signal being given they take down their tents and everyone packs up. No tent, however, maybe either taken down or set up before those of the tribunes and consul. The second signal they load the pack animals, and on the third, the leaders of the column must advance and set the whole camp in movement."

With the background of this description, it is interesting to note that in 1 Thessalonians 4:16, 17, reads, ". . . And the dead in Christ shall rise first: then we which remain shall be caught up together with them in the clouds." The third signal was the last. Is it possible that the apostle Paul built his message about the catching-away on this background knowledge that the recipients of the letter were familiar with?

2 – The order. When Paul speaks of the resurrection and catching-away in the first letter to the Corinthians, he speaks of these in direct connection with a definite order: "For as in Adam all die, even so in Christ shall all be made alive. But every man in his own order: Christ, the Firstfruits, afterward they that are Christ's at His coming: Then comes the end, when he shall have delivered up the Kingdom to God, even the Father; When he shall have put down all rule and all authority and power," 1 Corinthians 15:22-24.

Literally, the word for "order" here means "rank" or "turn." Again, Paul had taken this from the military terminology, as it was a common military expression. Everyone who has served in the armed forces knows, for instance, the command: "Company halt!" If Paul uses military terms in his chapter on the resurrection i e the catching—away, then we can also see the last trump in this connection—verse 52,—which clearly fits this context.

33

3 – A Command. In the chapter of the first letter to the Thessalonians on the catching—away, Paul writes of a command: "For the Lord Himself will come down from heaven, with a loud command," 1 Thessalonians 4:16, NIV. This term comes from the military vocabulary.

4 – The voice of the archangel. ". . . With the voice of the archangel . . ." 1 Thessalonians 4:16. This statement also can be compared with the military terms of that time, as we will see in our next point.

5 – The trump or trumpet. ". . . And with the trump of God." 1 Thessalonians 4:16. Surely, it is not by mere chance that Paul speaks here of a command that is directly connected with the voice of the archangel and the sound of the trumpet. Here, the commanding term is used, which was normal in the Roman army:

1. The command of the government.
2. The command of an officer.
3. The sound of the trumpet for the issue of the command to the army, whereby the third trumpet signalized the departure.

Something else occurs to us in this connection, however, namely:

6 – Military equipment. Paul, writing about the catching—away, explaining that the church does not belong to the night, meaning, the unlearned or illiterate, "Of the DAY OF THE LORD," but we are the children of the day, Ones who have "studied up, prayed up, and are ready to go up "We're moving on up to the East side . . ." remember that? George and Wezzie?:
"But let us who are of the day, be sober, putting on the breastplate of faith and love, for a helmet, the hope of salvation. For God has not appointed us to wrath, but to obtain salvation which

comes by our Lord Jesus Christ, who died for us, that, whether we are awake or are asleep, we should live together with Him. Wherefore comfort yourselves together and edify one another even as also you do, "already. 1 Thessalonians 5:811-. The words "breastplate" and "helmet" also belong to the terminology of the Roman army, namely, the equipment.

7 – The Army Tent. It is not without significance either that the taking down of tents, which also comes from the military scene, is explicitly used for the catching—away when Paul says, "For we know that if our earthly house of this tabernacle (NIV-Tent) were dissolved, we have a building of God, a house not made with hands, eternal, in the heavens (plural). For in this (tent) we groan, earnestly desiring to be clothed upon with our house which is from heaven: if so be that being clothed we should be found naked. For we, that are in this tabernacle do groan, being burdened, not for that we would be unclothed, but, clothed upon, that mortality might be swallowed up of life. Now he that has wrought us for the selfsame thing of God, who also has given to us the earnest of the Spirit."

2 Cor. 5:1-5

At that time, people no longer lived in tents. Only soldiers. Paul compares our bodies to a "tent." Military tent? And he would rather be "clothed" upon, that is, caught-up, than to be unclothed, which means die. But even they, the dead "shall rise first" in their immortal clothes, just as we "left standing here will be changed . . ." immediately in our immortal clothing.

Think! Think big! On the Feast of Tabernacles, Fall Feast, One of three Feasts of the Lord that He Himself said, "These are My Feasts and you shall keep them forever." Zecheriah chapter 14, explains what will happen to the nations who do not come up to Jerusalem each year to keep these Feasts of the Lord who declared "these are MY Feasts and you shall keep them forever."

The word "SHALL," is also a command.

Deut. 29:29, Job 15:8, Explain "Secret things belong to God."
Amos 3:7, Matt. 11:25, 13:35, Rom. 16:25, 2 Cor. 3:14, Explains
"Secrets are revealed by Him."
Psalms 25:14, "Secrets of the Lord is with them that fear Him."

Gods secrets were revealed to all these who studied Torah and Old
Testament and Paul had a Ph D in that. It's why he wrote these words:
"But, of the times and seasons . . ." "Feasts" are seasons. brothers,
you have no need that I should write them to you. Because you
yourselves know perfectly well that the DAY OF THE LORD
does so come as a thief in the night." 1 Thess. 5:1, 2.
The catching-away *is* the coming of our Lord, "As a thief in the
night." 1 Thess 4:16, 17.
Please read Matthew 12; beginning verse 24-28. To be able
to understand verses 29—Jesus was speaking of the *World*
being satan—"the strong man"—. And the strong mans goods
is the people living on or under the earth, born again and
His-Christs-secret coming, Christ will "bind that strongman,"
and steal each and every one of us away. 2nd coming.

Yom T'rooah—Feast of Trumpets—Preparing for Yeshua's Return

all over the world (2nd Corinthians 5:18)!

The Feast of Tabernacles (Lev. 23:42-43; Deut. 16:13-15; Zech
14:16) is the 7th and climatic feast. This feast is also called Ha
Hag (The Feast), The Feast of Ingathering and the Season of
Rejoicing; and it has many applications for our lives today.
To walk in the light of the Feast of Tabernacles is to:

- 1) Walk in an attitude of dependency.
- 2) Rely on our unseen God rather than relying on what
    is material.

- 3) Walk in faith of God's supernatural provision.
- 4) Walk in an attitude of thanksgiving & rejoicing.
- 5) Move when God moves.
- 6) Walk in an attitude of expectation & future blessing.
- 7) Walk in a spirit of giving & sacrifice.
- 8) Realize salvation is a process.
- 9) Live with an End Times mindset.

The Feast of Tabernacles speaks to us of God's provision, God's presence, thanksgiving and hope!

The Feast of Tabernacles from a Messianic perspective. I hope and trust that you will be built up in Messiah.

Walking In The Light Of The Feast of Tabernacles.

CHAPTER 4

JOHN THE BAPTIZER

John, the Baptist, lived and preached in the wilderness, wearing a cured camels' hide; hair still attached. Josephus said this hide came from behind the alter, where all the cured hides were laid after the process of slaying animals for sacrifice. How a camel's hide got there I don't know Josephus didn't say. Mark wrote about John in chapter one, beginning verse two; which parallels Isaiah 40:3, as well, "Behold I send My messenger before your face, which will prepare Your way before You. The voice of one crying in the wilderness, 'Prepare you the way of the Lord and make straight His pathes. John did baptize in the wilderness and preach the baptism of repentance for remission of sins. All the land of Judah and Jerusalem went to John, in the wilderness, seeking him and were baptised of him in the Jordan river, confessing their sins . . . He ate locust and honey and preached; "There is one mightier than I, that I am not worthy to tie or untie His shoes laces. I do indeed baptise you with water, but He will baptise you with the Holy Spirit (John 14:)." One day while John was busy baptising the people, he looked up to see the people waiting on the bank of Jordan to be baptised, then, upon seeing the Pharisees and Sadducees, he commanded in a somewhat harsh voice, "O you vipers! Hypocrites! Who has warned you to flee from the wrath to come!" More of a statement, rather than a question

What is the wrath of God? Seeing as how there are many kinds of wrath's mentioned in God's Holy Word.

38

Does everyone have to go thru the wrath of God we are talking about here? Is there a way to escape it?

Seeing as how, upon studying the different kinds of wrath's of the Living God upon people, all the people His wrath comes upon, are; evil people, rebellious people, people who will not accept our Savior, as Savior, or, even the One, the Only begotten Son of YHVH, the Creator of all things. In other words rebellious sinners. Even people attending churches who think they are a "Christian" are rebellious, at times. If they don't repent, then the Wrath of God we're talking about will come on them also.

All of Gods blessings and curses, even ways to escape God's Wrath that we are talking about, "to flee from the wrath to come," as John Baptist put it. Remember? In the wilderness Almighty God became very angry with the children of Israel, but Moses gave God, "a way of escape" from His own anger. So, Moses gathered all of these many millions of Israelites and said, "Who is on the Lords side? If you are then gather—with me—on the right side of the tabernacle door. Those who are not gather on the left side of the tabernacle door." There were many more on the Lords side than on the left. On the left there were 3,000. The Almighty God caused an earthquake to come, open up a giant chasm and swallow up all 3,000 Israelites. But, our Lord God had a way as only He can, of recovering all those 3,000 people. On the day of Pentecost, "when it had fully come and the 120 souls in the upper room hear a mighty rushing wind that filled all the house and cloven fire sat upon each of them. And they-all-began to speak in other languages. Some, outside on the street, from all these many nations under heaven said, mockingly, "These men are full of new wine." Peter stood up, with the eleven and said, These people are not drunk as you suppose seeing it is only the 3rd hour of the day (9am). But, this is that spoken of by the prophet Joel. "Acts chapter 2. The three thousand God brought back to Himself that day can be found in verse 41. From the 3,000 lost, at the left side of the tabernacle door in the wilderness.

Our Wonderful Father and His Son, our Savior, "Counted the cost" long before satan fell and Genesis 1:1 and 2, happened "And the earth was without form and void . . ." Void meaning empty in Greek. Recalling the Words of Jesus "For which of you intending to build a tower (or house) does not sit down—first—and count the cost whether he has sufficient funds to finish it . . ?" Luke 14:28-; Its as clear as the atmosphere on a rainy day when the sun comes out, our Father and Savior had sat down and counted their cost. Revelation 12: explains how satan and his demons were cast out of heaven. Is it any wonder the earth was without form and void, Greek for empty. Homer, in his book, "The Odyssey," was a Greek philosopher, wrote of Zeus' son, Vulcan, whom he called god of fire, hence, volcano's. Zeus cast his son out of heaven, wrote a poem then, saying it "took him all morning, noon and night just to land on the earth with a great thud."

John 3:35, 36, "The Father loves the Son and has given all things into His hand. All they that believe on the Son has everlasting life. All they that believe not on the Son shall not see life but the wrath of God abides on them." The same applies to angels who disobey as well.

1 John 5:11-20, "And this is the record that God has given us eternal life and that life is in Him-His Son. They that have the Son has life . . . All unrighteousness is sin . . . We know that whosoever is born of God does not sin, but he that is begotten of God keeps themselves and that wicked one cannot touch them. We know that we are of God . . . And we know that the Son of God is come and has given us an understanding that we may know Him that is true, and we are in Him that is true, even in His Son Jesus the Christ. This is the true God and eternal life.
"All they that believe on the Son of God already has the witness within themselves. All they that do not believe has made God a liar, because they believe not the record that God gave of His (Own) Son." 1 John 5:10.

". . . For which thing's sake the wrath of God comes on the children of disobedience. Mortify your members therefore which are upon the earth; fornication, uncleanness, inordinate affection, evil concupiscence, covetousness, all of which is idolatry."

Col. 3:6, 5

"But the Lord is the True God, He is the living God and an Everlasting King; at His wrath the earth shall tremble and the nations shall not be able to withstand His indignation." This is "He, that has made the earth by His power, He has established the world by His wisdom and has stretched out the heaven by His discretion." Jeremiah 10:10, 12.

The New Testament explains, "Its a fearful thing to fall into the hands of the living God." Here's why:

"A begger lay at the gate of the entrance of a kings palace. Everyday the king, upon leaving his castle, had to pass right by the begger . . ." Who was sick with some kind of disease that left him with sores and scabs that the neighborhood dogs put the only balm they had from their mouthes as they licked the beggers sorer, while he begged for food or even crumbs from the rich-mans table. The rich man just ignored the begger and went on his merry ol' way: ". . . It came to pass the begger at the rich-man's gate, died and was carried by the angels to Abraham's bosom. Then, the rich-man also died, was buried, and in hell he lifted up his eyes . . ."

This sounds very much like Paul whose wishes were; "We are confident, I say, and willing rather to be absent from the body and present with the Lord." 2 Corinthians 5:8.

Scripture says, "God rejoices over the death of His saints."

Num. 23:10, Ps. 23:4, 48:14, 116:15

So, if a saint's last breath here on earth puts them immediately in the presence of our Lord, doesn't it stand to reason that the last breath of the wicked then take their first breath in hell? As this very parable explains.

". . . Being in torment's—plural—seeing Abraham a long way off and Lazarus in his bosom, cried and said, "Father Abraham!

Have mercy on me. Send Lazarus so he may dip the tip of his finger in water and cool my tongue for I am in torment in this flame." Luke 16:22-31.

Most of us know this is a parable and most of us know parables are stories born out of a real happening of long ago. This parable happened in the days of Moses for Father Abraham explained to the rich-man begging for his five brothers—still—alive, "They have Moses and the prophets to listen to. If they won't hear them then they won't believe one though he rose from the dead."
Here's what "The American Heritage Dictionary—2nd College Edition" has to say of a parable:
"A true happening told in simple story form, illustrating a moral or religious lesson. To compare."

When the time and season had come—Passover—for our blessed Jesus to be and live out Isaiah 52 and 53 chapters and He was in the last stages of death, explained to the thief on a cross beside Him "Lord. Remember Me When You Come into Your Kingdom. Jesus replied, "Today you shall be with ME in Paradise." Luke 23:43.
No "IF's," "AND's", or "BUT's," about it. Abraham's Bosom was changed from underneath the earth to one heaven removed, below the true heaven where God lives, and called it PARADISE. Our Savior said PARADISE.

Strong's Executive concordance say's of PARADISE:
"Paradise is a Persian word and was applied to a garden or park connected (attached!) with *the* Royal residence. Owing to the Persian's regarding their King's or gods, which explains why the laws of the Mede's and Persians were unchangeable, the residence of the King and its' surrounding grounds were looked upon as a divine abode. Accordingly paradise came to mean the precients of the divine dwelling place." This same dictionary explains paradise is not heaven. "Heaven is the abode—place—where God lives."

Revelation 4:6, "Before the throne there was a sea of glass like unto fine crystal." So is our heavenly sky, like a sea of blue glass.
Revelation 6:9, 10, "When he had opened the fifth seal I saw *under* the alter, the souls of them that were slain for the Word of God and for the testimony which they held. They cried with loud voices, saying, How long O Lord, holy and true, do you not judge and avenge our blood on them that dwell on the earth?"

Please read Exodus, chapters thirty-seven, thirty-eight, and forty to learn about where the alter is placed, and where God sat when He came down, once a year to forgive the sins of the Israelites, in the temple. Either, Moses' tabernacle, Solomon or Herod's temple. Any of these three, to enlighten your understanding on how heaven—God's house—is laid out. His temple in heaven, that is.
Learn about the "Brasin Alter, and the "Brasin Sea." Ten of them placed strategically around the entrance's to the temple. Which they called "The sea of Blue." Mirrors were placed in each of them, heaven and paradise separated by a polished glass floor no one knows how many mile *BELOW* God's heavenly home. Only first Thessalonians, chapter four will put us in God's house, with His Son Jesus.

CHAPTER 5

GOING EAST? YOU'LL NEVER FIND IT

Each of us feel we were the Chief of sinners just as Paul felt—without doubt—he was, and had a scholarship to prove he majored in being the worst. Ever. None of us feel worthy of our Father's greatest sacrifice in all of time immemorial; His One, His Only Son and Firstborn at that, just so we could be out of the clutches of satan. Through no fault of our own, we were born into a sin nature, and it grieves me—still to this day—that My Redeemer, who knew no sin, had to die the most horrible of all death's for sin's of the world and not just yours and mine.

While He hung there on that horrible 'hill of death' cross, His thoughts were, "The sorrows of death compassed me, and the floods of ungodly men made me afraid. The sorrows of hell compassed me about; the snares of death prevented me. In my distress I called upon the Lord and cried unto my God, He heard my voice out of His temple and my cry came before Him, even into His ears. Then, the earth shook and trembled, the foundations also of the hills moved and were shaken, because He was mad. There went up a smoke out of His nostrils, and fire out of His Mouth devoured: Coals were kindled by it. He bowed the heavens also and came down, and darkness was under His feet . . . He made darkness His secret place His pavilion roundabout Him were dark waters and thick clouds of the skies. At the brightness that was before Him His thick clouds passed, hail-stones and coals of fire. The Lord thundered also in the heavens, and the

Highest gave His voice; hail-stones and coals of fire. Yea, He sent out His arrows and scattered them, and He shot out lightenings and discomfited them . . ." Psalms 18:3-14. It would be of great interest if you—the reader—would read the rest of this chapter for it is vital for everyone and not just you and I, to know what God did while His precious treasure was being mutilated, tortured and died, but arose from that death very victorious, three days and nights later.

"The earth is the Lord's and the fullness thereof." Ex. 9:29, Deut. 10:14, ". . . The World and they that dwell therein." Ps.24:1, 1 Cor. 14:21. Eccl. 1:4, "The earth abides forever." "Our Lord will shake the earth yet again one more time." Job 9:6, Ps. 46:3, 72:16, Isa. 2:19, 13:13, Hag. 2:6, 21, Heb. 12:26, Isa. 24:18, 52:2, 2 Sam. 22:8, Ps. 18:7.

A total of three times our Fathers Word speaks of shaking the earth. *The first* was between Genesis 1:1 and 2, when Revelation 12:7-9 ". . . That great dragon called satan was cast down into the earth . . ." "And the earth was without form and void." You've just read the beginning of this writing, which was *the second* shaking.

We read in Isaiah 14; beginning verse 9-17, but its always best to begin our reading with verse one on through to the end of the chapter. In speaking of satan:
"Hell from beneath is moved for you to meet you at your coming. It stirs up the dead for you, even all the chief ones of the earth, it has raised up from their thrones all the kings of the nations. All they shall speak and say unto you, 'Are you also become weak as we? Are you become like us? Your pomp is brought you down to the grave and the noise of your viols: the worm is spread under you. How are you fallen from heaven O Lucifer, son of the morning! How are you cut down to the ground, which did weaken the nations! For you have said in your heart:

45

I will—ascend into heaven—*I will*—exalt my throne above the stars of God—*I will*—sit also upon the Mount of the Congregation in the sides of the north:—*I will*—ascend above the heights of the clouds
—*I will*—be like The Most High.
"Yet you shall be brought down to hell, to the sides of the pit. They that see you shall narrowly look upon you and consider you saying, 'Is this the man that made the earth to tremble, that did shake kingdoms, that made the world as a wilderness, and destroyed the cities therein, that did not open the house of the prisoners?" This speaks of the way the world was before Genesis 1:1 and 2.

Hebrews 1:2, Parallel along side of these Scriptures, "Has in these last days spoken to us by His Son, whom He has appointed heir of all things, by whom He also made the world's." More than ONE world? No, its the same world, inhabited more than once.

Really, we do pray that you caught the Scripture in Isaiah, calling satan, A MAN? Ezekiel 28; also calls satan, "a man."

Isn't it wonderful, our Almighty God calls Himself a man when He said "I AM not a man that I should lie." Of course not! He is the Most High deity and He also said, "I can swear by no other," than Myself for there is none higher than He, Himself."

Scientists' say there was a tremendous blow to earth to knock it off its axes like that when satan and all his hells angels fell to earth.

I hypothesize Genesis 1:1, 2, was that giant blow. Not an asteroid as Scientists theorize.

A famous Scientist once said, "You can go North and find it. You can go South and find it. You can travel West and find it. But, my friend, when you travel East, you will never find it."

Dr. La Grassy.

Neil Armstrong said, while in space, "It suddenly struck me that this tiny pea, pretty and blue, was the earth. I put up my thumb and shut one eye, and my thumb blotted out the planet earth. I didn't feel like a giant. I felt very small."

CHAPTER 6

DEATHBLOW—TO SATAN'S PRISON

"For there is hope of a tree if it be cut down that it will sprout again, and that the branch, tender thereof will not cease though the root thereof wax old in the earth, and the stock thereof die in the ground, Yet through the scent of water it will bud and bring forth boughs like a plant." Job 14:7-9.

Job's words are like King Davids in the book of Psalms, full of mysteries that on the surface mean Job or David. Dig deeper though and a whole new set of mysteries appear. Take these words of Job and apply them to the words of Paul;
"Wherefore He said when He ascended up on high, he led captivity captive and gave gifts unto men. Now, that He ascended what is it that He also descended first into the lower parts of the earth? He that descended is the same that ascended up far above all heavens, that He might fill all things." Ephesians 3:8-10, 1 Peter 3:18-20.

John 3:13, "No MAN has ascended up into heaven, but He that came down from heaven, even the Son of God."

Romans 10:6, 7, "But the righteousness which is of faith speaks on this wise; Say not in your heart who shall ascend into heaven? (that is to bring Christ down from above): Or who shall descend into the deep? (That is to bring up Christ again from the dead)."

Many novices ask, "Why did Christ descend into hell, called the grave?"

Answer:

"For Christ also has once, suffered for sins, the just for the unjust, that He might bring us to God, being put to death—in the flesh—but quickened by the Spirit: By which also He went and preached to the spirits in prison which were sometimes were disobedient, when once the long suffering of God waited in the days of Noah . . ." 1 Peter 3:18-20.

Jesus' own Words will verify the words of Job, about the tree (see page one) ". . . The hour is come that the Son of Man should be glorified. Verily verily I say to you, except a corn of wheat fall into the ground and die it abides alone; but if it die it brings forth much fruit."

John 12:23, 24

"The corn of wheat" is Jesus for He did go into Abraham's bosom, preached to those locked up there and brought them *up* out of there, taking them, all, *up* to paradise. Therefore "it brings forth much fruit."

Job was before Moses, and is called "the oldest book in the Bible." Job spoke often of death and he left his readers with a slight tinge of fear about death that he imparted by his writings to us. Praise the Lord, God always provides us answers, "For as much then as the children are partakers of flesh and blood, He also Himself likewise took part of the same; that through death He might destroy him that had POWER over death that is, the devil; and deliver them who through FEAR of death, were all their lifetime subject to bondage."

Hebrews 2:14, 15

Why? Because satan bound those who died with locks, chains, doors and gates. Scripture verifies this.

49

David wrote of himself and, all of us know when he wrote of himself, nine out of ten times, it refers to Jesus as well; "There are terrors of death . . ." Ps. 55:4. Solomon also wrote in Proverbs 13:14, ". . . death has snares . . ." Snares are traps hunters use that has a chain on it anchored in the ground so their intended prey cannot run away with the hunters trap, even though the prey's foot is caught in it. When open the trap has large teeth cut in its iron jaws. Jaws that look exactly like the open mouth of a large shark.

BARS:	*CHAINS:*	*GATES:*
Job 17:16 bars of the pit 38:10, 40:18,	2 Peter 2:4,	Matt. 7:13, 16:18,
Psalms 107:16,	Jude 6,	Lk. 13:24,
Isa. 45:2 same	Lam. 3:33, 34,	Ps. 107:18,
147:13, 61:1,	Ps. 73:4,	Isa. 38:10,
Jer. 49:31,	Prov. 14:27,	
Jonah 2:6,		

There's lots of Scripture on the word "hell." When we read these Scriptures we must have wisdom to discern; is it speaking of hell where satan goes? Or is Scripture speaking of hell meaning—the grave—literal hell, or gehenna where trash and dead bodies were burned—outside—the city of Jerusalem:

hell's hell:

Deut.	32:22, fire burn to lowest hell
Job	11:8, deeper than hell
	22:6, naked before Him
Psalms	9:17, wicked turned into hell
	55:15, go down quick to hell
Prov.	9:18, guests are in depths of hell
	15:11, hell and destruction before Lord
	15:24, he may depart from hell
	23:14, deliver his soul from hell
	27:20, hell and destruction

Isaiah	5:14, hell has enlarged herself
	14:9, hell from beneath is moved
	14:15, shall be brought down to hell
	37:9, debase yourself to hell
Ezekiel	31:16, cast him down to hell
	31:17, went down to hell with him
	32:21, speak to him out of hell
	27, down to hell with weapons
Amos	9:2, dig beyond grave into hell
Jonah	2:2, out of belly of hell
Habb.	2:5, enlarges desire as hell enlarges
Matt.	5:22, in danger of hell fire
	5:29, body be cast into hell
	10:28, body into hell
Luke	12:5, body into hell
Matt.	16:18, gates of hell
	23:15, two—fold more child of hell
	23:33, can you escape damnation of hell
Luke	16:23, in hell he lifted up his eyes
James	3:6, set on fire's of hell
	2 Peter 2:4, cast angels down to hell

Revelation 1:18, "I Am He that was dead and am alive for ever more, and have the keys of death and hell." Jesus ". . . That through death He might destroy him that had power over death and hell, that is, the devil! And deliver them, who through FEAR of death, were all their life—time subject to bondage . . ." Of hells chains, bars, doors and gates.

David calls the bondage of death ". . . Terrors of death," and these terrors have been there since Adam—earthy man—sinned and gave control of earth to satan who chained dead bodies to the earth. Even King Solomon wrote of it when he said; when we die mans spirit goes back to God who gave it and the body back to dust.

Well, no more! satan is not controlling the earth any more with chains, bars, doors and gates. By the way during the time satan had control of these bondages, it was the righteous he—satan—set out to kill and bring to his prison. The wicked and the sinner he wasn't worried about, he had them already. Jesus came, lived, suffered, died and arose to live again, conquered death and the hell it caused in hell—the grave—. Isaiah 53; happened in all its awfulness. Christs life—death—resurrection is "Preach the gospel of the good news" to all the world.

The righteous, wicked and the sinner still die and yes, are laid in—hell—the grave, but there is no STING of death anymore. David put it "pains of death compass me about." Then we read in Acts 2:24, confirms Davids words "Jesus of Nazareth, a man approved of God among you by miracles, wonders and signs, which God did by Him in the midst of you, as you yourselves know: Him being delivered by the determinate counsel and foreknowledge of God, you have taken and crucified and slain: Who God has raised up, having LOOSED the pains of death: because it was not possible that He should be held to it (holden of it) . . ." David said and acts repeats, ". . . Therefore my heart did rejoice and my tongue was glad; moreover also (now) my flesh shall rest in hope because You will not leave my soul in hell, neither will You suffer Your Holy One to see corruption . . . let me freely speak to you of the patriarch David, that he is both dead and buried and his sepulchre is with us to this day. He seeing this BEFORE his death, David spoke of the resurrection of Christ, that His soul was not left in hell, neither His flesh did see corruption . . . For David is not ascended into the heavens . . ." Verses 27-33. Also found in the book of Psalms 110.
Sin reigned from Adam to Moses but was accounted to no one. Then Moses received the tablets on Mount Sinai, broke them, then received another set, this time the 10 commandments. Then everyone was accountable for their own sins.

CHAPTER 7

UNEARTH PROFOUND SECRETS

Our blessed Messiah, Jesus, in explaining how His secret catching away will be like: ". . . If I cast out devils by the Spirit of God then the Kingdom of God is come unto you. Or else how can one enter into a strong mans house and spoil his goods except *FIRST* He bind the strong man? And then He will spoil his house."

Matt. 12:28, 29

satan is the strong man. satan's house is the world. Jesus is the one who will come, bind the strong man and catch away His bride—the church. A secret catching away. Read Matthew 13:37-42, just remember every verse has more than one meaning. This Scripture also has another meaning, and that is found in: John 12:30-32,

"This voice came not because of Me, but for your sakes. Now is the judgment of this world now shall the prince of this world be cast out and if I be lifted up from the earth will draw all men to me."

Rightly so Christ was hung on a cross between heaven and earth, crucified, spent three days in hell (grave) loosing all the chains and locks on the righteous that had died from Adam unto Christs death and resurrection. Even opening the chains and locks of hells door's and gates too. Then, is when 1 Peter 3:18-21, happened; and Revelation 12:10, 11, happened, same time ". . . I heard a loud voice in heaven saying, "Now is come salvation and strength and the kingdom of our God . . ." The birth of our Messiah

First as a baby, grew up was crucified and God, 12:5, ". . . And she brought forth a man child who was to rule all nations with a rod of iron: and her child was caught up to God and to His throne."

". . . And the power of His Christ: for the accuser of our brethren is cast down, which accused them before our God day and night (Job 1:6, 7,). And they overcame him by the Blood of the Lamb and by the Word of their testimony . . ."

Scholars know that Revelation chapter twelve has two (and more) meanings of Messiah's comings. The first He came as a baby, the second is our catching away, and the Jewish peoples—third coming—found in Zechariah 14:4, when He comes with us to the Mount of Olives as a full-blown King and winning General of His own army.

Our secret catching away 1 Thess. 4:16-18, and Rev. 4:1.

Rev. 1:6, 7, is His coming of Zech. 14:4.

Matthew 22:1-14, The marriage of God's own Son, the Groom Jesus our Lord and the bride, the Church of Revelation 19, "The Kingdom of heaven is like unto a certain King which made a marriage for His Son. The King sent forth His servants to call them that were bidden (the Jews) to the wedding and they would not come. Again He sent forth other servants, saying, 'Tell them which are bidden, Behold, I have prepared my dinner: My oxen and my fatlings are killed, and all things are ready; come unto the marriage. But they made light (fun) of it and went their ways, one to his farm, another to his merchandise: And the remnant took His servants and entreated them spitefully and killed them . . . When the King heard thereof, He was angry, and He sent forth His armies and destroyed those murderers and burned up their cities (Zech. 14:4,). WHAT? Cooked meat in heaven?

"Then He saith to His servants, 'The wedding is ready, but they that were bidden were not worthy. You go therefore into the highways and as many as you shall find bid to come to the marriage. So those servants went out into the highways and gathered together all as many as they found both bad and good and the wedding was furnished with guests. And when the king came in to see the guests, He saw there a man which had not on a wedding garment:

"He said unto him, "Friend, how did you come in hither not having a wedding garment?" And he was speechless. Then said the king to the servants, "Bind him hand and foot, and take him away, cast him into outer darkness: there shall be weeping and gnashing of teeth." "For many are called but few are chosen."

Our Savior Jesus, left us with a mandate. Mandates come from the owner of the company you work for. Or a Monarchy, where there's a king reigning and all his "train," then the mandate would come from him. If it was disobeyed by you, who are just a lowly peasant, then the king would require your head. If it's a company and you disobeyed his mandate you'd be fired. If its Jesus you disobeyed, they'll cast you into hell.

John 3:3, 5, 7, 1 Peter 1:23, 1 John 4:5, 3:9, 5:4, 18, Jesus Himself gave this Mandate, "You must be born again," this, many times, so it's not like he said it *ONCE* so you could try and ignore it. There was a time you could claim ignorance of this fact and still enter in. But now, even Jesus said, "Thou art inexcusable O man." So heed the mandate so, "You may enter in." There is only one way, through the shed Blood of Jesus. No other way. Jesus said, "I Am the way, the truth and the life. No man comes to the Father except through and by Me, I Am the DOOR." John 14. Good works will not be enough. You have to have your garment washed in the Red Blood of Jesus to make them white as snow—Rev. 19.

Here's a little "What if:" There was a beautiful mansion, sat on a hill surrounded by a beautifully kept garden and forest. Many people came and were welcomed in by the door—keeper.
One day you say to yourself, "I'll pack my suitcase and go live there too. I'm a good person, keep all the commandments, don't smoke or cuss. Have done no one wrong or harmed them in any way. They'll let me in."

You arrive there with your little suitcase, walk up the long winding path, through the garden, the forest, enjoying all the animals, the birds singing. Finally, you arrive at the door and ring the door bell. The door opens and the doorkeeper says, "Yes?"

You go into this long speech you'd prepared, and ended with, "So, I've come here to move in with you."
The doorkeeper says, "The master and I don't know you. You don't have on the proper attire. You can't come in," and he shuts the door in your face without further ado.
What would you do then? Living like that your whole life through, without a born—again experience.

Our Father God does not send people to hell. Hell was created for satan and his angels.
People send themselves to hell. Our Father and His only Son have nothing to do with your sending yourself there.

In the days our Lord walked the earth, Jewish weddings were on this wise:
Young ladies gathered in the market place in Jerusalem. Young men, looking for a wife, would go to these gatherings to find the young lady of their dreams, and she him.

Once he found her, he rushed home to inform his father. Of course the father wanted to meet her as well, so all the arrangements were made for the son to bring the young lady, to meet her future father-in-law.

The two fathers talked, before this came about. You know, to see if her father and she had enough cash—money—wealth—or what—ever, in her—"hope—chest?—" Agreements were made and a time was set for the young man to bring his young maiden to his father for his approval as well as the approval of the young lady. Who knows? She might not like the young man at all.

Two glasses of wine were poured and sat in front of the father and the young lady. The father had the privilege of the first drink. This, after he had shown the young lady jewels and what ever that would be hers if she married his son, and he—the father approved, then he would take a sip.
Now it was the young ladies turn. To drink, or not to drink. If she drinks too, then the young man puts a ring on her finger, a tiny party for the three of them, happened for an hour or so. Of happiness.

She keeps the ring, the young man gathers her gifts, and the two of them go to her house, where another tiny party happens again, if her father approves.

For the next two years they don't see each other. The young man's father is building them a mansion of their own on his property. The father has assigned 10 virgins of his own whom he could trust, to live with and keep an eye on that the bride doesn't stray during those years. The reason—again—for this is, it might not take the father two years to finish their mansion. Thats the reason they, all 11 of them at evening time, looked up and down the road, looking for the bride—groom, "Watch, and pray for you know not what hour your Lord comes." Read the 10 virgins. Five wise. Five foolish.

Jesus said to His disciples "In My Father's house are many mansions. If it were not so I would have told you so." John 14:1-4. Christs disciples knew exactly what the Savior meant, for they knew the proceeding's of a Jewish wedding.

When the groom comes for the bride "No man knows *the* day or *the* hour your Lord shall come."
"But! of the times and the seasons brothers you have no need that I write to you (again). For you yourselves know perfectly well that the Day of the LORD so comes as a *thief* in the night." 1 Thess. 5:1, 2. Please read all the chapter to know what your

minister should be warning/teaching you about this great and awful day.

1 Thessalonians 4:14-17, is the one and only time we, the born—again are handed a written invitation to come to our Blessed Fathers house! And not just to paradise.

This mansion the Jewish father created for his earthy son, also parallels the heavenly Father and His Son Jesus' wedding. The groom comes to retrieve his bride, brings her to his fathers house, the wedding is performed, they party day and night for two weeks. Then the father escorts the groom and his lovely bride to their brand new mansion, equipt with everything, including men/women servants. The young couple do not leave the house for two years. Isn't that just amazing?!

Matthew 12:28, 29, explains just how secret this invitation is carried out.

There are two main purposes of Bible prophecy.
The first is that it enables us to understand God's purposes.
Secondly, Bible prophecy gives us warning and encouragement for the future.

Yom T'rooah—Feast of Trumpets—Preparing for Yeshua's Return

all over the world (2nd Corinthians 5:18)!

The Feast of Tabernacles (Lev. 23:42-43; Deut. 16:13-15; Zech 14:16) is the 7th and climatic feast. This feast is also called Ha Hag (The Feast), The Feast of Ingathering and the Season of Rejoicing; and it has many applications for our lives today.
To walk in the light of the Feast of Tabernacles is to:

- 1) Walk in an attitude of dependency.
- 2) Rely on our unseen God rather than relying on what is material.
- 3) Walk in faith of God's supernatural provision.
- 4) Walk in an attitude of thanksgiving & rejoicing.
- 5) Move when God moves.
- 6) Walk in an attitude of expectation & future blessing.
- 7) Walk in a spirit of giving & sacrifice.
- 8) Realize salvation is a process.
- 9) Live with an End Times mindset.

The Feast of Tabernacles speaks to us of God's provision, God's presence, thanksgiving and hope!
The Feast of Tabernacles from a Messianic perspective. I hope and trust that you will be built up in Messiah.

Walking In The Light Of The Feast of Tabernacles

This is a fact. The exact time for Christ return has been set. Matthew 24:36 states, "but of that day and hour (exact date and time) knoweth no man, not even the angels of heaven, but my Father only."

"For You created my inmost being;
You knit me together in my mother's womb.
I praise You because I am fearfully and wonderfully made;
Your works are wonderful, I know that full well.
My frame was not hidden from You when I was made in the secret place.
When I was woven together in the depths of the earth,
Your eyes saw my unformed body.
All the days ordained for me were written in Your book before one of them came to be."

CHAPTER 8

KNOWING VERSUS EXPERIENCING

Our Messiah Yeshua said "If I have told you earthly things and you believe not, how shall you believe if I tell you of heavenly things? And no man has ascended up to heaven but He that came down from heaven, even the Son of Man which is in heaven . . . They that believe on Him is not condemned, but he that believes not is condemned already because he has not believed in the Name of the *Only* Begotten Son of God." The Living God of Abraham, Isaac and Jacob. John 3:12, 13, 18.

"For David is not ascended into the heavens: but he says of himself, THE Lord said unto MY Lord, Sit you on My right hand until I make your foes your footstool." Acts 2:34, 35. Psalms 110:1, bears witness to this statement.

There is multiple Scripture's that explain we, the born again will escape the many "Wraths" of God. The following are just a few: *WRATH*—Lk. 21:23, Rom. 2:5, 8, 5:9, 13:4, 5, Gal. 5:20, Eph. 2:3, 1 Thess. 1:10, 2:16, 5:9, Rev. 6:16.

DAY OF WRATH: Job 20:28, 21:30, Ps. 110:5, Prov. 11:4.

WRATH OF GOD: Jn. 3:36, Rom. 1:18, 2:5, Rev. 6:17, 14:10, 19, 19:15, Eph. 5:6, Col. 3:6, Jer. 10:10.

As for myself, I'm thrilled beyond worde we do not have to endure all that. Life has been, "hell on earth" for some of us, almost from birth to the grave. Others suffer very little, if any at all. As the song says in our asking, why? "We will understand it better" when we are called home at last, "in the sweet by and by."

"For if we believe that Jesus died and rose again, even so they also which sleep in Jesus will God bring with Him."
What is God bringing with Him when He returns? Eccl. 12:7, Zech. 12:1, 1 Cor. 2:11, say, "When a man dies his spirit goes back to God who gave it, and the body goes back to the dust (earth)." If you, the reader have read any of the work we've done on the human brain, know that our spirit is what makes us, us. Our spirit and soul live in our brain. So, our Lord is bringing our physicy back to enter a brand new glorified body; of the old one, that all preachers call "soul sleep" when a person dies.

". . . For this we say unto you by the word of the Lord, that we which are alive and remain unto the coming of the Lord shall not prevent them which are asleep. For the Lord Himself shall descend from heaven with a *shout* with the voice of the archangel and with the *trump of God*: and the dead in Christ shall rise first: Then we which are alive and remain shall be caught up together with them in the clouds, to meet the Lord in the air: and so shall we ever be with the Lord." 1 Thess. 4:14-17, Eph. 1:10, Luke 9:27, Matt. 16:27, 28, Jude 9:27.

With all our heart's we pray, you, the reader, really were paying close attention to the wording of these Scripture's. Not once did any of them say He would touch His feet to the ground, or the Mount of Olives. The angel told the disciples and some few hundreds standing there in Jerusalem when, "A great cloud caught Jesus up to paradise." A *cloud* of spirits of those who arose when He did and walked the streets of Jerusalem. Those in Jerusalem and those of 1 Peter 3:18, 19. "And behold, the vail in the temple was torn into two from the top to the bottom, and the earth did quake and the rocks split, and the graves were opened and many of the bodies of the saints which slept arose, came out of the graves after His resurrection and went into the Holy City and appeared to many." Matt. 27:51-53.

Only the redeemed in Christ will be able to hear the *shout* and the *trumpet*. How do we know? We're so glad you asked:
"Then a *voice* . . ." could this be the shout? We know its the trumpet. ". . . Father, glorify Your Name. Then there came a voice from heaven saying, I have both glorified it, and will glorify it again. The people therefore, that stood by, said that it thundered: others spoke saying, An angel spoke to Him. This voice, Jesus said, came not because of me but for your sakes."

John 12:28-30

Jesus said in another place, "My sheep know my voice and another they will not follow." Also while He was dying, while hanging on that cruel cross, He shouted, "With a loud voice, My God My God! Why have You forsaken Me!?"

One time in my life I was outside in the rain heading toward the car. Suddenly the parking area was as bright as day—it was night where I was at. The next thing, I heard a terribly loud crack of thunder, right over my head! Made my ears ring. "Someone answer the phone! It won't stop ringing!" A metaphor for *you* to ponder.

By the above we know that only the dead in Christ, and those in Christ who are still alive, will hear His voice, hear His trumpet and *go up* to meet Him in the air. If that isn't secret I don't know what a secret is or the meaning of the word.

"But of the times and seasons brethren, you have no need that I should say it to you . . ." For you know full well what season it is He comes. ". . . For yourselves know perfectly well that the day of the Lord so comes as a thief in the night."

1 Thess. 5:1, 2

THE FEAST OF TABERNACLES

Is the last of seven Feasts established by YOD'HAY'VAV'HAY—phonetically—meaning "I AM that I AM" found in Leviticus 23, Almighty God and there is none other.

This concluding celebration climaxes with a great rejoicing and is sometimes called "The Season Of Joy."

Teshuvah, meaning repentance, comes first, God calls this "The 40 Days of Awe," and ends on the Day of Atonement which is called YOM KIPPER, and as all Israel is forgiven, they can now rejoice with great joy. Refreshing always follows repentance. Acts 3:19, "Repent therefore and be converted that your sins may be blotted out so that times of refreshing may come from the presence of the Lord." The King James version explains, "So that," in this verse it is literally saying, "In order that." Peter is advising, "in order for a refreshing to come, you must first repent."

Of all these seven Feasts, God said, "Of three of these; they are MY Feasts and you shall keep them forever." These three are:
Feast of Passover
Feast of Pentecost
Feast of Tabernacles.
Almighty God also said, again, "These are My Feasts but only three will you keep forever.

Already we have given you Scripture of 1 Thessalonians 5:1, 2, but will repeat once more, here, "But of the times and the seasons brethren, you have no need that I write to you, again, For you yourselves know perfectly well that the Day of The Lord so comes as a thief in the night."

Because God heard Israel's prayer of repentance, the season had arrived to rejoice and celebrate, which occurs only on the Feast of Tabernacles. This Feast reminded all Israel of their living in tents for 40 years and the faithfulness of God, who brought them into the promised land.

The Feast of Tabernacles, also known as, The Feast of Ingathering, occurs at the time of the major fall harvest of crops. The autumn harvest of crops was greater than the Spring harvest. Just as the latter rain, or, autumn harvest, of the outpouring of the Spirit would surpass the early rain of the outpouring of the Spirit.

Deuteronomy 11:13, 14, explains, "And it shall be that if you earnestly obey My Commandments which I command you today, to love the Lord your God and serve Him with all your heart and with all your soul, then I will give you the rain . . . in its season, the early rain and the latter rain."

The Feast of Tabernacles was the final season of ingathering and rejoicing over the harvest. It is also listed in the fruit harvest, Exodus 23:17, as one of the three feasts, including Passover and Pentecost all males had to attend every year. The celebration begans five days after The Day of Atonement, of the fifteenth day of the seventh month which is our months of September and October. It continues for seven days. After the scattering of the Jews to "the four corners of the earth," and they began coming back to Israel in 1942-43, they added an eighth day, final day, thus ending the Feast as it had begun, on a Sabbath Day of rest.

During the Feast of Tabernacles, the Hebrew people were instructed to dwell in a sukkah, or booth, a temporary structure build somewhere near their homes. The roof of the structure is referred to as sekhakh, meaning, a covering. A covering loosely woven so that at night, when they lay down to sleep they could view the stars of Gods heaven.

The material used had to be something that grew from the ground and was cut off. Mostly these are palm frons., tree branches, corn stalks, bamboo reeds, sticks or, maybe even 2x4's. It was according to the family budget, just as at Passover, a Lamb is required, but the poor could use two turtle doves.

During the Feast of Tabernacles, Jews were commanded to take Arbat Ha Minim, or small branches from four species of trees, and wave them as they rejoice before the Lord. The four trees were Etrog-or citron a citrus fruit similar to a lemon tree and native to Israel. LuLav, a palm branch, Hadas, a myrtle branch and Arava, a willow branch.
The palm—Myrtle, and willow branches were bound together and referred to as the LuLav, carried in the right hand, and the citrus was carried in the left hand. In praise to God, they were waved in six directions: north—south—east—west—up—down.

One of the highlights was the drawing of water ritual, in which the priest would lead a procession to the pool of si'loam. Dipping a golden pitcher in the fresh water, he would carry this golden vessel back to the Temple, with a "pid-piper" multitude following him. On the priest's arrival he would pour the water on the brass alter

The meaning of the pouring of water was an illustrated prayer for God to send rain to Israel during winter and prepare the ground for next years harvest. Jesus made a spiritual reference to this ritual. He said the water being poured on the alter parallel the Holy Spirit being poured out and flowing through the innermost being of all believers. John 7:37-39,
"On the last day, that great day of the feast of Tabernacles, Jesus stood and cried out—If anyone thirsts, let him come to Me and drink. He who believes in Me, as the Scripture has said, out of his heart (belly) will flow rivers of living water." By this He spoke concerning the Holy Spirit who, those believing in Him would

receive, for the Holy Spirit was not yet given, because Jesus was not yet glorified," by the Father.

All my life or at least half of my 72 years of age, have tried to look back over my "growing up" time to learn, understand and explain to all who ask, about these amazing types, shadows and patterns, even cryptic notes. In Scripture about our blessed and wonderful Savior. A lot are hidden in these seven feasts. We have explained before about 1 Thess. 5:1, 2, where the very learned Apostle, Paul, said to the Thessalonians "You brethren, have no need for me to reiterate to you the Feast of Tabernacles. For you know the times and seasons. We just don't know the day or the hour."

"Ask Marilyn" column in each Sunday's Parade magazine, a question was asked: "When a clock chimes 12 am (midnight), which tone indicates the storied "stroke of midnight"?" Robert Gist, Co. Sprs., Colorado.

Answer: "The FIRST is the Charm! Chiming clocks typically have a mechanism synchronized with the clock face. As soon as the hands reach the hour, they trigger the strikes to begin."

Does any of this sound familiar to you? The readers? In the days of when Aaron was priest, Moses gave all the signs and sounds of the trumpet, to be sounded at certain events. For instance: At all the Feasts there are certain procedures the trumpet blower must sound the trumpet—with that certain sound. That's why, in the wonderful book of Psalms David said, "I was glad when they said it was time to go into the house of the Lord." Lest we forget theres a trumpet sound called "jubilee," which means eating, drinking, dancing, making merry. Just as David, "Danced before the Lord, gym*, with all his heart," and one of his relatives saw it and despised David with all *HER* heart.

Passover was at the barley harvest and the offering of a lamb. Pentecost was the time of the wheat offering, along with fruit. Tabernacles came during the final ingathering.

At none of these Feasts were the Jews to attend empty-handed. In those days it was First-fruits of their harvests. Today, these first-fruit offerings would be money. From our paychecks. No, it is not our tithes. It is over and above our tithes. A "thankful" offering. Since Passover and Pentecost have passed, the Feast of Tabernacles, a fall feast, this would be a wonderful time for you to start obeying Gods Word and do the same. After all, it is the Jews who taught us about God. God taught them, they taught us, and as Jesus said; a mandate—"Go ye into all the world and preach the gospel . . ." The gospel of the crucifiction, *PLUS* how it all came about.

*GYM, in Greek means "Naked."

Christs first appearing was as a baby who grew up; Matthew, Mark, Luke, John.
His second coming is found in 1 Thessalonians 4:16-18, Revelation 4:1, 2.
His third coming will happen as Zecheriah 14:1-5, "Behold the day of the Lord comes and the spoil shall be divided in the midst of you . . . Then shall the Lord go forth and fight against those nations as when He fought in the day of battle . . ." meaning in the day Joshua fought the battle of Jericho. ". . . And His feet shall stand in that day upon the mount of Olives which is before Jerusalem on the east, and the Mount of Olives shall split into two—toward the east and toward the west and there shall be a great valley . . . And the Lord my God shall come and all His saints with Him." Joshua fought the giants! And won.
Other Scripture that parallel these in Zechariah are Isaiah 64:3, Psalms 2:6, Ezekiel 39:11, Matthew 24; Mark 13; and 1 Thessalonians 3:13.

"And it shall come to pass that everyone that is left of all the nations that came against Jerusalem shall even go up from year to year to worship the King—the Lord of Hosts—and to keep the Feast of Tabernacles. And it shall come to pass that who so shall not come up of all the families of the earth to Jerusalem to worship the king, the Lord of hosts, even upon them there shall be no rain." Zechariah 14:16, 17, Isaiah 66:23. There are two types of rain mentioned here; the rain of water—natural—and the rain of the Holy Spirit—spiritual. "Let no man deceive you by any means; for that day shall not come except there come a falling away first . . ." and WOW! Was there ever a "falling away," since Constantine unto now. Within these past five to ten years, God has opened the eyes of many Christians to see the *truth* in Scripture, concerning—The God—of Abraham, Isaac and Jacob, and that—even—HE—is Jewish! Wow! Who'd have ever thought that!

". . . And that man of sin be revealed, the son of perdition: Who opposeth and exalteth himself above all that is called God showing himself that he is God. Don't you remember that when I was yet with you I told you these things?
And now you know what withholds that he might be revealed in his time. For the mystery of iniquity does already work: Only He who lets will let, until He be taken out of the way. Then shall that wicked be revealed, whom the Lord shall CONSUME with the SPIRIT of His MOUTH, and shall destroy with the brightness of His coming. Even HIM whose coming is after the working of satan with all power, signs and lying wonders." 2 Thess. 2:3-9, Zech 14:4, 5, Amos 9:5, Rev. 13:

Hebrews 4:12, "The sword of the Lord is sharper than any two-edged sword." Eph. 6:17, Rev. 1:16, 19:15, Jer. 12:12.
Jesus Himself said, "I Am not come to send peace but to bring a sword." Matt. 10:34

"He who lets," is the Holy Spirit "Until He be taken away." Where? Is the Holy Spirit? John 14; He lives *inside* us. God *never* takes away His gifts no matter how evil you become. Or good. Holy Spirit is a GIFT!

The Israelites have two calendars, one is a religious calendar and the other is a civil calendar. The first calendar, naturally, was established by Almighty God, and begins in the spring, in the month called Nisan, which appears in our calendar of the months of March and April. The 14th day of Nisan begins the first Feast of our Lord, who commanded the world; "three times a year shall you go up and keep these Feasts in Jerusalem" Zecheriah chapter 14.

There are seven Feasts of God, to be quiet literal about it, but Passover is the very beginning of them all, and was established in Egypt when the Hebrews were under Egyptian bondage. On the night of Passover, the Hebrew father had to kill a lamb Leviticus 23; and place its shed blood on the left and on the right, and on the lental—meaning the top of the door frame—of the door entering into each Jewish families home. Naturally, this blood would drip on to the threshhold of each door. The lamb would then be roasted and eaten in the house before midnight, Exodus 12;. The lamb's blood kept the destroying angel out of the Israelites homes, and eating the flesh of the lamb brought healing to every person living in the house, Psalms 105:37. Plus strength to every fiber of their clothing and their shoes.

The first oblation—meaning offering—occurred at noon on that day, and a major oblation again around 6 pm. of the same day. Between the evenings would be at 3 pm. Which, in our Saviors day and time was called, the ninth hour, the very time when Yeshua died on the cross during the Passover season, Matthew 27:46.

The next day, following, which would be Nisan 15, was the beginning of "Unleavened Bread." The Israelites departed on that day from Egypt and it was swift. They had no time at all to bake a regular loaf of bread, so they ate unleavened bread. A good thing too because Pharaoh, the King of Egypt had changed his mind and wanted—all of them—back. Back in the bondage they were so accustomed to. Throughout the years, from then to now, the Jews developed the custom to remove all leaven from their homes during this season of Passover as a memorial to their ancestors Exodus from Egypt. Leviticus 23:6, 7, is a foreshadowing of Christ, the sinless, spotless precious Lamb of God, without leaven, crucified and His body laid in a tomb.

During this same season, on the day after the Passover Sabbath, another feast was developed wherewith it is called the Feast of First Fruits. Going back to Genesis chapter four. Satan tried his level best to fool God by causing Cain—his own son—to offer his first fruits from his garden, to God, and thereby satans son, Cain, would become Gods first fruits. Our Almighty God is worlds apart in intelligence, wisdom and knowledge from satan and any ploy he can or ever could "dream up" to fool Him. Cains fruit was fresh and undefiled and yet Scripture says "God despised Cains offering." How much easier it would have been for Cain to have traded—equal for equal—his fruit and vegetables with his brother Abel, for a precious little lamb. After all, Adam and Eve taught them what Almighty God acquired of them from the time each were born. After all, Almighty God taught Adam and Eve from the moment He slew the first animals for the alter He taught Adam to build to how to roast the meat of the first Lamb "slain from the foundation of the world" to forgive them of their sin of disobedience and made clothes for them to wear, Genesis 3:21. What? You've never heard of God's Word that says "God *hides* His meaning in Scripture. Its up to kings to search it out.

During this time of the Feast of First Fruits, a sheaf of barley, hence First Fruit—representing the first harvest of the year, was cut from the field, and counted until the Feast of Pentecost. This was called the counting of the Amer. On the Feast of First Fruits, the sheaf was waved—side to side—up and down—horizontally and vertically respectively. This, to represent the cross on which Yeshua would die, of whom He Himself said, "If I be lifted up, I will draw all men to me." Christ, the First—Fruit's of all those who sleep. 1 Corinthians 15:20-23.

During these three spring feasts of Almighty God, He instructed His people, "You shall keep the feast of unleavened bread: you shall eat unleavened bread seven days as I have commanded you, in the time appointed of the Month of Abib; for in it you came out from Egypt (meaning SIN) and none of you shall appear before me empty handed," Exodus 23:15. Now-a-days this would mean "from our pay checks. Over and beyond your tithes.

During all of the seven feasts, all males over 20 years of age were to go to Jerusalem each year during three of these seven feasts:

The Feast of Passover
The Feast of Pentecost
The Feast of Tabernacles

Spring, summer, and fall, respectively. Every families offerings had a threefold purpose:
Obedience to Gods Word.
His blessing in the pasts deliverance.
The belief that God would bless them during the coming year.

Passover   April-May Eight days
Pentecost   May-June
Tabernacles   September-October

These feasts begin at sundown on their first days, and at sundown on their last day.

CHAPTER 9

MATRIARCH: THE MOTHER–ELECT

"Behold, My Servant whom I upheld, Mine elect, in whom my soul delights, I have put My Spirit upon Him and He shall bring forth judgment to the Gentiles." Isaiah 42:1.

This is speaking of the end time after 1 Thessalonians 4:16, 17; of all the Gentile nations that have come against the Jewish Nation to "Wipe them off the face of the earth," as the little Hitler of Iran is always claiming.

"For Jacob my servant's sake, and Israel my elect, I have even called you by My Name, I have surnamed you though you have not known Me. I Am the Lord and there is none else, there is no God other than Me, I girded you though you have not known Me. That they may know from the rising of the sun and from the going down in the West, that there is none beside Me, I Am the Lord and there is none else. I form the light and create darkness. I make peace and create evil, I, the Lord, do all these things." Isaiah 45:4-7.

"And I will bring forth a seed out of Jacob and out of Judah an inheritor of my mountains, and my elect shall inherit it, and my servants shall dwell there." Isaiah 65:9.

The prophet Isaiah, in speaking to the gentile nations who come against the Jews one last time AFTER Christ's bride—the Church—has been taken out of this world, "Therefore thus sayeth the Lord, look, my servants shall eat but you shall be hungry. Look, my servants shall drink but you shall be thirsty. Look, my servants shall rejoice but you shall be ashamed," Isaiah 65:13.

These Jews are the original "Mother—Elect" Jews. The Matriarch who taught—us—the grafted-in-wild-olive. Having often wondered about the original olive and the grafted in wild olive. In reality, I wanted to know why? This? In reality I understood the spiritual meaning, as everyone else. I just wanted more and who better to explain this, not only to me but to the whole Christian—believing—believer's all over the world.

One day while watching a Christian program on Christian television, a pastor was interviewing a Rabbi Professor from Hebrew University in Israel. Having missed half the telecast already and was forlorn about that, this Rabbi had my full attention, for the rest of the program at least. The pastor ask this Rabbi the very thing I'd been wanting to know for quite a few years, at this time:

"Rabbi, could you explain to all of us, and those who are watching, when you walk through an olive grove and all the trees are healthy. Well, maybe one or two need help, how do you bring it back to it's healthy state? Or do you just let it die?"

The Rabbi said, "No, we don't just let them die, we treat them by grafting in a branch from a healthy olive tree. Not just any olive tree branch will do. It has to be a healthy branch from a wild olive tree. The nutrients from the wild one is health to the "old—sickly—olive tree" growing in the olive grove."

Praise the Lord! The Rabbi answered my question of many years, in the spiritual and the reality. That, beloved readers, is the reason for the title of this section. Israel *is* the Matriarch Mother of Christiandom. She said YES when God called and asked "Who will go for me to teach the world about me?" Even Isaiah, in his very first chapter, repeated this command saying, "I'll go, Lord." Isaiah was a Jew speaking to Jews. The Torah is the WIFE of God. Hence—the mother Matriarch, teaching her siblings. Her siblings being—US!—dear friends. The wild olive grafted in to the Mother of Christiandom. US! The bride of our blessed Groom Jesus, whom our very soul loves with all our being.

The parents, always, in any marriage have to "give away" their son, or their daughter. In our case we are the bride—the church. Our Groom is THE ONE THE ONLY Son of God and Israel—His Wife—*MUST* perform their Son's wedding.

Just one more reason why our precious Father is causing His children—the Jews—to come into our blessed Savior's sheep—fold. He who said to His disciples, Jews, by the way, "If I be lifted up, I will draw all men to me." John.

The still disbelieving Jews; the one third Torah speaks of "will be saved," are these that Jesus and His bride come back to help save from total destruction, Zechariah 14:4, 5. "And it shall come to pass that in all the land (of Israel) saith the Lord, two parts therein shall be cut off and die, but the third shall be left there in. And I will bring the third part through the fire and will refine them as silver is refined, and will try them as gold is tried. They shall call on my Name and I will hear them. I will say, "It is My people." And they shall say, The Lord is My God." Zechariah 13:8-9.

"And the dragon (satan) was angry with the woman and went to make war with the remnant of her seed which keeps the Commandments of God and have the testimony of Jesus Christ." Rev. 12:17

Rev:2:17

One must read the whole chapter to understand: The woman is the remnant of Israel. V-II, explains they've finally learned, through the two witnesses of Rev. 11:4-12. If you read chapter II also, you'll realize these happenings are in the thick of the horrible war of the great tribulation, end part, just before Zechariah 14:4, 5.

Paul, the apostle sent to bring in the Gentiles, said to the Romans concerning God's remnant, "Isaiah also cried concerning Israel; Though the number of the children of Israel bear the sand of the sea, a remnant shall be saved." Rom. 9:27.

As we've written earlier, these are they that come through the tribulation period. They are not the Jews we are seeing today coming to Christ realizing He actually is *their* real Messiah of Isaiah 53. Paul wrote of these born again Jews "For the Scripture says whosoever believes on Him shall not be ashamed, for there is no difference between the Jew and the Greek (Gentiles), for the same Lord is Lord over all and is rich unto all that call upon Him." Romans 9:11, 12.

While our Savior was here on earth among His people the Jews, His 12 disciples, also Jews, took Him aside and asked Him to explain to them, privately, "When shall these things be." Matthew 24:21,22, "For then shall be great tribulation such as was not since the beginning of the world to this time, no, nor ever shall be. Except those days be shortened there should no flesh be saved, but for the elects sake those days shall be shortened." Christ was speaking to Jews about Jews.

". . . No flesh be saved . . ." Flesh is matter. Matter is flesh. Flesh means birds of the air, fishes of the sea, and man as well as animals of all sorts walking on the face of this earth Flesh is made of earth. Satan is still in charge of-dirt-the earth. Isaiah chapter 14, explains how satan has already destroyed-all-that was on this earth once before.

Here's the sign we've spoken of before but never mentioned. The sign of Zechariah 14:4, 5:
Verse 27 of Matthew 24, "For as the lightening comes from the East and shines even to the West, so shall also the coming of the Son of Man be." Paralleling with Mark 13:20, 22, 27.
Verses 30, 31, "Then shall appear the sign of the Son of Man in heaven: Then shall all the tribes of the earth mourn and they shall see the Son of Man coming in the clouds of heaven with power and great glory."

Zechariah 12:8-11, "In that day shall the Lord defend the inhabitants of Jerusalem and he that is feeble among them at that day shall be as David, and the house of David shall be as God, as the angel of the Lord before them. And it shall come to pass in that day that I will seek to destroy all the nations that come against Jerusalem. And I will pour out upon the house of David and upon the inhabitants of Jerusalem the Spirit of grace and of supplications, and they shall look upon Me whom they have pierced and they shall mourn for Him as one mourns for His only Son and shall be in bitterness for Him as one that is in bitterness for His First born. In that day there shall be a great mourning in Jerusalem . . ."

Revelation 1:7, Confirms these words of the prophet Zechariah; "Behold, He comes with clouds and every eye shall see Him and they also who pierced Him, and all kindreds of the earth shall wail because of Him. Even so, Amen." "CLOUDS" represent people. "A crowd of people."

John the beloved knew the Torah, for he—being so young, 15-17 scholars say—wouldn't let Jesus out of his sight, he was so in love with Him. Just as I am. And anyone who has ever been truly born-again. So, John knew there were quite a few resurrections and not just two, our Lord Jesus' and ours of 1 Thess. 4:16, 17.

And now to finish the last verse we intended to use of Matthew 24:31, "And He shall send His angels with a great sound of a trumpet and they shall gather together His elect from the four winds, from one end of heaven to the other." His elect being the remnant of Jews numbered as the sands of the sea.

"And shall not God avenge His own elect which cry day and night unto Him? Although He bears long with them?" Luke 18:7

Romans 8:31-33, "What shall we say then to these things? If God be for us who can be against us? He that spared not His own Son but delivered Him up for us all, how shall He not, with Him also, freely give us all things? Who shall lay anything to the charge of God's elect? It is God that justifies."

Colossians 3:10-14, "All have put on the NEW man which is renewed in knowledge after the image of Him that created Him, where there is neither Greek nor Jew; circumcism nor uncircumcision, Barbarian, Scythian (Italy), bond or free: but Christ is all, and in all" of us. "Put on therefore as the elect of God, holy and beloved, bowels of mercies, kindness, humbleness of mind, meekness, longsuffering, forbearing one another and forgiving one another, if any man has a quarrel against any; even as Christ forgave you, so also do you. And above all things put on charity which is the bond of perfectness."

Paul loved Gods elect just as much as he loved the Greek—Gentiles for he was both himself, both Jew and Gentile. His father a Roman Jew bought and paid for his son Saul later Paul to be "born Jew." Read your history people. 2 Timothy 2:10, "Therefore I endure all things for the elects sake, that they may also obtain the salvation which is in Christ Jesus with eternal joy."

"Paul, a servant of God and an apostle of Jesus Christ, according to the faith of God's elect, and the acknowledging of the truth which is after godliness." Titus 1:1.

Peter, another apostle of our Lord Jesus the Christ, explained in 1 Peter 1:1, about the "saved in Christ Jesus" Gentiles, of some five nations. His explanation: verse 2, "The elect according to the foreknowledge of God the Father through sanctification of the Spirit unto obedience and sprinkling of the Blood of Jesus Christ, Grace unto you and peace be multiplied." Peter was called to preach the gospel of the cross to his Jewish brothers and sisters.

John, also an apostle, though not John the beloved who wrote the book of Revelations, wrote to a certain honorable lady and her children, "The elder unto the elect lady and her children whom I love in the truth, and not only I, but also all they that have known the truth . . . The children of your elect sister, greet you, Amen." 2 John 1:1,13. The Jews.

CHAPTER 10

WHY A CROWN OF THORNS?

A surprising connection between Passover and the Crucifixion sheds light on who Yeshua really is and His importance to the world.

"Its a little known fact that there are several Rosh Hashanah's each year. Rosh Hashanah means "Head of the Year" or "New year." The Rosh Hashanah that most people are familiar with is the holiday that starts on the first of Tishrei, in the fall of the year. This is the traditional first day of the Jewish New Year, also known as the Feast of Trumpets," found in Leviticus 23:24.

"The second one we celebrate is the Rosh Hashanah for the Trees. When the Jewish people entered the Land of Israel, they were instructed not to take of the fruit of the trees for the first three years." Lev. 19:23. "Tu B'shvat is the New Year for the purpose of calculating the age of trees."

"The third is Rosh Hashanah for the kings, the New Year for the Kings. That day the Kings of Israel were crowned. This has great significance regarding the Crucifixion and the Messiah. To understand the full importance and meaning, you must realize that although He is called "Messiah" or "Mashiach", in Hebrew, Mashiach is not a detached word. We say "Melech haMoshiach"—or—"King Messiah." Melech means "King." Using this title immediately raises the thought, "How could

79

someone be a King without being crowned?" A King must be crowned."
So it was with every king in the history of Israel and the world. The Messiah, as understood by Israel being Melech haMoshiach, King Messiah, needed to be crowned.

"Before the crucifixion something was missing for Yeshua to be considered the True King Messiah and that was the crowning." This is the most important moment in the history of the world. The first crucial moment was when Israel was led out of Egypt and eventually into the "promised land." Israel is not just a little Nation in the Middle East. Israel is the reason that Christians and Muslims in the world today believe that there is only One God. Its not just another Nation. Israel brought the truth to the world that there is One God. There were two kinds of people in the world: Idol worshippers, pagans who believed in multiple gods, and then there were Jews, "The People of the Book," the people of Israel who believed in One God. It was Israel's purpose in history to bring the nation of One God to the world. Do you know how this happened? It was through Yeshua, you may know Him as Jesus.

"This is an uncomfortable statement for a Jewish person to consider, but when I am teaching, I ask, "Do you like the Bible Verse that says 'Israel is a light for the Nations?' Of course. Do you like Isaiah 2:3, "From Zion Torah comes forth and the Word of the Lord from Jerusalem?" Now, tell me 'Did the Word go out'?"

"Everyone from Israel to Europe to the world accepts that there is One God. By the means of whom did this happen? Isaiah? No. Moses? No. Perhaps it was through "The Word," Yeshua? It is unavoidable—it is a fact that must be acknowledged. Because of Him, people the world over came to believe that there is One God. Whether you like Him or not, you must admit, that, is a historical fact."

"The second crucial moment in the history of the world was the Moment of Crucifixion. At that moment Yeshua was about to be taken out of this world. But if we believe that He is the Messiah, then where was the Crown? A crowning is a very formal act that must take place at the appointed time. It can't be done at any arbitrary time, but the "Appointed Time." This time appointed in history that the kings are crowned is Passover Rosh Hashanah for the kings."

How do we know that Passover is Rosh Hashanah for the Kings? It is in the Tenakh's, though somewhat hidden. How do we know that the Kings of Israel are crowned at Passover? In the Book of One Kings, it reads, ". . . In the fourth year of Solomon's reign over Israel, in the Month of Ziv, which is the second month, that he began to build the House of Adonai." 6:1. It is repeated in 2nd. Chronicles 3:2, as well. The second month of the reign of King Solomon was crowned the month BEFORE! The month of ZIV is now known as the month of Iyar, which comes after the month of Nisan, when Passover is from this understanding, we can check it with the other Kings of Israel as well. There was a debate between the house of Hillel and the house of Shamai whether it was on the 15th or the 1st of the month, but the 15th was Passover night and this became the common understanding.

AND WHO SHALL
ANNOUNCE HIM?

So, now, how does the crowning relate to Yeshua, Jesus? If He truly is the Messiah, He could not depart from this world without being crowned. So who would do it? The Jews who believed in Him could not do it, so who did God pick for this time? When God pronounced His blessing upon Israel, He used an idol worshipper by the name of Ba'laam who did not even know what he was doing. This time?

"God picked the Roman soldiers. They didn't know what they were doing either. They were mocking Yeshua when they fashioned a crown of thorns and placed it upon His head. Do you remember what happened next? He was named and announced. The plaque that was placed above His head, in Hebrew read, "Yeshua Hanotgri Melech Ha'yehudim"—"Yeshua of Nazareth, King of the Jews!" He was crowned on the day of the Crowning of the Kings of Israel. He departed, fulfilling the WORD, King Messiah. Oh how I love and worship Him.

I, myself, am more guilty than anyone of repeating preacher after preacher on this very same subject. Why? Because I did not believe my own earthly dad was telling us kids *all* of the truth of Scripture. In my "ancient of days" now, believe me, now! I believe, I believe, I believe, please forgive me My own true Father in heaven. You Father, the God of Abraham, Isaac and Jacob, in Yeshua's holy Name, Amen (Hebrews say Ah-mean. The correct pronunciation).

"Blotting out the handwriting of ordinances that was against us which was contrary to us and took it out of the way nailing it to His (Roman) cross," by doing so, "having spoiled principalities and powers, He made a show of them openly, triumphing over them in it." Colossians 2:14, 15.

"And we are complete in Him which is the head of all principality and power." Col. 2:10. Col. 1:16, 17, "For by Him were all things created that are in heaven and in earth, visible and invisible whether they be thrones, or dominions, or principalities or powers; all things were created by Him and for Him: and He is before all things and by Him all things consist."

"Put on the whole armor of God that you may be able to stand against the wiles of the devil, for we wrestle not against flesh and blood, but against principalities, against powers, against the rulers of the darkness of this world, against spiritual wickedness in high places. Therefore take unto you the whole armor of God, that you may be able to withstand in the evil day, and having done all to stand. Stand therefore having your loins gird about with truth, and having on the breastplate of righteousness, and your feet shod with the preparation of the gospel of Peace. Above all, taking the shield of faith wherewith you shall be able to quench all the fiery darts of the wicked. And take the helmet of salvation and the sword of the Spirit which is the Word of God. Praying always with all prayer and supplication for all of the saints Eph. 6:11-18.

Romans 8:38, 39, "For I am persuaded that neither death, nor life, nor angels, nor principalities, nor powers, nor things present, nor things to come. Nor height nor depth, nor any other creature, shall be able to separate us from the love of God which is in Christ Jesus our Lord."

THE REST OF THE STORY

And even yet, that is not the whole picture. It is known that Yeshua took upon Himself the sins of the world and removed the curse by His Blood atonement. Which, by the way was the Father Adonai's BLOOD. It could not and did not touch the earth, an angel caught it in a heavenly utensil belonging in the heavenly tabernacle to be sprinkled on God's heavenly alter. After that, Revelation 8:1, happened, "And when He had opened the seventh seal there was silence in heaven about the space of half an hour." That was when the earthly flesh was burnt on the heavenly alter in Gods heavenly tabernacle. Christ's earthly "MAN" body.
Everyone remembers the picture of Mary, walking in the garden, finding the tomb empty, seeing a man dressed in "gardener's Clothing" and asked Him where "they have lain my Lord." Jesus said "Mary," She recognized Yeshua's voice, falling at His feet she would have touched Him but He said, "Don't touch me for I have not yet ascended to My Father and your Father." That accounts for the half hour.

Adam was created on the eighth day after God planted His "Garden in Eden" and had "no man to tell it" so He created Adam to tend, till and cultivate it. Now, think on this Crown—it is made of thorns. What is a thorn? The curse on the earth, Genesis 3:17-19, ". . . Cursed is the ground for your sake, in sorrow you shall eat of it all the days of your life; Thorns and thistles also shall it bring forth to you and you shall eat the herb of the field. In the sweat of your forehead shall you eat bread until you return to the ground, for out of it you were taken. For dust you are and unto dust you shall return."
Adam was created a Jew and so was his wife Eve. All the other races were created on the sixth day Genesis 1:26.

Yeshua redeemed not only the curse upon mankind from the disobedience in the Garden of Eden, but also with His Blood upon the Crown of thorns—He took away the curse of the earth. Not only that, but when Zechariah 14:4, 5, happens this whole-old-earth will be renewed to a new earth and it will be "Paradise on Earth." A wonderful pleasure gift for all of us who have "having done all, to stand" on the faith measured to all who have overcome until the very end.

Note: Paragraphs in parentheses are the words of Ya'acov Ben—Israel, Native Israeli & Hebrew Scholar at Hebrew University, Israel. 2006, Others are my earthly dads'. It goes without saying, Scripture is Scripture and it will be—word for word—forever.

CHAPTER 11

THE ORDER OF A MONARCHY

KING:
A male monarch. One that is the most powerful or eminent of a particular group—category—or place. (God-Christ)

KINGDOM:
A political or territorial unit that is ruled by a King or Queen. The eternal spiritual sovereignty of God. The realm over which the sovereignty extends.

PRINCE:
A hereditary ruler: King—The ruler of a principality. A male member of a royal family other than the Monarch. A nobleman of varying status or rank.

PRINCIPALITY:
A territory ruled by a prince or from which a prince derives his title. The position, authority, or jurisdiction of a prince, sovereignty. One of the nine orders of angels.

DUKE:
A nobleman with the highest hereditary rank especially a male of the highest grade of the peerage in a monarchy. A Duke ranks immediately below a Prince.

MARQUIS:
A nobleman ranking next below a Duke and above an Earl. Marquis' are rulers over various track's of land.

EARL OR A COUNT:
Equal in status. Noblemen of a rank below a Marquis and next above that of a Viscount. They are Governors of one of great divisions of the territories of a Marquis.

VISCOUNT:
A nobleman next below an Earl or a Count, and next above a Baron. A Viscount is a deputy of a Count or an Earl. A sheriff.

BARON:
A member of the lowest grade of Nobility. A nobleman just below a Viscount, and just above a Vassel. Holding—being a landlord—of land's under a direct grant from the King. A Baron is a member of the House of Lords. An important financier or industrialist, especially one with great power in a particular area, such as 'An Oil Baron.' A financial institute such as a Bank. A Banker.

VASSEL:
(In a Feudal system). A person granted the use of land in return for which he rendered homage, fealty and usually military service, or its equivalent to his Lord or other superior. A feudal tenant. A servant or a slave, usually a male.

FEUD OR FEUDAL:
Pertain to a feud: The holding of land for a fee. A bitter, continuous hostility especially between two families, clans, etc., often lasting years, generations, or centuries. To engage in a feud, an argument.

Satan is a vassel, the lowest of lows on the ladder of Monarch's. "The holding of land for a fee." Land is earth, dirt, dust, matter.

Flesh is all of these. Matter. Matter is substance a person can feel-touch-handle. Matter is flesh.

This order of a Monarchy should *open* many people's spiritual eyes as well as their Carnel ones. Carnality is an enemy towards' Adonai. Enmity is sinful jealousy, and it is what filled satan to the brim many millennia ago, and continues—still—to over flow his brim of hate for the Living God of Abraham, Isaac and Jacob, and all who love and worship Him. I bow to You Father. I salute You. I am forever in Your debt for paying such a horrible fee to set me free from this mad man satan, in Jesus holy Name. A Name above all Names named among men, Amen.
Is it any wonder we must be born-again? There are no two ways about it! We must be born-again!

> *He personally carried our sins in his body on the cross so that we can be dead to sin and live for what is right.* ***By his wounds you are healed*** *(NLT).*
>
> 1 Peter 2:24:

Ephesians 1:7 tells us that we have redemption through His blood—one translation says that He *purchased our freedom with the blood of His Son* (NLT).

God responds to faith. In fact, we can do nothing to please Him, NOTHING, unless it is done in faith (see Hebrews 11:6).

Remember this, satan is a vassel granted use of the earth and he rules it in a military way. Now, look back and understand the "Testimony of Paul." A military man himself. *We* must serve Jesus militarily. Understand your enemy, my old sarq. used to say.
King, Kingdom and Prince, all belong to Yeshua, and yet we still call Him Lord. I wonder why? Maybe its because all through the New Testament, all the apostle's called Him, "Lord." For this

reason I would say, so do we call Him Lord. Even a Lord in the order of the monarchy has everyone bowing their knee to them while they pass by or stand in front of you.

Satan was—past tense—lord of this earth after Adam and Eve ate the evil fruit of the "tree of good and evil fruit," that was in the Garden of Eden. Almighty God so plainly said in Genesis, chapter two, "You shall not eat of its fruit."

Our Savior so humbly went to the cross, died and arose again, taking away that part of the monarchy from satan. Making him now a vassel: "A person granted the use of the land in return for which he renders homage, featly, and usually military service, or its equivalent to his Lord (Lord Yeshua now made King)." A feudal tenant now on this earth. ". . . A servant or a slave, usually male." Ezekiel 28; the prophet of old calls satan, "a man." Such a horrible shame our Savior had to suffer such horrific agony to pay satan's ransom, he put on our heads. But Jesus agreed with His heavenly Father to endure all that, just to buy us back, and He handed all of us back over to the Father, when He fulfilled Calvary and Revelation chapter eight at the, "half hour of silence in heaven." We need no earthly, mortal, priest to take the blood of our lamb behind the veil into the holy of holies to redeem us of our sins for one more year, forward. We can now cry "Abba," which means "Father," for our own selves any place, any time, we have a need to and ask for our own sins to be forgiven. Praise our Lord Yeshua for that huge big favor. Yeshua is our very own personal lawyer to go before God and plead our cause for us. That is why God, at Calvary, split that two foot thick, cloth veil in the holy of holies, when Yeshua Himself, cried with a loud voice, while on the cross, "Abba! Abba! Why have You forsaken Me." Hung His head and died only to be resurrected.

For all these reasons, satan can no longer—himself "Come, and stand before God and accuse us" any more as he did before. Read the first chapter of Job for this to enlighten yourself.

This monarchy WILL be practiced in the New Earth called paradise. So, get used to it! Call Yeshua by His rightful Name—King Yeshua—and show Him all the honor He so rightly deserves!

CHAPTER 12

BOOKS

". . . All that dwell upon the earth shall worship him (antichrist), whose names are NOT written in the Book of Life of the Lamb slain from the foundation of the world. If any man has an ear, let him hear." Revelation 13:8, 9, Gen. 3:21, Rev. 17:8.

20:12, ". . . And the Book's were opened, and another Book was opened which is the Book of Life . . ."

21:27, ". . . There shall in no wise enter into it (New Jerusalem) anything that defileth, neither whatsoever works abomination or which makes a lie; but they which are written in the Lamb's Book of Life."

These are they that have survived the horrible holocaust of the Great Tribulation who were never saved or believed on our Savior. They may never have heard of Him in this life, or accepted or rejected His wonderful offer. But now, in this new earth they will have that chance to do just that. For they will live as long as trees. Rev. 22:19, "And if any man shall take away from the Words of the Book of this prophecy, God will take away his part out of the Book of Life, and out of the Holy City, and from the things written in this Book."

Phil. 4:3, ". . . I entreat you also true yokefellow, help those women which labored with me in the gospel with clement also, and with other my fellow-laborers whose names are in the Book of Life."

Malachi 3:16, 17, "Then they that feared the Lord spoke often one to another: And the Lord hearkened and heard it and a Book of Remembrance was written before Him for them that feared the Lord and that thought upon His Name. And they shall be Mine saith the Lord, in that day when I make up My jewels, and I will spare them, as a man spares His own Son that serve Him."

"And in that day shall the deaf hear the Words of the Book, and the eyes of the blind shall see out of obscurity and out of darkness." Isaiah 29:18.

"Then said I, 'Lo, I come: In the volume of the Book, it is written of me." (Yeshua) Psalms 40:7.

"You tell of my wanderings, you put my tears into Your bottle: Are they not in Your Book? Psalms 56:8.

"Let them be blotted out of the Book of the Living and not be written with the righteous." Psalms 69:28.

"Your eyes did see my substance yet being imperfect; and in Your Book all my members were written, which in continuance were fashioned, when, as yet, there was none of them." Psalms 139:16.

"Before I formed you in the belly I knew you and before you came forth out of the womb I sanctified you, and I ordained you a prophet to the nations."

Jeremiah 1:5

Moses pleads with Adonai to not be angry enough to destroy all the Israelites. He said to the Father, "Yet now If You will forgive their sin—; And if not, blot me, I pray You, out of Your book which You have written. And the Lord said to Moses, Whosoever has sinned against me, him will I blot out of My Book." Exodus 32:32, 33.

"... Until He that lets be taken out of the way ..."

91

"But in connection with the coming of our Lord Yeshua the Messiah and our gathering together to meet Him, we ask you brothers, not to be easily shaken in your thinking or anxious because of a spirit or a spoken message or a letter supposedly from us claiming that the Day of the Lord has already come. Don't let anyone deceive you in any way.

"For the Day will not come until after the Apostasy has come and the man who separates himself from Torah has been revealed, the one destined for doom. He will oppose himself to everything that people call a god or make and object of worship. He will put himself above them all, so that he will sit in the Temple of God and proclaim that he himself is God.

"Don't you remember when I was still with you, I used to tell you these things? And now you know what is restraining, so that he may be revealed in his own time. For already, this separating from Torah is at work secretly, but it will be secretly only until He who is restraining is out of the way. Then the one who embodies separation from Torah will be revealed, the one whom the Lord Yeshua will slay with the breath of His mouth and destroy by the glory of His coming." 2 Thessalonians 2:1-8.

"And now you know what is restraining." The restrainer is the Holy Spirit. The Holy Spirit is embodied in the human temple's of the Church of our Lord Yeshua the Messiah. When 1 Thessalonians 4:14-18, happens; the blessed hope all Christians hope and pray to happen, on an almost daily basis, these days:

". . . For since we believe that Yeshua died and rose again, we also believe that in the same way God, through Yeshua will take with Him those who have died. When we say this, we base it on the Lord's own Word: We who remain alive when the Lord comes will certainly not take precedence over those who have died. For the Lord Himself will come down from heaven with a rousing cry, with a call from one of His ruling angels and with God's shofar. Those who died united with Messiah will be the first to rise: then we who are left still alive will be caught up with them in the clouds to meet the Lord in the air, and thus we will always be with the Lord. So encourage each other with these words." Luke 9:27, Jude 14, Eph. 1:10, Matt. 16:27, 28.

Before we continue, there are a few things we must learn, just a little—wee tiny bit—more about. We will begin with God's very own, Garden of Eden:

Adam and Eve were cast out of The Garden of Eden. A Rabbi from Hebrew University in Israel explains they are of the opinion; and there are many scholars at Hebrew University. Not just there, but every University one can think of in many, many countries, so, yes, I am with the Rabbi on this one. He is of the opinion, "The Garden of Eden" was in Jerusalem, just as the spiral ladder of Jacob was there also. Many other things and people were there too, in earthly Jerusalem.

The nations of the world were created on the sixth day Genesis 1:26. Genesis 2:1-6, "God saw that it was good and He rested from all His labors." On the *seventh* day, He awoke on the eighth day and planted the seeds and things He had with Him, then, "He found that He had not made a man to till, tend, create and cultivate this newly made Garden He'd planted for Himself." Verse 7, explains then God formed the man of the dirt *outside* the Garden of God, breathed into his nostrils and the man became a "living soul." This was the beginning of the Jewish nation. Later He created Eve to be a companion to Adam.

Ezekiel, the prophets explains a bit more about the man and woman God wanted to tend His wonderful Garden:6:2-15.

"Son of man." Have you noticed—at—all-through Scripture, our Savior is called "Son of Man?" Not only that, He Himself calls Himself "Son of man." This is one of those rare—in your face"—subtle "heads up" our Father gives us every so often that I truly love, and want you, the reader, to love also.

"Son of man, Thus says the Lord God of Jerusalem, Your birth and your nativity is of the land of Canaan Your father was an Amorite and your mother was an Hittite. As for your nativity in the day you were born your naval was not cut, neither were you washed in water to comfort you. You were not salted at all, nor swaddled at all . . ."

We are praying, you, the reader, do remember what a salt covenant was. In the days of David and Saul was King, his son Jonathan and David made a salt covenant among themselves. Each of these families had a "family crest," used to seal letters to other people. If the seal was broken the receiving party was not to receive the letter and were to kill the messenger. Jonathan carved his "Crest of Israel" on Davids wrist, and David carved his "family Crest" into Jonathan's wrist. If was deep and would scar, but scar even more if they put an irritant in the newly carved flesh. That irritant was salt. It was called "Cutting a Covenant," according to Josephus.

". . . No one around you pitied you, to do any of these things unto you, to have compassion upon you, but you were cast out into an open field, to the loathing of your person in the day that you were born . . ."

Adam and Eve were cast out of the Garden of Eden. Neither Adam or Eve had their umbilical cords cut. Any land around Jerusalem is called Israel.

". . . And when I passed by you and saw you polluted in your own blood, I said unto you when you were in your own blood—LIVE—yea, I said unto you when you were in your own blood LIVE. I have caused you to multiply as the bud of the field and you were increased and waxed great and you are come to excellent ornaments: your breasts are fashioned, and your hair has grown, whereas before you were naked and bare . . ."

Solomon's Temple? Josephus wrote, "people of all nations came just to marvel at it, it was so beautiful" (Book of wars).

". . . Now when I passed by you and looked upon you, behold, your time was the time of love, and I spread my skirt over you . . ."

The Song of Solomon explains the beauty of the temple and how much Solomon loved "her." He explains about the temple the way a male poet would explain his love affair with "his fair one."

The book of Ruth a Gentile, slept at the feet of Boaz, a Jewish "type of Christ" gentleman who redeemed the Gentiles by "spreading his skirt" over the Gentile lady, Ruth, later, marrying her. As Jesus our Groom is going to marry us, Jesus a Jew. Us! We are the Gentile Jewish Church, the bride of Christ.

". . . And covered your nakedness; Yea, I swear unto you and entered into a Covenant with you. Saith the Lord God and you became Mine. Then I washed you with water, yea, I thoroughly washed away your blood from you, and I anointed you with oil . . ."

Mary, in the New Testament poured an alabaster bottle of oil on our Savior's feet, anointing them for the day of His burial, our Savior said. She washed His precious feet with the oil, her tears, and dried them with her long flowing hair.

Our Savior is a high priest, but not after the order of Aaron, of whom Moses and others poured a whole bottle of oil on Aaron when they anointed him to be high priest.

". . . I clothed you also with broidered work and shed you with Badger skin and I girded you about with fine linen and I covered you with silk. I decked you also with ornaments and I put bracelets upon your hands and a chain on your neck . . ."

Exactly what a king would wear. The temples of Solomon and Herod were dressed in these fine arrays.

". . . And I put a jewel on your forehead and earrings in your ears, and a beautiful crown upon your head. Thus were you decked with gold and silver, and your raiment was fine linen and silk and broidered work, you did eat fine—flower, and honey, and oil, and you did prosper into a kingdom. And, you, renowned, went forth among the heathen for your beauty, for it was perfect through my comeliness which I have put upon you, saith the Lord . . ."

The last verse of Matthew 23, our Savior, from a high place overlooking Jerusalem, said, "O Jerusalem, Jerusalem! How often would I have gathered you together under my wings as a chicken does her chicks, but you would not. You will not see Me again until you say, "Blessed is He who comes in the Name of the Lord."
That will certainly come to pass during that holocaust called the great tribulation. Zechariah chapters 12 and 13, explain just that, and they will be saying "Blessed in He who comes in the Name of the Lord," Zechariah 14.

But first the bride and the Groom must have their day in the Father's house. We only have *ONE* invitation to enter our Father's house, that of 1 Thess. 4:15, 16.

In speaking of the oil, Mary of the New Testament poured oil on the Savior's feet. There are three pressings of oil from the olive oil and used for various things in order of those three pressings. First pressing, is used for salads, perfumes, and anointing. Second, is mixed with flour for baking cakes, breads, crackers and for cooking. Third pressing is for oiling the feet after washing them from a long trek in the desert. They wore sandals! Used also for the burial of a body, three day's after death. The 2nd, pressing is also used for lighting the lamps.

CHAPTER 13

BRIDE-GROOM

Yeshua is our wonderful lovely and handsome bride-Groom. We, who are born-again, love Him and worship Him with every part of our being. With Adonai God's Agape love.

AGAPE: Is a Greek word for the God of Israel's love for His own. Webster's says this of God's Agape Love: "The love of God, Christ for mankind. The brotherly love or spiritual love of one Christian for another, corresponding to the love of God for man."

When we surrender all-everything-our lives, our love, our spirit, soul, all our mind to Jesus upon our born-again experience to the Father through His Son Yeshua, we-in turn—fall whole-heartedly in AGAPE love with Jesus. Who—in their right mind—would NOT love someone who gave His all so we could call God ABBA again without shame. Christ paid a horrible price for our freedom to love Him and Yeshua with (again) all of our being. Agape love, unconditional love.

The Romans called the love of a married couple: EROS love, identified with cupid; a winged figure of a child with the power to shoot arrows at them filled with sexual love. Psychiatry calls this our libido.
Is it any wonder we are so in love with Jesus?

"Their line has gone out through all the earth, and their words to the end of the world. And in them He has set a tabernacle for the sun, which is as a bride-Groom Coming out of His chamber . . ." Psalms 19:2-5. This is fulfillment of Zechariah 14:4, 5.

"I will greatly rejoice in the Lord, my soul shall be joyful in my God: for He has clothed me with the garments of salvation, He has clothed me with the robe of righteousness as a bride-Groom decks Himself with ornaments, and a bride adorns herself with her jewels." Isaiah 61:10.

"For as a young man marries a virgin, so shall your sons marry you: And as the bride-Groom rejoices over the bride, so shall your God rejoice over you."
Isaiah 62:5

All these wonderful Scriptures speak of our blessed Savior. Our Groom of Revelation Chapter 19.

"Then the disciples of John came and said to Jesus, why do we and the Pharisees fast often, but Your disciples do not? Jesus replied, 'Can the children of the bride-Chamber mourn as long as the bride-Groom is with them? But the days will come when the bride-Groom shall be taken from them and then they shall fast." Matt. 9:14, 15, Mark 2:19, Luke 5:24, 34.

John Baptist said, "You yourselves bear me witness that I said 'I am not the Christ, but I am sent before Him. He that has the bride is the bride-Groom which stands and hears Him, rejoices greatly because of the bride-Grooms VOICE: this, my joy, therefore, is fulfilled." John 3:29.

Matthew 25:1-11, explains about the ten Virgins, five were wise, five were foolish. The foolish wasted their oil wanting to borrow oil from the five who were wise. But no ONE can SHARE their infilling of the Holy Spirit (John 14:) with evidence you've received it by your speaking in an unknown language. Book of Acts.

Our Jesus said "My sheep KNOW my VOICE and another they will not follow."

Scripture requires two or three witnesses to establish a thing written in it. We've just given you seven witnesses (Above) of our Savior Jesus being the bride-Groom. Plus six more on the witnesses themselves: Num. 35:30, Deut. 17:6, 19:15, Matt. 18:16, 2 Cor. 13:1, 1 Tim. 5:19.

"The heavens declare the glory of God and the firmament shows His handiwork. Day unto day utters speech and night unto night shows knowledge. There is no speech nor language where their voice is not heard. Their line is gone out through all the earth and their words to the end of the world. In them has He set a tabernacle for the sun. Which is as a bridegroom coming out of his chamber and rejoices as a strong man who runs a race." And wins. Ps. 19:1-5
"I will greatly rejoice in the Lord, my soul shall be joyful in my God; for He has clothed me with the garments of salvation, He has covered me with the robe of righteousness, as a bridegroom decks himself with ornaments and as a bride adorns herself with her jewels." Isaiah 61:10.

"For as a young man marries a virgin, so shall your sons marry you; and as the bridegroom rejoices over the bride, so shall your God rejoice over you. I have set watchman upon your walls O Jerusalem, which shall never hold their peace day or night. You that make mention of the Lord, do not keep silent, and give Him no rest until He makes Jerusalem a praise in the earth." Isaiah 62:5-7.

These Scriptures speak of the land. The land where Almighty God said-and has proved—He has set His Name in Jerusalem and "Jerusalem is mine saith the Lord." Jerusalem belongs to

God and has set His One, Only Begotten Son Yeshua as King over it. Remember what the thief on a cross beside Yeshua said, "Remember me Lord, when You come into Your Kingdom." Kings are the only people on earth, in heaven or elsewhere, who have Kingdoms.

"Can the children of the bride chamber mourn as long as the bridegroom is with them? But the days will come when the bridegroom shall be taken from them and then shall they fast." Matthew 9:15.

Where were these people and Yeshua when the disciples of John Baptist asked Yeshua about fasting? Where was the "bride chamber" Yeshua spoke of? Jerusalem. They were standing in Jerusalem. On the soil of Jerusalem. Letting all of us know just where our worthy King Yeshua, has His Kingdom. This Scripture can also be found in Mark 2:19, and Luke 5:39.

Matthew 25:1-18, explains of the ten virgins-in Jerusalem—five which ran out of oil for their lamps. While they went to buy more oil to burn in their lamps the bridegroom came and swept the bride away.

The oil for the burning in their lamps was the second pressing of the olive oil. The oil used for cooking, baking, frying, and burning of the proverbial, "burning of the midnight oil." "Oh," you say, "Now I get it." I thought you would.

Then, we have this in John 3:29, 30, the words of John the Baptist testifying how he is a witness to THE bride-Groom, Yeshua, ". . . I am sent before him. He that has the bride is the bridegroom: but the friend of the bridegroom which stands and hears Him rejoices greatly (meaning himself) because of the bridegroom's voice: therefore, this my joy is fulfilled. He must increase, but I must decrease." As for myself, I too exalt our Savior far above myself, who is nothing but dirt. He is made of heavenly material, I too say, and try to live life as though Yeshua has increased so greatly in me, that I am nothing. All I want people to see when they look at me, is Yeshua, Yeshua, Yeshua.

CHAPTER 14

A SHORT HISTORY LESSON

"And God said, 'Let us make man in our image,
After our likeness and let them have dominion over the fish of
the sea, over the fowl of the air, over the cattle, over all the earth
and over every creeping thing that creeps upon the earth.' So God
created man in His own image,
In the image of God created He him;
Male and female created He them.
And God blessed them. And God said 'Be fruitful and multiply
and replenish the earth, subdue it, have dominion over the fish
of the sea, over the fowl of the air, over every living thing that
moves upon the earth. And God saw everything that He had made
and behold, it was very good.
And the evening and the morning were the sixth (6) day."

Genesis 1:26-28,31

Six—6—times God said these words "image" and "create."

"The heavens and the earth were FINISHED, and *ALL* . . .—
ALL—ALL—the host of them.
"And on the seventh (7th) day God ENDED-ENDED-ENDED
His work which He had made, and He rested on the seventh (7th)
day from all His work which He had made." Genesis 2:1, 2, Heb.
4:4-10, "For He spoke in a certain place on this wise; And God
did rest the seventh (7th) day from all His work. And in this place
again, if they shall enter into my rest. There remains therefore a

rest to the people of God. For he that is entered into his rest, he also has ceased from his own works as God did from His."

What was it our Lord Jesus said to the thief on the cross—dying—right beside Him? "Today you shall be with me in paradise."
"Seeing then, that we have a Great High Priest that has passed into the heavens Jesus the Son of God. Because we have not a High Priest that cannot be touched with the feeling of our infirmities; but was in all points tempted like as we are yet WITHOUT sin." Wow! "Then let us therefore come boldly to the throne of grace, that we may obtain mercy and find grace to help us in time of need." V's 14-16.

The Lord God Adonai said, "But the seventh is the Sabbath of the Lord your God. In it you shall do no work, nor your son, nor your daughter, your man-servant, your maid-servant your cattle nor your stranger that is in your gates." Exodus 20:10.

"You speak to the children of Israel saying, 'Verily My Sabbaths you shall keep for it is a sign between Me and you through-out your generations so that you may know I AM the Lord that does sanctify you. It is a sign between me and the children of Israel for ever . . . And on the seventh day He rested" Exodus 31:13, 17.

"It shall be a Sabbath of rest unto you and you shall afflict your souls, by a mandate forever."

Lev. 16:31

". . . The seventh day is the Sabbath of rest, a holy convocation, you shall do no work therein, it is the Sabbath of the Lord in all your dwellings."

Lev. 23:3

". . . In the seventh month, in the first day of the month you shall have a Sabbath, a memorial of the blowing of trumpets, a holy convocation. Nine days after this on the 10th day of this seventh month there shall be a day of atonement: It shall be a holy convocation to you. You shall afflict your souls and offer an offering made by fire to the Lord . . . (V-31) You shall do no manner of work. It shall be a statute for-ever throughout all your generations in all your dwellings." Lev. 23:24.

The seventh month is Tishri.
The first day of the month is the 15th until the 22nd It is the Feast of Tabernacles, sometimes called the Feast of Ingathering, or the Feast of Harvest. The people were required to build and live in booths, their roof's loosely woven with palm branches, so they could view the stars at night. Days of fun, laughter, eating and drinking. These are our months of September/October.

"In the 15th day of the seventh month, when you have gathered in the fruit of your land, you shall keep a Feast to Me the Lord for seven days. On the eighth day shall be a Sabbath. And you shall, on the first day of it, you shall take the good boughs of goodly trees, branches of palm trees, and the boughs of thick trees and willows of the Brook, and you shall rejoice before the Lord for seven days. And you shall keep a Feast unto the Lord seven days in the year. It shall be a statute *forever* in your generations. You shall celebrate it in the seventh month Tishri. Verse 42, You shall live in booths seven days, all that are Israelite born shall dwell in booths." Lev. 23:39. Verse 43, "That your generations may know that I made the children of Israel dwell in booths when I brought them out of the land of Egypt. I AM the Lord your God."

"And on the Sabbath day, two lambs of the first year without spot, and two tenth deals of flower for a meat offering, mingled with oil and the drink offering thereof. This is a burnt offering of every Sabbath, beside the continual burnt offering, and His drink offering. Verse 8, . . . It is a sweet savor to the Lord." Numbers 28:9, 10.

The Sweet Savor of the sacrifices, Genesis 8:21, Ex. 29:18. Type of Christ, 2 Cor. 2;14, Eph. 5:2, a sacrifice to God a sweet savor. Gen. 27:4, Matt. 16:23, Mark 8:33.

"And remember you were a servant in the land of Egypt, and the Lord your God brought you out with a mighty hand and by a stretched out Arm. Therefore the Lord your God commanded you to keep the Sabbath day." Deut. 5:15.

"The Lord God of Israel said, "All who come to the Lord, no matter what type you are; Blessed are they, the man who keeps the Sabbath and the son of man that takes hold of the meaning of it to keep their hand from doing evil. Includes the sons of strangers, eunuchs, even to them, I will give in My house and within my walls a place, and a name better than of sons and of daughters, I will give them an everlasting name that shall not be cut off. The sons of strangers themselves, all they who join themselves to the Lord to serve. Him, to be His servants who keeps His Sabbath from polluting it and takes hold of My covenant. Even all they will I bring to my holy mountain, make them joyful in My house of prayer. Their burnt offerings and their sacrifices shall be accepted upon My alter for My house shall be called a house of prayer for all people. The Lord God which gathers the outcasts of Israel says, Yet will I gather others to Him beside those that are already gathered to Him." Isaiah 56:1-8, Eze. 20:10-12.

We had to give you these 18 Scriptures so you would know and understand Genesis 2:2, "And the Lord God rested from all His labor, blessed it," and repeated "The Lord God rested from all His labor on the seventh day."

Now, we must learn WHO the Lord of the Sabbath is *AND* was made for; "The Son of Man is Lord even on the Sabbath day." Matt. 12:8.

105

"The Sabbath was made for man, and not man for the Sabbath, therefore, the Son of man *is* Lord also on the Sabbath." Mark 2:27, 28, Luke 6:51.

Isaiah said of the Israelites, "Except the Lord of the Sabbath had left us a seed . . ."

Paul an apostle, wrote about the Sabbath day; "For you yourselves know perfectly well that the day of the Lord . . ." Read again all the aforementioned Scripture to refresh your memory, "The Day of the Lord" is the Sabbath day. ". . . So comes as a thief in the night." 1 Thess. 5:2. Have you "taken hold" of it yet?

In speaking of the Israelites, Peter preached this to them, in Acts 2:20, "The sun shall be turned into darkness, the moon to blood before that Great Notable Day of the Lord (Sabbath)." The Sabbath day.

"For the Great Day of His Wrath . . ." Rev. 6:16, 17, 16:4-7, James 5:4.

"He who has an ear let him hear . . ."

Websters is great at expounding on Words. Some, we feel we know enough about to get by. But really? Do we? How many of us really want to know the alpha and omega of a word. Not just any word. For this we must return back. Sometimes we have to take a few steps back just to go forward one step.

Beginning, once again, at Genesis 1:26, 27, "And God said, 'Let us make man in our own image . . . in the image of God He made man and woman . . ."
In another place in Scripture it reads, "What is man that You are so mindful of him?"

For this we must consider the word ANTHROPOLOGY. Oh, sure. We know it means something that a trained Archaeologist would use in their "everyday" speech. But, what do I know? I'm just a simple layman trying to get by, day by day.

ANTHROPOLOGY: "The science that deals with the origins, physical, and cultural development, racial characteristics, and social customs, and beliefs of Mankind. The study of man's similarities to and divergence from other animals. The science of man and his works. The study of the nature and essence of man, also called philosophical Anthropology."

ESSENCE: "The basic, real, and invariable nature of a person or thing, or its significant individual feature or features."

THIS, dear friends is what God and Messiah made on the sixth day of His Creating, "Let us make man in our image . . . So He created man and woman in His image."

Taking notice of part of the definition of anthropology, "the study of man's similarity to and divergence from other animals." We are lumped into the category of "animals?" Yes! Well, you say, what is animal, and why are we different? Why does God call us creatures?

So glad you asked that!

ANIMAL: "Any living thing . . ." Wow! "Any living thing having certain characteristics distinguishing *it* from a plant, as in having the ability to move voluntarily, having the presence of a nervous system and greater ability to respond to stimuli. Pertaining to the physical or carnel nature of man, living, breathing air, breath."

From this we learn man animal. There's no difference except for a nervous system. If any of you have read anything we've written on our brain, would know everyone's nervous system is spread throughout our whole body and more so in our brain. Our bodies just carry us—our spirit and soul—around where ever we wish to go. We—our bodies—are just clay vessels. Consider a pot. We use them to hold "stuff" in, whether it be liquid or solid, only with legs and arms and not handles. It is our spirit and soul, that lives in our brain that satan wants and spends our whole live trying to get into his possession knowing our vessel, our carnel bodies will follow. Our spirit and soul lives in our brain. That's why Solomon wrote when we die our spirit—our breath—goes back to God who gave it. Then Paul wrote in the New Testament when we die our soul sleeps. Job said, our bodies go back to the earth, because everything we put into the earth try's to grow itself. Adonai explained to Adam "dust you are and to dust you shall return."

Another word we must learn and that is this *ANTHROPOGRAPHY:* "The branch of Anthropology that describes the varieties of mankind and their geographical distribution."

Genesis 1:20-26, "And God said . . ." Everytime God speaks, things come into existence. That is another of the many reasons He needed an earthy-clay vessel—for our Savior to inhabit while here on earth. Jesus said "Every Word I speak is of my Father," John 14.

"And God said let the waters bring forth abundantly, the moving creature that has life and fowl that may fly above the earth in the open firmament of heaven. And God created great whales, and every living Creature that moves, which the waters brought forth abundantly, after their kind, and every winged fowl after their kind, and God saw that it was good and God blessed them saying, Be fruitful and multiply and fill the waters in the seas and let fowl multiply in the earth. And the evening and the morning were the fifth day. And God said, let the earth bring forth the living creature after his kind, cattle and creeping thing and beast of the earth after his kind: and it was so. And God made the beast of the earth after his kind, and cattle after his kind, and everything that creeps upon the earth after his kind and God saw that it was good. And God said let us make man in our image after our likeness and let them have dominion over the fish of the sea and over the fowl of the air and over the cattle and over all the earth and over every creeping thing that creeps upon the earth."

From these Scriptures and Websters definition of several Anthropo's that man and animals were created on the sixth day. Birds and fish on the fifth day. Adonai God and our dictionaries agree, together man and animal are lumped together in one category, ANIMAL. With one difference, our nervous system throughout, that animals don't have. And yes, they too have a nervous system, else how could they also feel pain. Its just different. But, what do I know, I'm not a doctor.

Animals, birds and many fishes were distributed throughout the world. Some in warm to hot climates, some to cold and or freezing climates and of course, some to intermediate countries. THEN men and women (plural) were created into the many race's to be distributed throughout where ever the animals had also been placed.

ANTHROPOGENESIS: "The Genesis-or-development of the human—race (s), especially as a subject of scientific study. Also ANTHROPOGENETIC, the study of DNA." Is it any wonder the sages of old, the prophets, questioned God on, "What is man that you are so mindful of him?"

And YES! These races, created on the sixth day *were* distributed into their proper places around the world. And NO! Adam or Eve were not created in this first creation. Lets examine the Scripture and see: AGAIN? "Line upon line, precept upon precept . . ."

"And Adonai God saw everything that He had made and looked, it was very good. And the evening and the morning were the sixth day." Gen. 1:31.

"And God saw EVERYTHING . . ." Everything means just that. ALL. There's nothing else. Zip.

"Thus the heavens and the earth were FINISHED!" The end. NO more. Nada.

". . . Finished and all the host of them. And on the seventh day God ENDED His work which He had made and He rested on the seventh day from all His work which He had made. And God blessed the seventh day and sanctified it because that in it He had rested from all His work which God created and made.

"These are the generations of the heavens and the earth when they were created in the day that the Lord God made the earth and the heavens, and every plant of the field *before* it was in the earth and every field be-it grew: for the Lord God had not caused it to rain upon the earth . . ." Genesis 1:31, 2:1-5.

Scolars say, "When God mentions something. Anything. No matter how miniscule it may seem to you, He wants us to STOP, back up and read it again." In this case we will read Genesis 1:29,30, Although we did not add it. Yet. We will now, for you, dear readers, to understand this tiny little nugget of cryptic note our Father wants us to "Search the Scripture and see that, "I Am good." And in another place "Rightly divide" My Word. And in-still-another place—WISDOM—is given by Adonai God Ex. 31:3, 1 Kings 3:12, 4:29, 1 Chr. 22:12, 2 Chr. 1:10, Ezra 7:25, Prov. 2:6, Eccl. 2:26, Dan. 2:20, Acts 6:10, 7:10, 2 Pet. 3:15. Wisdom obtained in answer to prayer, 1 Ki. 3:9, 10:6, Prov. 2:3, Dan. 2:21. Oh how our heavenly Father knows the many times I've agonized in pray because I could not figure out a verse, or for that matter, a whole chapter! On the other hand I am eternally grateful for what amount He has blessed me with, AND the knowledge to put it together like "Pieces of a Puzzle" lying loosely on the ground. There's a virtual "Other World" in Scripture for all those willing, and do, search out the "way down deep" meaning of, not just one, but a myriad of hidden messages in His Word if we just want to "seek and you shall find."

Genesis 1:29, 30, "And God said-look-I have given you every herb, bearing seed, which is upon the face of the earth . . ." Not just some small little plot of land over here "for you," and, "you can have that one over there" NO! "The face of the whole earth!" Earth is round and there is no end to round. Round is round and no matter how you try to make round in any other configuration, it is still ROUND.

". . . upon the face of all the earth, and every tree in the which is the fruit of a tree yielding seed. To you it shall be for meat. And to every beast of the earth, and to every fowl of the air, and to everything that creeps upon the earth, where in there is life I have given every green herb for meat and it was so. And God saw everything that He had made and behold! It was very good, and the evening and the morning were the sixth day."

By these words of these three verses we know God had everything on this round earth for all the birds, fishes, animals and people (who are lumped in the "animal" section) needed to survive, forever. How do we know this? As we said earlier "anything we put into the ground tries to grow itself. A cycle of RE-growth. For everything.

The plants, herbs and seeds God is speaking of in Genesis 2:5, 6, is what was "left over," or some of what was left over for His garden He had planned for when He had finished His house. When one plans to build or RE-build a house, as with a car, truck, van, the accessories are added *after* the thing one is working on is FINISHED! You have *nothing* to add accessories to if it isn't finished. Therefore God wanted a garden He could come and relax in, in "the cool of the evening." Gen. 3:8. Verse 5, 6, "And every plant of the field before it was in the earth, and every herb of the field before it grew: for the Lord God had not caused it to rain upon the earth, and there was not a man to till the ground . . ."

111

The Key Word here is an action word and it is *TILL:* "One who tills, a farmer."

FARMER: "A person who farms. A person who undertakes some service, such as, the care of children or the poor, at a fixed PRICE?"

HUSBANDMAN: "The cultivation and production of edible crops or of animals for food. Agriculture, farming. The science of raising crops or food, or animals. The management of domestic affairs, or of resources. "Or raising children!

Oh people! I'm at a loss for words if you cannot read into these explanations of our Messiah Yeshua!

1 – He redeemed us "at a fixed price."

2 – Messiah said "Suffer the little children to come to Me."

3 – Messiah said "Blessed are the poor . . ."

4 – Isaiah said of Messiah ". . . Unto us a child is born, unto us a Son is given and the government . . ." domestic affairs and resources. ". . . shall be upon His shoulder: and His Name shall be called Wonderful, Counselor, The Mighty God, The Everlasting Father, The Prince of Peace." A garden is PEACEful. "Of the increase of His government and peace there shall be no end, upon the throne of David and upon His Kingdom to order it, and to establish it with judgment and with justice from henceforth, even forever. The Zeal of the Lord of hosts will perform this." Isa. 9:6, 7, Gen. 13:10 EZE. 28:13, 36:35, Joel 2:3, John 18:1.

5 – ". . . Because they have taken away My Lord and I know not where they have lain Him. When she had said this she turned around and saw Jesus standing and knew not that it was Jesus . . . She supposing Him to be the GARDENER.?!" John 20:13-15. Wow! If the eyes of our heart and soul are still not open after these Words then we must, without doubt be deader than the "doorknob" so famously spoken of.

"Death reigned from Adam to Moses even over them that had not sinned after the similitude of Adams transgression who is the figure of Him that was to come . . . And so it is written, The first man Adam was made a living soul; the last man Adam was made a quickening spirit. Allbeit that was not first which is spirit (Yeshua), but that which is natural (Adam); and afterward that which is spiritual. The first man is of the earth, earthy: the second man is the Lord from heaven. As is the earthy, such are they also that are earthy, and as is the heavenly, such are they also that are heavenly. As we have borne the image of the earthy, we shall also bear the image of the heavenly. Now this I say, brethren, that flesh and blood cannot inherit the kingdom of God, neither does corruption inherit incorruption." 1 Cor. 15:45-50. Top, Rom. 5:14. But! Flesh and bone *can* enter into the heavenlies, Luke 24:39. A glorified bag of flesh and bones that is.

Genesis 2:5-14, ". . . And there was not a man to till the ground. But there went up a Mist from the earth and watered the whole face of the ground . . ." Face of *the* ground wherewith God had picked to design, plan and plant His restful place to relax in "the cool of the evening." ". . . And the Lord God formed man:" Ah Ha Dam (A man) to till the plot of land Zion which means Jerusalem, ". . . Formed the man of the dust of the ground and breathed into his nostrils the breath of life and man became a living soul. And (then) the Lord God planted a garden eastward in Eden and there He put the man (the Ah ha Dam = the man) who He had formed. And out of (that) the ground, the Lord God made to grow every tree that is pleasant to the sight and good for food; the tree of life also in the middle of the garden and the tree of knowledge of good and evil fruit. And a river went out of Eden to water the garden . . ."

Remember now, the garden is planted outside of Eden. ". . . And from there—the river in Eden—parted and (split) became into four heads. The name of the first is PISON, that is (the one) which compasses the whole land of Havilah where there is gold,

113

and the gold of the land is good: there is BDELLIUM and the onyx stone.

"The name of the second river is Gi hon: the same is it that compasses the whole land of Ethiopia. And the name of the third river is Hiddekel: that is it which goes toward the east of Assyria. And the fourth river is Euphrates. Then the Lord God (again) took the man and put him into the garden of Eden to dress it and to keep it."

We do pray you see the wide difference between the men and women of all races of Genesis 1:26, 27. Both man and woman created in ONE day. THE MAN THE WOMAN of each race of the whole world, "And God said be fruitful and multiply and replenish the earth . . ." The earth is dirt. The earth is round. Yes, ROUND. ". . . And have dominion over the fish of the sea, the fowl of the air and every living thing that moves upon the earth." Earth is round.

Now, never again do we have to wonder why our precious Messiah, "Then shall the Lord go forth and fight against those nations as when He fought in the day of battle (Joshua's battle). And His feet shall stand in that day upon the Mount of Olives which is before Jerusalem . . . And the Lord my God shall come, and all the saints with Him." Zech. 14:4, 5, Isaiah 64:1-3. "Yet have I set My King upon My holy mountain My holy hill Zion." Ps. 2:6, 1 Thess. 3:13. Which is Jerusalem.

Remember Cain? "And Cain said unto the Lord, 'My punishment is greater than I can bear. Behold you have driven me out this day from the face of the earth, and from Your face shall I be hid; and I shall be a fugitive and a vagabond in the earth, and it shall come to pass that everyone . . . ? EVERYONE?? Who are these "everyone?" Of course, now, you the reader, surely do know who these "everyone's" are, now. Where before you wondered all your life who were these people in Nod where Cain went, and took a wife." Genesis 4:13-17.

Adam/Eve were the beginning of the Jewish Nation.

What follows next is the genealogy of Adam to Noah. Our Bible does not give the genealogy of the 6th day race distributed throughout the world. Reason for that? Each country keeps its own records, even Israel. Read Josephus. When God names-names, its important to pay attention and find out why. And now, as Paul Harvey used to say at the end of each broadcast, "And now heres the rest of the story."

Father	Years	Son	Meaning of Their NAMES
ADAM	130 + 800 = 930	SETH	Man of red tint
SETH	105 + 807 – 912	ENOS	Man
ENOS	90 + 815 = 905	CAINAN	Possessor
CAINAN	70 + 840 = 910	MAHALALEEL	Praise of God
MAHALALEEL	65 + 830 = 895	JARED	Low Ground
JARED	162 + 800 – 962	ENOCH (walked with God)	Raised to heaven. Teacher—Perfected humanity
ENOCH Then he was not	65 + 300 = 365	METHUSELAH	Man of offspring died yr. of the Flood
METHUSELAH	187 + 782 = 969	LAMECH	POWERFUL
LAMECH	182 + 595 = 777	NOAH	To rest/give comfort
NOAH	500 + 350 = 950 + 100 to build the ARK	SHEM/HAM/ JAPHETH	*SHEM* Special blessing is Promised.

HAM AFRICA
warm (dark) ica is identified with Jupiter Ammon & Zeus. These words mean hot, Fervent, Sunburnt. ART Literature and science,

Alphabetic writing, weaving of cloth, architecture, astronomy plastic art, sculpture, navigation, agriculture, painting, music.

*JAPHETH:*nd son.
Correct spell. YAPHAH meaning FAIR like the root-wood meaning Light-Complexion, races from Greece's shores & islands, coasts of the Great Sea, Asia Minor, Asia and Europe "Man of red tint. Man, possessor, praising God. (lives at) low ground—raised to heaven: (was) a teacher, perfected humanity. Man of offspring died year of the flood. POWERFUL. To rest, to give comfort.

SHEM: "special blessing is promised."

Ham: "Dark ica Africa, warm. Is identified with Jupitar (Greek) AMMON (Egypt) and Zeus (Greek again) These words mean HOT, FERVENT, SUNBURN. Master of Art, literature and science, Alphabetic writing, weaving of cloth, architecture, astronomy, plastic art, sculpture, navigation, agriculture, painting and music."

JAPHETH: Second son: "Correct spelling YAPHAH, meaning fair skinned like the root-wood meaning light complexion races of Greece's shores and Islands, coasts of the Great sea, Asia Minor (Turkey) Asia and Europe."

CHAPTER 15

DNA? GENES?

"I will greatly rejoice in the Lord, my soul shall be joyful in my God; for He has clothed me with the garments of salvation, He has covered me with the robe of righteousness, as a bride—Groom decked Himself with ornaments, and as a bride adorns herself with her jewels."

Isaiah 61:10

This next verse speaks of Christ's Church, His bride, as the daughter of Zion, and we are for our Mother—the Elect Mother is Israel; "Behold the Lord has proclaimed to the end of the world, say you to the daughter of Zion Behold, your salvation comes, behold. His reward is with Him and His Work before Him." Isaiah 62:11. Verse 12, goes with it; "And they shall call them, The holy people The redeemed of the Lord: and you shall be called, Sought Out, a city not forgotten."

These Scriptures are the fulfillment of 1 Thess. 4:16, 17. Isaiah 63; is the fulfillment of Revelation 19:13, when We, of Isaiah 62:11, come back with Him in Zechariah 14:4, 5.
"When You did terrible things which we did not look for, You came down, the mountains flowed down at Your presence." Another fulfillment of Zechariah 14:4, 5.

Isaiah 64:3

". . . Because the former troubles are forgotten, and because they are hid from My eyes. For behold, I create new heavens and a new earth: and the former shall not be remembered nor come into our mind. You, be glad and rejoice for ever in that which I create: for behold, I create Jerusalem a rejoicing and her people a joy. And I will rejoice in Jerusalem and joy in my people: and the voice of weeping shall be no more heard in her, nor the voice of crying. There shall be no more thence an infant of days, nor an old man that has not filled his days, for the child shall die a hundred years old; but the sinner, being a hundred years old shall be accursed. And they shall build houses and live in them, they shall plant vineyards and eat the fruit of them."

Isaiah 65:16-21

These Scriptures are speaking of all those who survived the great tribulation and lived to tell about it. They still will have their mortal bodies, and that is why they will live and die at a hundred years old. They will, unbelievably, have a second chance to know and serve our precious Messiah, or reject him and end up in hell. God does not send people to hell. People send themselves to hell. They have free-will, just as we did here on this earth as Mortals. YOU and YOU alone choose where you will go when your life is over. No one chooses for you. Just you decide that.

"The wolf and the Lamb shall lie down together, and the lion shall eat straw like the bullock, and dust shall be the serpent's meat (still?!). They shall not hurt or destroy in all My holy mountain saith the Lord."

Isaiah 65:25

"Thus saith the Lord, the heaven is My throne and the earth is My footstool . . ." Isaiah 66:1.

"Then will I cause to cease from the cities of Judah, and from the streets of Jerusalem the voice of mirth, and the voice of gladness, and the voice of the bride Groom and the voice of the bride, for the land shall be desolate." Jeremiah 7:34, Ezekiel 38.

118

Earlier in these writings we explained to you how Scripture read "antichrist cannot reveal himself until "He that let's will let until He—Holy Spirit—be taken out of the way? Well, this is that, that was holding this world together until now.

"... For in the wilderness shall waters break out, and streams in the desert. And the parched ground shall become a pool and the thirsty land springs of water: in the habitation of dragons, where each lay, shall be grass with reeds and rushes. A highway shall be there, and a way, and it shall be called The way of holiness; the unclean shall not pass over it but it shall be for those, the wayfaring men, though fools shall not err therein . . . But the redeemed shall walk there, and the ransomed of the Lord shall return and come to Zion with songs and everlasting joy upon their heads: they shall obtain joy and gladness and sorrow and sighing shall flee away."

Isa. 35:6-10

You, the reader, may think this is complicated, but bear with us, and you'll see how neatly it unfolds before your spiritual eyes.

Isaiah 26:17-20, In speaking of the one third remnant of the Jews in Israel during the great tribulation. Of course we know the Church has been taken out a few years earlier. We will get to that a little later:
"Like as a woman with child, we have been in pain. We have, as it were brought forth wind, we have not brought any deliverance in the earth, neither have the inhabitants of the world fallen. Your dead men shall live together with my dead body shall they arise. Awake and sing you that dwell in the dust: for your dew is as the dew of herbs, and the earth shall cast out the dead. Come, my people, you enter into your chambers, and shut your doors behind you. Hide yourselves as it were for a little moment, until the indignation is over-past." Matt. 24:15, Dan. 11; Rev. 14:10, 20:16.

As we can see from what the writer is trying to say, is—to the dead—as well as those alive who are wise enough to escape the great tribulation period. Of course he is writing to the Jews.

Revelation 12:1-12, Genesis 37:1-9, "And there appeared a great wonder in heaven, a woman clothed with the sun and the moon under her feet, and upon her head a crown of twelve stars. And she, being with Child cried, travailing in birth and pain to be delivered. And there appeared another wonder in heaven; and look! A great red dragon having seven heads and ten horns and seven crowns upon his heads . . ." Verse nine (9) gives a clear definition of who this "dragon" is. SATAN! ". . . And his tail drew a third part of the stars of heaven, and cast them down to earth, and the dragon stood before the woman which was ready to be delivered for to devour her child as soon as it was born. And she brought forth a man child who was to rule all nations with a rod of iron . . ." Read Jer. 47: also. (Job 21:9, Ps. 2:9, 23:4, 110:2, Prov. 10:13, 26:3, 13:24, 29:15), ". . . And she brought forth a man child . . . And her child was caught up to God and to His throne."

The great wonder in heaven: A woman . . . Israel. Spiritual Israel, not Carnel Jacob. Jerusalem is in Israel and is Israel's capital. Josephus explains in his book of Wars (of Israel), that Herod's temple as well as Solomon's temple were like a crown set on a hill, decked out like the shining sun during the day and a bright full moon at night to guide way farers coming to Jerusalem.

The woman's man Child is Jesus—our King—who lived 33 to 33½ years before He was "caught up to God and His throne," . . . "To devour her child as soon as it was born."
The woman, Israel, has not yet "fled into the wilderness, where she has a place prepared of God for her, that they should feed her a thousand two hundred and three score days . . ." 1,260 days.

A year has 365 days. 3 years adds up to 1,095 days. A half a year is 182½ days. This is the last half of the seven years of tribulation. And we know without doubt this has not happened. Yet-Israel is still occupied by the precious people of God. Read Daniel 11; for more information on the seven year tribulation that Jesus Himself said, "Except those days be shortened there would no flesh be left to rescue." Matthew 24; is for the Jews for it was 12 Jews asking A JEW, our Savior "Lord, tell us when these things shall be?"

Scholars tell us the hidden City of Petra in Jordan is the, "hidden place, prepared by God" for the woman to flee to, that satan sends a "flood" after her to destroy her remnant. "Flood in Scripture means people.
Who built Petra?

Mark 3:8, Gen. 25:29-34.

"The country was settled by the descendants of Esau. The ruddy hue of the mountains may have given the name Edom which is "red" in the original . . ." Isn't it ironic the first Jew—Adam—was made of red clay and the last place on earth for the Jews to be rescued is in a RED CITY? Is this a win-win situation or what!

". . . The ancient name was Mt. Seir. Seir means rugged. On the E. side of W. Arabah from Elath, on the S. to Moab on the N. at the brook Zered, Deut. 2:13, 14, 18, about 100 miles long by 20 miles long. The whole country is wild, rugged and full of deep glens, but is also very fertile on the Mesa's; while the desert on each side is barren. The people dwell amid the rocky heights, in caves and houses perched on dizzy crags like eagles in their nests, living by their swords, Gen. 27:40, Jer. XLIX:16, yet, as Isaac promised, this land possessed "the fatness of the earth and of the dew of heaven" Gen. 27:39. The ancient capital was Bozrah—"Sela" (Petra) was the stronghold, and Ezion-geber its seaport, where Solomon built a fleet, 2 Sam. 8:14, 1 Ki. 9:26. The crusaders built a fortress 12 miles N. of Petra on Mons Regalis now a ruin, called Shobek. The people were always idolaters, 2

121

Chr. 25:14, Jos. Antiquities 15:17. The rock temples and dwellings of Edom were cut into softrock (soapstone); were large and airy, well lighted and dry, and a safe protection against robbers."

Smith's Bible Dictionary.

We know that Revelation 12:6, has not happened yet. John wrote the words of Jesus as He said them to him, "Write the things you have seen, the things which are . . ." happening right now while you are on this island. ". . . And the things which shall be here after." Rev. 1:19.
Our God bestows on all those who pray for Wisdom, the Wisdom to discern the Scripture's to "Rightly divide them" with His Knowledge to do so. This is exactly what we are doing in these writings. From beginning of these to the very end of the same.

This next verse of Rev. 12:6, and also verse 7 as well, happened in Genesis 1; between verses one and two. More Scripture to bear this out Jeremiah 4:23-26, Psalms 90:2.

". . . That they may see, know and consider, understand together that the Hand of the Lord has done this, and the Holy One of Israel has created it. Let them bring forth . . ." their causes. ". . . and show us what shall happen, let them show the former things, what they be that we may consider them, and know the latter end of them. Or declare us things for to come. Show the things that are to come hereafter that we may know . . ." Isaiah 41:20-23.

"Howbeit for this cause I obtained mercy that in me first Jesus Christ might show forth all longsuffering for a pattern to them which hereafter believe on Him to life everlasting."
1 Tim. 1:16
John, on the island of Patmos, having a deep revelation of what was to come in the future of himself: "I Am Alpha and Omega. The beginning and the ending says the Lord which is and which was and which is to come, the Almighty . . ."

"I Am Alpha and Omega, the First and the Last. What you see write in a Book and send it . . ."

"Write the things which:

You have seen,
The things which are,
And the things which shall be hereafter."

Rev. 1:8, 11, 19

After this I looked and beheld a DOOR open in Heaven: And the FIRST Voice I heard was as it were of a trumpet talking to me which said "Come up Here, and I will show you things which must be Here After." Rev. 4:1, 1 Thess. 4:16, 17.

"If we receive the witness of men, the witness of God is greater, and this is the witness of God which He has testified of His Son. They that believe on the Son of God has the witness within themselves; they that believe not God has made Him a liar because they believe not the record that God gave of His Son. And this is the record that God has given to us, His eternal life, and this life is in His Son. They that have the Son has life and they that have not the Son of God has not life.
"These things I have written to you that believe on the Name of the Son of God that you may know that you have eternal life and that you may believe on the Name of the Son of God." 1 John 5:9-13.

Christ has in His Name His Father's Name and that Name is YAH. Yeshua pronounced phonetically YAH SHUA. Just like Joshua. His Name is YAH—shua and "all they that call upon the Name of the Son of God and believes in that Name shall be saved and have eternal life." Otherwise you are dead in your sins-still-.

Jesus said "You must be born-again" or you will never and I mean NEVER enter into the New Earth or into paradise or into heaven where God in heaven is.

By this we know without doubt we have the very DNA GENE of the Father who infills us with the very Mind of Christ, Gods very own One and Only Son.

CHAPTER 16

MIDNIGHT OIL? BURNT FAR TOO' LONG

Jesus Himself said, "Go you into all the world and preach the gospel to every CREATURE." Mark 16:15. Creature being the operative word here.

"This is the law of the beasts, and of the fowl and of *every* living Creature that moves in the water and of *every* Creature that creeps upon the earth" Leviticus 11:46.

"In whom we have redemption through His Blood . . ." ONLY if we ask with a broken heart and broken spirit. ". . . even the forgiveness of sins; Who is the image of the invisible God, the First born of every Creature." Colossians 1:14, 15

"For the earnest expectation of the Creature waits for the manifestation of the sons of God . . . Because the creature itself shall be delivered from the bondage of corruption into the glorious liberty of the children of God . . . Nor height, nor depth, nor any other Creature shall be able to separate us from the love of God, which is in Christ Jesus our Lord." Romans 8:19, 20, 21, 39.

"For He spoke in a certain place of the seventh day on this wise, And God did rest the seventh day from all His works" Hebrews 4:4, Gen. 2:2, "After creating all the Creatures of the land furry ones and human ones Genesis 1:24-30. Then, verse 31, "And

God saw everything He had made and LOOK! It was very good. The evening and the morning were the sixth day."
"Saying with a loud voice, Worthy is the Lamb that was slain to receive power, riches, wisdom and strength, honor and glory and blessing, And every Creature which is in heaven and on earth, and under the earth, such as are in the sea, and all that are in them . . ." Revelation 5:12, 13.

All these Scriptures—we pray—let you, the reader, know our very own Father in heaven and His Son calls us! We—people—Creatures. Who am I to try and dispute Their Word? Or any Word from them? No, I will not, since I'm a nobody anyway and I like it this way, if this is the only way I can magnify the Only One who ever loved me and taught me how to love.

Since we've learned about the genealogy of the first Man Ah ah Dam the first Hebrew, all the way to Noah where "Only eight righteous souls were saved." Be very careful of every word of God you read for we can "mess-up" royally in no time at all. The operative Word here is righteous, meaning, these eight creatures were the only ones in all the world, with "A Clean, undefiled, without spot or wrinkle, DNA Blood line." Brush up on your history.

This Scripture we are about to give is as beat up, messed up, most deceiving, for every one in the whole world that our Father has drawn my attention to, to try and correct for Him. Having had this terrible pain in my heart each and every time I hear people as well as preachers mutilate Gods Word—here in this particular Scripture, and the other is about Adam. Noah was a "pure bred, elite, stallion Jewish Man. Proof found in his generations we've already given you, the reader his genealogy.

Am so sorry to have to say this; Its my belief Noah drank a lot and became drunk more than once, according to Scholars, Josephus, and a Syrian historian. Even so, "Noah found grace in the eyes of the Lord . . . Noah was a just man and perfect in his generations . . . And God said to Noah, the end of all flesh is come before Me for the earth is filled with violence through them . . . I will destroy them with the earth." Genesis 6:8, 9, 13.

"And the Lord said to Noah, You come now, and all your house into the ark, for you, have I seen righteous before Me in this generation. Of every clean beast you shall take to you by sevens, the male and female and, and of beasts that are not clean by two; one male one female. Of fowls of the air, by sevens, the male the female to keep seed alive upon the face of the earth. And they went in unto Noah into the ark, two and two of ALL flesh . . ." Genesis 7:1-3, 14, 15.

FLESH: "The soft substance of an animal or human BODY, consisting of muscle and fat. The BODY as distinguished from the spirit and soul. Man-kind, living Creatures."

Man. Animal. Both are lumped into ONE Word Creature." ". . . All flesh wherein is the BREATH of LIFE." All the race's created on the sixth day. Notice if you will, furry Creatures were created FIRST, then "Male and female created He them. In the image of God created He male and female," breathing life into all of them, furry ones and smooth skinned ones. Adam, father of the Jewish race, created the 8th day, "And God breathed into the man and he became a living soul." A smooth skinned creature.

In light of all this, it still remains a mystery to me why people and preachers do not know or cannot see that one male one female from every race from around the world God had placed them in the climate most suitable to their flesh. Just as God distributed each animal to the climate most suitable to them. Two—a male, a female of every race were on that ARK with Noah and his family! Don't believe it? Even after all these Scriptures, dictionary definitions an everything? Only God can help you now. Even with God's help I was unable to open your spiritual eyes? Sorry.

What has taken me a life-time to learn, you will learn in just a few hours. IF you read these writings with an open mind. Other-wise the covering is still over you as heavy as before.

So, Now. All of us had better, "fish or cut bait," as the old fisherman says.
"As it was in the days of Noah . . ."

CHAPTER 17

STOP–LOOK–LISTEN

". . . Then we which are alive and remain shall be caught up together with them in the air . . ." 1 Thess. 4:6, Eph. 1:10, Lk. 9:27, Matt. 16:27, 28, Jude 9:27.

This does not mean "we who are alive when Jesus comes" will not die. Of course we will! Its just that the dead will get to witness how it was when they fell asleep in Jesus. Before our mortal bodies hit the ground in an instant of a second, we—with our mortal bodies—will be changed to immortal. Just that quick is all it takes to have an incorruptible body. "In one twinkle of an eye." It takes 20 twinkles to bat an eye. ONCE!

My older brother who pastured a Church in Columbus Ohio, had to go and be fitted for glasses some years before his death. I hope I remember this correctly. While there, waiting, he felt he would ask the doctor what a twinkle in the eye was. Was it like—or close to—a flutter when one closes or bats their eye? This doctor explained to him that it was like batting the eye once, but not really. "It takes 20 twinkles or flutters to bat one's eye ONE time." Wow! If that isn't a secret coming I don't know what is. "When light hits the pupil, it reflects back like a mirror Also a twinkle." ". . . He comes in a cloud . . ." A "cloud", means a whole host of people who need to pick up their mortal—to immortal—in one of 20 twinkle bat's of our eye—bodies.

When our Lord stood outside of His friend Lazarus' tomb, there were quite a few living people standing around as well, waiting, to see a miracle. So, for their sake, and the sake of all the dead in Christ all around Lazarus' tomb, our Lord Savior shouted, with a loud voice the earthly name of Lazarus, who awoke instantly and came out of the tomb. Jesus had said earlier, to Mary and Martha that Lazarus was not "dead but asleep." Martha misunderstood so our Lord had to rephrase His sentence. How many times have we read where doctors have said to a grieving family "Your loved one is brain dead and it would be merciful for you to make the decision to unplug their life support." One or two, statistic's say, out of 10, go on living on their own. In the days of our Savior they had no life support machines, and no way of telling-at all—if a person was dead or still alive, their breathing was slow to nothing if there was any at all. It was only in the 17th Century, in England and America, they began using a mirror next to or on that persons nose to see if there was the slightest bit of fog on it to know if they were still alive. How many times have I read in documents and literature of the United Kingdom where grave-diggers had dug up many bodies where fingernails had dug into the lid of a coffin—on the inside—where the person had been buried alive but no one knew. How could they? It was required reading for me, along with a myriad of other literature, to acquire my degree.

". . . In the mouth of two or three witnesses, let every Word be established." 2 Cor. 13:1.

"For the Lord Himself shall descend from heaven with a shout, with the voice of the arch angel, and with the trump of God . . ." 1 Thess. 4:16.

"For if the trumpet gives an uncertain sound, who shall prepare himself to battle?" 1 Cor. 14:8. Military.

The dead shall rise first, then the living shall rise . . . And in another place . . . And we shall all be changed . . ." From mortal to immortal, in the twinkling of an eye.

Isn't this wonderful? Now, when Scripture is rightly divided to edify His Church, it just fits together—like—well, tailor made.

When John had the vision of the unfolding of the book of Revelation, my feeling is, he was scared. When our Savior gives me visions, sometimes I am a bystander, sometimes I'm in the thick of it trying to escape. Is it any wonder Paul was scared? And had to be taken out of the equation so he wouldn't faint again from the horrors being shown to him.
"After this I looked and beheld, a door was open in heaven. And the first voice I heard was as it were a trumpet talking with me, which said, 'Come up here and I will show you things that must be hereafter. And immediately I was in the spirit, and behold, a throne was set in heaven and ONE sat on the throne." Revelation 4:1, 2. Our 1 Thess. 4:16, 17.

There being only ONE on the throne, where was our Savior? Seeing as how Scripture itself says "He ascended on high to sit on the right side of the throne of God until God has/had put all (evil) things under Jesus' feet." Revelation chapter one tells us where Jesus was. With John, showing him many wonders. Dear readers, this is 1 Thessalonians 4:16. The catching away of Christs Church. What happens next you say? We are so glad you asked.

"And after these things I heard a great voice of much people in heaven saying, AL-Le-Lu-JaH, Salvation and glory and honor and power unto the Lord our God: For true and righteous are His judgments for He has judged the great whore which did corrupt the earth with her fornication and has avenged the blood of His servants at her hands. And again they said, AL-Le-Lu-JaH. And her smoke rose up for ever and ever."

Rev. 19:1-3

Jesus Himself said in the very first chapter of this book; "John. Write the things which you have seen, the things which are and the things which shall be hereafter." Rev. 1:19.

Take, for instance, Revelation 8:1, ". . . There was silence in heaven about the space of half an hour."

We have been through this earlier, so we will only touch on a couple of things here. One, Genesis 1:1, 2, Earth was made perfect in verse one, in verse two "and the earth was without form and void (empty)." What happened? Isaiah chapter 14 is what happened along with Ezekiel Chapter 28.

Number two is, Matthew, Mark, Luke and John's account of our blessed Savior giving His life—literally—for all of us. And just as Aaron the high priest and all the other high priests after unto our Savior, always took a vessel from the temple to catch the blood of the innocent lamb shed for the family in Israel offering that precious lamb, caught that blood in a vessel they could not set down. It was made for that purpose, to keep the blood from coagulating so it could be placed on Gods alter in His Holy of Holies behind the curtain wall. God did not want lumps of blood thrown on His alter. He wanted it sprinkled. God has the same identical temple-tabernacle—in heaven, with Him, that is full scale. Alter and everything.

Isaiah explains how satan fell and why.

Genesis explains when satan fell and displaced the earth. Isaiah said satan made it empty.

The angels caught our Saviors Blood of God to keep it from touching the earth and contaminating heaven once again, Revelation Chapter 8:1.

Matt. Mk. Lk. Jn. tell of Mary wanting to touch the "gardener" she found out was Jesus instead. Jesus said to her, "touch me not for I have not yet ascended to my Father and your Father yet." Lamb's were bled. Blood caught in a vessel. High priest poured it on the four corners of the alter, the Rams horns. Then the lambs

body burn on that alter, "for a sweet savor for Gods Nostrils."
Line upon line, precept upon precept.
All this happened to our Savior (Isa. 53). Then Rev. 8:1, happened
to purify heaven as well.

Jesus, who is the spoken Word of God, said, "Can a man build a
house without FIRST sitting down to count the cost." Isn't that
exactly what God and Jesus did? Maybe even before the war in
heaven Rev. 12, and satan was cast out in Gen. 1:1, 2. You'd better
believe He—They—did, and the plan has been being fulfilled
ever since, praise the Lord.

We, who write these nuggets for you, pray you have noticed how
we had to "rightly divide Scripture," from Genesis to Revelation
and all in between, just to enlighten our readers on one simple
subject, that is not worthless at all. No! It is the main—most
important one of all. Our Father "building a house" of the earth,
no less! Magnificent! Bravo! Way to go Father!

"And a voice came out of the throne (one? on the throne?)
saying, Praise our God all you His servants, and you that fear
Him both small and great. Then I heard as it were the voice of a
great multitude, and as the voice of many waters, and the voice
of mighty thundering saying, Al-le-lu-JaH for the Lord God
omnipotent reigneth. Let us be glad and rejoice, and give honor
to Him: for the Marriage of the Lamb is come, and His wife hath
made herself ready. And to her was granted that she should be
arrayed in fine linen, clean and white: for the fine linen is the
righteousness of saints (Ps. 149:1, 7, 8).
And He said unto Me—Write—Blessed are they which are called
to the marriage supper of the Lamb. And He said unto me, These
are the true sayings of God.

"And I fell at his feet to worship him, and he said unto me; see
thou do it not: I am your fellow-servant, and of your brethren,

that have the testimony of Jesus. Worship God. For the testimony of Jesus is the spirit of prophecy.

"And I saw heaven opened (again), and beheld a white horse, and He that sat upon him was called Faithful and True and in righteousness He does judge and make war . . ." also found in Zech. 14:4, Eze. 38:39; and Isa. 24:17-23.

"His eyes were as a flame of fire and on His head were many crowns. And He had a Name written that no Man knew but He Himself. And He was clothed with a vesture dipped in blood: (Joel 2:16, Ps. 2:9, 11:4, Isa. 63) And His name is called 'The WORD of God! And the armies which were in heaven followed Him, clothed in fine linen white and clean. And out of His mouth goes a sharp sword, that with it He should smite the nations: and He shall rule them with a rod of iron: and He treads the winepress of the fierceness and wrath of Almighty God (Isa. 63). And He has on His vesture and on His thigh a name written KING of KINGS and LORD of LORDS." Rev. 19:1-16.
Revelation 2:16, 19:15, same. Let your tallit drop over your shoulders, straddle a horse, and see where the names of God on your tallit fall. On your thigh. Can't be any other way.
All the things the bride and Groom do, spiritually, in heaven, the Father's house. Its time now we follow our Lord King into Zechariah 14.

CHAPTER 18

28 CARAT TRUE BLUE

"In the month of Tammuz (June-July on our Calendar), the fourth month, in the fifth day of the month, as I was among the captives by the river Che'bar that the heavens opened and I saw visions of God . . . Upon looking, I beheld a whirlwind come out of the North, a great cloud and a fire in-folding itself, and a brightness was about it. Out of the midst thereof as the color of Amber, out of the midst of the fire . . . And the likeness of the firmament upon the heads of the living Creature was as the color of the terrible crystal stretched forth over their heads above . . . And when they went I heard the noise of their wings, like the noise of many waters, as the voice of the Almighty, the voice of speech, as the noise of a host: when they stood, they let down their wings . . . And above the firmament that was over their heads was the likeness of a THRONE, as the appearance of a Sapphire stone: Upon the likeness of the throne was the likeness as the appearance of a man above upon it. And I saw as the Color of Amber, as the appearance of fire round about within it, from the appearance of His loins even upward, and from the appearance of His loins even downward, I saw as it were the appearance of fire and it had brightness round about.

"As the appearance of the bow that is in the cloud in the day of rain, so was the appearance of the likeness of the glory of the Lord. And when I saw it I fell on my face and I heard a voice of one that spoke."
Eze. 1:1-28, sporatically

135

Ezekiels wheel in the middle of a wheel and the living Creatures.

Then, we have the book of Job and what he saw when heaven opened; "He stretched out the NORTH over the empty place and hung the earth upon nothing. He holds back the FACE of His throne and spreads His Cloud upon it." Job 26:7-9.
These speak of The Living God's throne in heaven sitting on a polished sea of Sapphire colored crystal. 1 Kings 22:19, "And he said, hear you the Word of the Lord I saw. The Lord sitting on His throne and all the host of heaven standing on His right and on His left."
Then, we have our Savior Yeshua's throne, on this earth, "Thus spoke the Lord of Hosts, saying, Behold, the Man whose Name is: "The Branch," and He shall grow up out of His place, and He shall build the temple of the Lord. Even He shall build the temple of the Lord and He shall bear the glory, and shall sit and rule upon His throne, and He shall be a priest upon His throne and the counsel of Peace shall be between them both."

Zech. 6:12, 13

Zechariah was speaking of the throne of David, set upon this earth, "My covenant I will not break or alter the thing gone out of My lips. Once I have sworn by My holiness that I will not lie to David. His seed shall endure forever, and his throne as the sun before Me. It shall be established for ever as the moon and as a faithful witness in heaven." Psalms 89:34-37.

"The Lord reigns, let the earth rejoice; let the multitude of isles be glad thereof. Clouds and darkness are round about Him. Righteousness and judgment are the habitation of His throne." Psalms 97:1, 2."
"The Lord has prepared His (YHVH's) Throne in the heavens, and His Kingdom rules over all." Psalms 103:19.

"Christ shall sit on the throne of David." Acts 2:30.

136

There's a world of difference between The Father's throne in heaven, and our Savior Yeshua's throne and where each are placed.

All those who've died before this date May 14, 2012, have died this day and all the days past this date until our Lord catches us away to be with Him, all, are in Paradise and not in Almighty God's heaven.

"How say they that Christ is David's son? When David himself sayeth in the book of Psalms (110:1) 'The Lord said unto My Lord, Sit thou on My right hand till I make thine enemies thy footstool." David therefore calls Him Lord, how then is He his son?" Lk. 20:41-44.

"For David himself said by the Holy Spirit, The Lord said to My Lord, Sit thou on My right hand, till I make thine enemies thy footstool." Mark 12:6, Matthew 22:44

"For David is not ascended into the heavens: but he himself said; 'The Lord said unto my Lord, Sit thou on My right hand until I make Your foes Your footstool.'"

Acts 2:34, 35

"God, who at different times and in various places and manners spoke in time's past unto the fathers by the prophets.

Has in these last days spoken to us by His Son, whom He has appointed heir of all things by whom also He made the worlds (plural!); Who being the brightness of His glory, and the express image of His person, upholding all things by the Word of His power. When He had by Himself purged our sins, sat down on the right hand of The Majesty on high. Being made sooooo much BETTER than the angels as He has—by inheritance—obtained a more excellent name than they." How? "For to which of the angels did He—God—say at any time, "You are My Son, this day I have begotten (conceived) you? 'And again, 'I will be to Him a Father, and He shall be to Me a Son?' And again, when He brings in The First Begotten into the world He said, 'And let _ALL_ the angels of God worship Him." Hebrews 1:1-6.

"How shall we escape (Wrath of God) IF we neglect so great salvation . . ." Hebrews 2:3.

Our Father, God, said, of Himself, "You have put all things in subjection under His feet. For in that He put all in subjection under Him, He left nothing that is not put under Him. But! Now we see *NOT YET* all things put under Him." Hebrews 2:8.

"But this Man—Jesus—after He had offered ONE sacrifice for sins forever, sat down on the right hand of God; From henceforth expecting until His enemies be made His footstool." Hebrews 10:12, 13. That, dear people, will happen after Zechariah 14:4, and our own earth then becomes Paradise. Paradise on earth, for a thousand years. Same earth. Just refurbished.

". . . By the resurrection of Jesus Christ, Who is gone into heaven and is on the right hand of God; angels and authorities and powers being made subject to Him."

1 Peter 3:21, 22

"Now, of the things which we have spoken, this is the sum: We have such a high priest who is sat on the right hand of the throne of the Majesty in the heavens: A minister of the sanctuary, and of the TRUE tabernacle which the Lord pitched and not man."

Heb. 8:1, 2

"Looking to Jesus the author and finisher of our faith, who, for the joy that was set before Him endured calvery, despising the shame and is sat down at the right hand of the Throne of God."

Heb. 12:2

"If you then be risen with Christ, seek those things which are above, where Christ sits on the right hand of God." Colossians 3:1.

CHAPTER 19

JERUSALEM
WORLD'S CAPITAL

During those horrible years of tribulation, Zechariah wrote of Gods elect in Jerusalem Israel, "And I will bring the third part through the fire and will refine them as silver is refined, and will try them as gold is tried. They shall call on My Name (Yud Ha Vav Ha) and I will hear them. I will say, It is My people, and they shall say, The Lord is my God."

Zech. 13:9

Our Father YHVH is the, I mean *THE* Master Artist. The very first artist of any sort or any kind. Henry Ward Beecher once said, "Every artist dips their brush FIRST into their own soul." And really. Isn't that exactly what YHVH did when He put His very own BLOOD in the veins of His One Only Son Yeshua? Jean Richer, another Christian artist wrote, "Art is indeed not only the Bread but the Wine of life as well." Lets not be mistaken here. These artists were so good in their field of expertise, they made their living painting. They were rich and therein lies the only reason their "pearls of wisdom" were written down. No "starving artist," on the street, trying to sell their "Art in the Park," would have anything they ever said written down for posterity, no matter if it was wisdom akin to Solomon, the absolute wisest person ever lived in his era.

"Behold, the day of the Lord comes and your spoil shall be divided in the Midst of you." Zech. 14:1. This is speaking of Jew and Gentile alike in those horrible seven years. It was Jew and Gentile alike who murdered our Savior and, at His very feet, they gambled for who would get what of His clothing.

"But I will gather all nations against Jerusalem to battle; and the city shall be taken, the houses rifled, the women ravished and half the city shall go forth into captivity, and the residue of the people shall not be cut off from the city itself." Zech. 14:2.

But Israel itself is a "Whole 'Nother" story.
"Then, let them which be in Judea (Israel) flee into the Mountains: Let him who is on the house-top . . ." Repairing the roof, or fixing palm-friend's on the roof of their Booth on the Feast of Tabernacles.

". . . On the house top not come down to take anything out of his house. Neither let him which is in the field . . ." What does one do in a field? They are doing one of two thing's, either planting, which would be Feast of Passover, or they are harvesting which is the Feast of Tabernacles. Yeshua is our Jewish Messiah. Twelve Jews ask this Jewish Messiah "tell us when these things shall be? Master." Matt. 24.

Rev. 12:5, "And she brought forth a man child who was to rule all nations with a rod of iron and her Child was caught up unto God and to His throne." This, we all know, is the birth, life, and death/ resurrection of Messiah.

Rev. 12:6, now we are at least two thousand years or more, later: Into Matthew 24, "and the woman fled into the wilderness, where she has a place prepared for her of God, that they should feed her there 1,260 days (3½ years)." Verse 7 happened between Genesis 1:1 and 2.

". . . Neither let him which is in the field return back to take his clothing. And woe to them that are with Child, and to those women whose babies are not weaned." Matthew 24:15-19.

The end of verse 15 reads "Whosoever reads, let him understand." I hear my Savior say "Whosoever reads please! I beg of you, please understand, not just this, but everything you read in this book."

Isaiah, a prophet, saw this day that was coming, and fearing God as he did (we all do!), "O that You would read the heavens, that You would come down, that the mountains might flow at Your presence, as when the melting fire burns, the fire that causes the water to boil, to make Your name known to Your adversaries that the Nations May tremble at Your presence! 64:1-3.

This Scripture parallels Zech 14:4, 5, "Then shall the Lord go forth and fight against those Nations, as when He fought in the day of bottle (Joshua's battle at Jericho). And His Feet shall stand in that day upon the Mount of Oliver, which is before Jerusalem on the east, and the Mount of Olives shall split in the middle thereof toward the east and toward the west, and there shall be a very great valley; half of the mountain shall remove toward the north, the other half of it toward the south. And you shall flee to the valley of the Mountains, for the valley shall reach unto Azal, Yeah! You shall flee like as you fled from before the earthquake in the days of Uzziah King of Judah:

"And the Lord My God shall come and all the saints with You."

Isaiah saw the mountain melt, the melting fire burned down the melted mountain to the waters causing them to boil. A volcanic eruption.

Zechariah saw an earthquake the instant Yeshua's feet touched the earth on top of Mount Olives.

Matt. 23:39, The very last verse before Matthew 24, we have just been reading about:

"For I say to you . . ." O Jerusalem! ". . . You shall not see me henceforth until you shall say, Blessed is He who comes in the Name of the Lord.'"

Zech 12:1-12, Verse 3, "And in that day." Verse 4, "And in that day." Verse 6, "And in that day." Verse 7, ". . . Jerusalem shall be inhabited again in her own place, even in Jerusalem. The Lord also shall save the tents . . ."

Save the tents?? The only time Jews live in tents is at the fall feast of Tabernacles. Well! Who would have thought that!??

". . . Save the tents of Judah first, that the glory of the house of David and the glory of the inhabitants of Jerusalem: and "in that day" shall the Lord defend the inhabitants of Jerusalem, and he that is feeble among them at "that day," shall be as David, and the house of David shall be as God, as the angel of the Lord before them. And it shall come to pass in "that day" that I will seek to destroy all the nations that come against Jerusalem.
"And I will pour upon the house of David and upon the inhabitants of Jerusalem, the Spirit of grace and of supplications: And they shall look upon Me whom they have pierced and they shall mourn for Him as one mourns for His *only* Son, and shall be in bitterness for His First born.
"In "that day" shall there be a great mourning in Jerusalem as the mourning of Ha-dad-rim-mon in the Valley of Megiddon. And the land shall mourn, every family apart; the family of the house of David apart and their wives apart . . ."

All this before Zechariah 14:4, 5, And then it happens: "Then shall the Lord go forth . . . And His feet shall stand in "that day" upon the mount of Olives . . ." A great earthquake happens. "And You, the Lord my God shall come and all Your saints with You." Zech 14:8, 13:16, "And it shall be in that day that living water shall go out from Jerusalem . . ." And in that day there shall be a fountain opened to the house of David and to the inhabitants of Jerusalem for sin and for uncleanness . . . And one shall say to Him, What are these wounds in Your hands? Then He shall answer them 'Those of with which I was wounded in the house of my friends."

Rev. 1:7, 8, "Behold, He comes with clouds (saints) and every eye shall see Him, and they also which pierced Him: And all Kindreds of the earth shall wail because of Him. Even so, Amen. I AM Alpha and Omega, the beginning and the ending, says the Lord which is, which was, and which is to come, the Almighty."

"Jerusalem: Foundation of Peace. First mentioned in Genesis 2:7, named Salem. Gen. 14:18, whose King was Melchizedek who Rabbi's say was Shem the patriarch. The name Shalaim Ps. 124:2, means two cities, and is applied to the cities or quarters on modern day Zion (Jerusalem) and in the Tyropoeon Valley. At the conquest of Canaan the name of its King was Adonai-Zedek, meaning Lord of Justice Joshua 10:1-3, almost the same as Melchizedek, meaning King of righteousness, Joshua speaks of its occupiers. In the time of the judges the name was Jebus 29:10, 11, and the City only became the capital of the nation after 450 years from the time of Joshua, when David made it his royal residence John, the author of Revelations, 21:1—wrote, And I saw a new heaven and a new earth . . ." He saw this after Jesus and all His saints with Him, Zechariah 14:4, 5, Job 19:25. Scripture says "The earth abides for ever," Eccl. 1:4. Our Father, Son, Holy Spirit and us, have our work cut out for us, as far as "cleaning" is concerned, if John felt what he saw was a brand new heaven and new earth. Everything satan and his demons touch turn to trash, since he and all his, has free range all over our atmosphere and the earth polluting both to an unrecognizable heap.

Our Father knows—for He is THE Creator of all things—that the sanctuary, near the center of his Kingdom Eza. 5;5, leaving Hebron where he had reigned for 7½ years. The seat of the religion had been before this, at Shechem Shiloh, Gibeah, Nob, and Gibeon. Zion was not called the City of David, and was soon enlarged by

143

walls, strengthened by towers, and beautified by a palace for the King, built by the Mechanics of Hiram, King of Tyre.

David's son Solomon's three great works were the Temple, with its East Wall and Cloister, The Palace and wall of Jerusalem (Josephus). Also read; Robinson and Barclays "City of the Great King 526 AD, and Smith's Bible Dictionary, of which these writings were taken.

Fire is a cleansing agent. NO!! Absolutely not! Satan and his demonic fallen angels and every creature on earth who took their mark and followed them into hell, will *NEVER* EVER be cleansed. There's a Church who like to call themselves an origination. I call it an out and out *CULT* that only the "mind-controlled" members could ever—in this lifetime or the next—believe. They believe "A body can burn only so long before its burned up. And, so what if I don't make it into the New Earth and die first. I can only burn so long and I'm through." Oh no! You are not getting off that easy.

Jesus said, in the four gospels, "Be cast into hell where the worm never dies. "And in another place" Fear Him who can separate your spirit *and* soul and cast it into hell." What was it Paul wrote in one of his letters to all the churches he and others had started, "When we die in Christ, it is our soul that sleeps." If any of you, dear reader, have read anything I've written about our Mind, know that I have studied nearly everything ever written on our minds. And have concluded, yet not I, but Scripture, and what others have written about our mind, being Christian themselves, plus six, eight or more, learned scholars, who've earned their professor-ship, on our mind. Had to say all that, just to say this: "I have learned-positive proof, our spirit and soul live in our brain. Heres what Websters has to say about a WORM: anything living or dead without arms or leg's. A worm is a creature with a mind. Anything with a mind a soul lives in." Eccl. 7; explains when we die "Our breath . . ." which is our spirit, ". . . goes back to God who gave it and the body back to "dust you are and to dust you shall return." Only our soul that lives in our brain will survive, either in Paradise, or hell. When we die our soul goes to one or the other place. One with peaceful Paradise sleep. The other to eternal hell. How do we know this? "And the *sea* gave up the dead which were in it, And *death* and *hell* which were in them, and they were judged every Man according to their works . . ." They did while alive on this earth. ". . . And death and hell were cast into the lake of fire."

People, we are put here, on earth, with a mind of our own, and free-will of our own. *We* alone decide where we will spend eternity. Born-again Christians have set up God's standard in their lives. They are banner carriers for Yeshua who paid one horrible price, not just for us. No. For each and every human creature from Gen. 1:26, 2:7, to now and even beyond after all is said and done and we leave this earth for an eternity with Him. Saint or sinner alike. Yeshua died for all of us defeating the devil and arose again on the third day.

". . . For the first heaven and the first earth and all therein was no more sea.
"And I. John. Saw the holy City—New Jerusalem—coming down from God out of heaven prepared as a bride adorned for her husband. And I heard a great voice out of heaven saying. Beheld, the tabernacle of God is with men and He will dwell with them, and they shall be His people, and God Himself shall be with them and be their God. And God shall wipe away all tears from their eyes, and there shall be no more death, neither sorrow, nor crying, neither shall there be any more pain, for the former things have passed away. And He sat upon the throne and said, Behold, I make all things new."

Rev. 20:13, 14, 21:1-5

"And it shall come to pass in the last days, that the Mountain of the Lord's house shall be established in the top of the mountains, and all nations shall flow unto it. And many people shall go and

145

say, come, let us go up to the mountain of the Lord, to the house of the God of Jacob, and He will teach us of His ways and we will walk in His paths, for out of Zion shall go forth the law and the Word (Yeshua) of the Lord from Jerusalem. And He shall judge among the nations and shall rebuke many people, and they shall beat their swords into plow-shares and their spears into pruning hooks: Nation shall not lift up sword against nation, neither shall they learn war any more." Isaiah 2:2-4.

YHVH said of His only Son Yeshua, "Yet have I set My King upon My Holy Hill." Psalms 2:6.

". . . And the government shall be upon His shoulder, and His Name shall be called Wonderful, Counsellor, THE Mighty God, The Everlasting Father, The Prince of Peace. Of His government and peace there shall be no end, upon the throne of David and upon His Kingdom to order it, and to establish it with judgment and with justice from henceforth even for ever. The zeal of the Lord of Hosts will perform this." Isa. 9:6, 7.

"And there shall come forth a rod out of Jesse, A branch shall grow out of his roots. The Spirit of the Lord shall rest upon Him, the Spirit of Wisdom and understanding, the Spirit of counsel and might the Spirit of Knowledge, and of the fear of the Lord shall make Him of quick understanding in the fear of the Lord, and He shall not judge from what His eyes see, neither reprove after the hearing of His ears. But with righteousness shall He judge the poor and reprove with equity for the meek of the earth, and He shall smite the earth with the rod of His Mouth, and with the Breath of His lips shall He slay the wicked (Rev. 19:15,), And righteousness shall be the girdle of His loins (preparing for war), and faithfulness the girdle of His reins." Isa. 11:1-5.

"And the Lord said, 'I will remove Judah also out of My sight, as I have removed Israel and will cast off this city, Jerusalem which I have chosen . . .'" 2 Ki. 23:27.

This verse happens before Zechariah 14:4, 5.

"Since the day that I brought forth My people out of Egypt, I chose NO City among all the tribes of Israel to build a house, in that My Name might be there; neither did I chose a man to be a ruler over My people Israel: But I have chosen Jerusalem that My Name might be there and have chosen David to beaver My people Israel." 2 Chr. 6:5, 6.

"Our feet shall stand within your gates O Jerusalem."

Ps. 122:2

"If I forget you O Jerusalem, let my right hand forget her cunning." 137:5. David, who agonized over these words, was a Mighty warrior and that explains ". . . let my right hand forget how to make war."
"Praise the Lord O Jerusalem, praise your God O Zion." Ps. 147:12.
"Behold, I lay in Zion, saith the Lord God, for a foundation a Stone, a tried Stone, a precious Corner Stone, a sure foundation, he that believes shall not make haste." Isa 28:16.

In the New Earth ". . . They shall see the glory of the Lord and the excellency of our God. Strengthen you the weak hands and confirm the feeble knees. Say to them that are fearful of heart, Be strong, fear not; behold your God will come with vengeance, even God with a recompense; He will come and save you (Zech. 14:4,5,). Then eyes of the blind shall be opened, and the ears of the deaf shall be unstopped. Then shall the lame man leap as a hart, and the tongue of the dumb sing; for in the wilderness shall waters break out and streams in the desert. And the parched ground shall become a pool and the thirsty land springs of water, in the habitation of dragons where each lay, shall be grass with reeds and rushes (a swamp).
"And a highway shall be there, and a way, and it shall be called—The Way of Holiness—the unclean shall not pass over it

(Revelation 22:14, 15,), but it shall be for those, the way faring men, though fools shall not err therein, No lion shall be there, nor any ravenous beast shall go up there on; it shall not be found there, but the redeemed shall walk there. And the ransomed of the Lord shall return and come to Zion with songs and everlasting joy upon their heads: they shall obtain (work for) joy and gladness and sorrow and sighing shall flee away."

Isaiah 35

"O Zion that brings forth good tidings, you get up into the high mountain. O Jerusalem that brings good tidings lift up your voice with strength, lift it up! Don't be afraid. Say to the cities of Judah, Behold, your God! Behold, the Lord God will come with strong hand, and His arm shall rule for Him; behold, His reward is with Him (1 Thess. 4:16, 17,) and His work before Him. He shall feed His flock like a shepherd, He shall gather the lambs with His arm, and carry them in His bosom, and shall gently lead those that are with young. Who has measured the water in the hollow of His hand . . ?" Isa. 40:9-11.

Joel 3:20, ". . . The Lord" dwells in Zion." "The Lord yet shall comfort Zion, and shall yet choose Jerusalem." Zech. 1:17. "Thus saith the Lord; I Am returned unto Zion, and will live in the middle of Jerusalem." Zech. 8:3.

". . . But Jerusalem shall be safely inhabited . . . And it shall come to pass that every one that is left of all the Nations which came against Jerusalem shall even go up from year to year to worship the King, the Lord of hosts, and to keep THE FEAST OF TABERNACLES." Zech. 14:11, 16, Isa. 66:23.

This Feast of our Lord is one of three Feasts our Father said would be "kept forever for they are My Feasts." Feast of Passover, Feast of Pentecost, and the Feast of Tabernacles.

"And it shall be that whose will not come up of all the families of the earth to Jerusalem to worship the King, the Lord of hosts, even upon them shall be no rain . . ." Book of Joel, "the former rain and the latter rain. ". . . And if the family of Egypt does not go up, and comes not, that have no rain, there shall be the plague (verses 12-15), wherewith the Lord will unite the heathen that come not up to keep the Feast of Tabernacles . . . this shall be the punishment of all nations that come not up to keep the Feast of Tabernacles."

Zech. 14:11-19

"I Yeshua have sent My angel to testify to you these things in the Churches . . . And the Spirit and the bride say COME. Let him that hears, say, COME. Let him that is thirsty, COME. And whosoever will, let him take the water of life freely . . . Surely I come quickly." Even so, come Lord Jesus." Rev. 22:16, 17, 20. AMEN

CHAPTER 20

THE BRAZEN ALTER

"And you shall make an alter of acacia wood, five cubits long, and five cubits wide. The alter shall be foursquare, and the height of it shall be three cubits. You shall make the horns of it upon the four corners of it. His horns shall be the same and they shall overlay it with brass. You shall make his pans to receive his ashes and his shovels, and his basons, and his fleshhooks (tongs), and his firepans, all the vessels thereof you shall make of brass. You shall make for it a grate of network of brass. Upon it the net shall you make four brazen rings in the four corners thereof. You shall put it under the compass of the alter beneath, that the net may be even to the midst of the alter. And you shall make staves for the alter, and you shall make them of acacia wood, and overlay them with brass. And the staves shall be put into the rings, and the staves shall be upon the two sides of the alter, to carry it. Hollow with boards shall you make it, as it was showed to you while you were on the Mount (Sinai), so shall they make it."

Exodus 27:1-8

Biblical Archaeology. What a wonderful profession to choose for one's life-long career. There's a bi-monthly with that name and we receive it. A wonderful article of an archaeological find in or near Jerusalem, November/December 2010 issue, they unearthed a room or rooms:

"The rooms apparently held a reddish clay alter covered with a thick layer of ash and bones. The remains of the sacrifices not completely burnt on the alter were apparently deposited here. This may have been the MAQUM ha-deshen, "the place of the ashes," mentioned in Leviticus 1:16, as part of the temple. The area around this building was full of animal bones.

"The sacred nature of the compound is further confirmed by several large cisterns used for purification and washing of the sacrificial animals. Some other finds, small, reflect the sacred Nature of this precint. A small gold bell with a silver clapper must have belonged to the EPHOD of the High Priest, decorating the hem of his skirt. The Bible mandates that the skirt of Aaron's ephod shall be decorated with alternating pomegranates and "bells of gold" (Exodus 28:33, 34). The sound of the bells eased the minds of the other priests and temple worker's that the High Priest, Aaron was still alive behind the thick veil where the Brazen Alter was, that Aaron sprinkled the blood of the sacrifice; seven times on it, plus applying it to the four horns of the alter."

We feel its wonderful the archeologists have unearthed at least ONE place where the Brazen Alter was carried, here—there—everywhere, to be placed, once again. There are six articles that resided in Moses. Tabernacle and Solomon's Temple:
The Ark of the Covenant with the Mercy Seat resting atop it;
The Menorah, or Golden Candlestick;
The Alter of Incense; The Table of Shewbread;
The Brazen Laver and the Brazen Alter.

Of course we will not examine each of them in detail because each is a study within themselves. What we want to do is look at the positioning of these articles for they show how incredibly detailed and orderly our God is in all that He does.

In Exodus 40, God specifically dictated where these items were to be placed in the house of the Lord.

"He took the testimony and put it into the ark, insert the poles through the rings of the ark, and put the mercy seat on top of the ark. And he brought the ark into the tabernacle, hung up the veil of the covering, and partitioned off the ark of the testimony (covenant), as the Lord had commanded Moses." 20, 21.

The Ark of the Testimony, or Covenant, was positioned behind the veil in the Holy of Holies in the Tabernacle.

"He put the table in the tabernacle of meeting on the North side of the tabernacle, outside the veil; and he sat the bread in order upon it before the Lord, as the Lord had commanded Moses. He put the lampstand (Menorah) in the tabernacle on the south side of the tabernacle, and he lit the lamps before the Lord, as the Lord had commanded Moses.

"He put the golden alter in the tabernacle of meeting in front of the veil and he burned sweet incense on it, as the Lord had commanded Moses. He hung up the screen at the door of the tabernacle.

"He put the alter of burnt offering before the door of the tabernacle of the tent of meeting, and offered upon it the burnt offering and the grain offering as the Lord had commanded Moses.

"He set the laver between the tabernacle of meeting and the alter, and put water there for washing and Moses, Aaron and his sons would wash their hands and their feet with water from it. Whenever they went into the tabernacle of meeting and when they came near the alter they washed as the Lord had commanded Moses.

"And he raised up the court all around the tabernacle and the alter, and hung up the screen of the court gate. So Moses finished all the work that the Lord had commanded." Exodus 40:22-33.

If we were a bird or a helicopter, up above looking down on this scene, we would see the position of a cross. Each piece of sacred furniture represents another aspect of the redemption plan that would be fulfilled by our precious Messiah.

The positioning of these articles in the Tabernacle God revealed His One, His Only begotten Son and the purpose of the Word who was to become flesh and dwelled among us as the presence of God dwelt among men in the earthly tabernacle.

For instance:

1 – The brazen alter represented judgment fire Acts 10:42, Jesus is the judge of the living and the dead.
2 – The brazen laver contained cleansing water John 4:10-14, Jesus is the living water springing up to eternal life.
3 – The alter of incense represented prayers of the saints, prayed. 1 Timothy 2:5, refers to Christ as the One Mediator.
4 – The Menorah gave light in the Holy Place. John 8:12, describes Jesus as the light of the world.
5 – The table of shewbread held 12 loaves representing the 12 tribes of Israel. John 6:35, Our Savior is the Bread of Life.
6 – Finally, the Ark of the testament held the Law given on tablets of stone to Moses on Mount Sinai. Jesus is the Word Made flesh and dwelt among us." John 1:14.

"Then the Temple of God was opened in heaven and the ARK of His Covenant was seen in His Temple." Revelation 11:19. No one can deny even if they tried: THE ARK OF THE TESTAMENT is in God's Heaven! Psalms 78:24, 25, speaks of Bread coming down from heaven:

"God had rained down Manna on them to eat and given them of the bread of heaven." Men ate angel's food. He sent them food to the full.

Clearly there is heavenly bread that angels eat, just as there was bread on the table of showbread in the Tabernacle on earth.

B.J. Cline-Woodruff

There is a Menorah—Candlestick in the Temple in heaven:

"Then I turned to see the voice that spoke with me. And having turned I saw seven golden lampstands, and in the midst of the seven lampstands, One like The Son of Man clothed with a garment down to the feet and girded about the Chest with a golden band." Revelation 1:12, 13.

These seven lamps are a picture of the seven branched Menorah built by Moses and placed in the Holy place in the wilderness Tabernacle. In the heavenly Temple, they represent the seven main churches in John's day and the seven periods of Church history. My belief is we are in the Laodicean church age, ". . . I know your works that you are neither cold or hot . . ." Rev. 3:14, 15.

John saw an Alter of Incense in the temple of heaven:
"Then another angel, having a golden censer, came and stood at the altar. He was given much incense, that he should offer it with the prayers of all the saints upon the golden alter which was before the throne. And the smoke of the incense, with the prayers of the saints ascended before God from the angels hand." Revelation 8:3, 4.

Each morning in the earthly tabernacle and the earthly Temple, the priest offered burnt incense on the golden alter. It was believed the prayers of God's people mingled with the smoke of the incense as it ascended from the golden alter.

Yes, there is an alter in heaven as well. Revelation 6:1, 9, "And I saw when the Lamb opened one of the seals, I heard, as it were the noise of thunder . . . And when He had opened the fifth seal I saw under the alter . . ." Rev. 20:9 ". . . And fire came down from God out of heaven . . ." An alter and fire.

154

This is only one of several examples of judgment fire originating in heaven. Revelation 14:18, also speaks of an angel who controls fire. Since the earthly brazen alter had three fires burning on it, there may be three fires burning on the heavenly alter as well. Just as cleansing water was also available in the earthly tabernacle, as the Law required, so a river of life-giving water is located in heaven.

"And he showed me a pure river of water of life, clear as crystal, proceeding from the throne of God and of the Lamb. In the middle of its street and on either side of the river was the tree of life, yielding its fruit each month. The leaves of the tree were for the healing of the nations." Rev. 22:1, 2.

God ordered Moses to construct the wilderness Tabernacle, even paying close attention to the measurements of it. A scaled—down model of the true Temple Tabernacle and all its furniture in heaven, to make God comfortable and to feel at home when He came down to visit with His people whom He so dearly loved. So Moses actually built with earthly material what has existed in heaven since the beginning of time.

John—The Beloved—described a huge throne of God, like jasper. Jasper is a beautiful amber colored stone, opaque, Rev. 4:3. Glory emanated from God's presence, brighter than the sun, Revelation 1:16. Makes us wonder what John meant when the said "Brighter than the sun?"

Job also saw Gods Throne; "He stretches out the North over the empty place, and hangs the earth upon nothing. He binds up the waters in His thick clouds and the cloud is not torn under them. He holds back the FACE of His THRONE and spreads His cloud upon it." 26:7-9.
By this statement alone it implies people on earth could look up and see into heaven before God decided to cover it with many water filled clouds. Which also explains why "Now there was a

day when the sons of God came to present themselves before the Lord, and satan came also among them. The Lord said to satan where did you come from? Satan answered the Lord and said, from going back and forth in the earth, and from walking up and down in it." Job 1.

Our heavenly Father and Jesus, long ago laid out the blue-print for planet earth to be "replenished," immediately after satan had committed his heinous act and was cast out of heaven, he and all his fallen angels of Revelation chapter 12 (Job 1:7).

What you've read of the clouds filled with water Job saw covering up the earthly sight of God's throne in His heaven, happened long after Job 1:7, "and satan came also." That was when satan could still go "up, down, back, forth" in the earth "seeking whom he may devour." Never again, since that time in Job was satan ever allowed back into heaven. Yet he still accused the brethren. Rev. 12:11, 12.

John, the beloved; Revelation 4:3 "Saw a rainbow behind God's throne." Scientists say light bends. And its so. If you've ever put a large prism on a window seat in the bright early (or late) sun, you see the light actually bend creating a rainbow *without* the presence of water. "God gave us the rainbow in the sky as a covenant sign He would never destroy the earth again by water" Genesis 9:13-16.

Scientists say, "that in the beginning, when the earth was just forming, the sun was much, much hotter then, than it is now (Scientific American 2011).
Our Father God has special reasons for everything He does. He is never chaotic. He creates and He commands everything on earth to follow this special plan of His and we do.

The Ark in heaven was built on the giant blueprint plan Jesus and our Father laid out when satan and his one third evil angels were cast out of heaven. Gen. 1:1, 2, "In the beginning God created the heaven and the earth." How long and how old? No one knows except God and our Savior. After this verse a catastrophic event happened. That event was Revelation 12:7-9, "And there was war in heaven . . ."

Then Genesis 1:2, happened and Rev. 12:11 then came into existence. For all the races of people were created on the sixth day and instructed to go and replenish the earth. The Jewish race created on the eighth day. But then, that is another book, not belonging here, in this one on the BRAZEN ALTER on earth, the smaller one and the much larger one in heaven.

Leviticus 16 explains, once a year, on Yom Kippur the Day of Atonement, the high priest was allowed into the Holy of Holies. He would sprinkle the blood of a bull and a goat seven times on the east side of the lid of the Ark, called the Mercy Seat. This yearly atonement of sacrificial blood was necessary for the remission of sins.

Blood is unique among the substances in our bodies: "For the life of the flesh is in the blood, and I have given it to you upon the Alter to make atonement for your souls; for it is the blood that makes atonement for your soul," Leviticus 17:11.
Animal blood was used during the Temple services. God would not allow, tainted, corrupted animal blood to be placed in the Temple in heaven, because animal blood was only a pattern of what was fulfilled through Messiah. Old Testament sacrifices were a temporary substitute, pointing people to the coming Redeemer. Remember God's gigantic blueprint?

When God made His heavenly Temple and all the furniture there in, heaven was so pure it needed no blood. Then, that was before satan fell and all those that followed him. You can read about satans true name in Isaiah 14:12.

The word Lucifer comes from a Hebrew Word HALEL, which is the same word found in HALLELUJAH, which means "May I enter to praise YAH." Enter to praise the Lord.

From the time satan rebelled against God; and was expelled and cast down from heaven to earth (Rev. 12:). From that moment, the Temple was violated in heaven, by angelic sin and would need to be cleansed. God's plan all along arranged, "From the foundation of the world" that would not only provide cleansing blood for the heavenly holy of holies, but would also give mankind access back to the presence of God.

When Adam and Eve sinned we all know what the first thing God did was to take two animals—pure, clean, spotless,—under two years old, made skin clothing for the two of them, *AND* created the substitute "Lamb slain from the beginning of the world." Revelation.

Gen. 3:21

Moses sprinkled both the tabernacle and all the vessels of ministry in it with blood, Hebrews 9:21. He did this why?
"According to the law almost all things are purified with blood, and without shedding of blood there is no remission of sin." 9:22.

Adam and Eve passed down to their children how to make sin sacrifices but to make clothing from them as well, just as God had showed them the very first time.

"The life of the flesh is in the blood, and I have given it to you upon the alter to make atonement for your souls." Lev. 17:11.

Our Father made a decree, a mandate, if you will, that because life is in the blood, the law of justice would be for life, Genesis 9:6. But God the Father couldn't allow one human, any human, to be offered up for another humans sin's. That sacrifice would be totally unacceptable. Human for human? NO!

God refused to allow one human's blood to act as atonement for another's sins because everyone has the same kind of blood: "Therefore, just as through one man sin entered into the world, and death through sin, and thus death spread to all men, because of sin," like a plague. Romans 5:12.

This is why even a righteous person cannot atone for another. When Abel's blood was spilled on the ground, it would have redeemed all mankind if the only requirement was a righteous Man's blood. Sin passes down from generation to generation because of Adam's transgression: "For all have sinned and fallen short of the glory of God," Romans 3:23.

Joseph was not our Savior's father. God, the Father was His Father, Luke 1:35. His Holy Spirit filled Mary's womb with Wisdom and knowledge because that is what God is: "Therefore when He came into the world He said "Sacrifice and offering You did not desire, but a body You have prepared for Me." Heb. 10:5.

The church thinks "the body You have prepared for me" was Mary's body, and that's true to a certain extent. Lets "extend" that a little further "A body You have prepared for Me." The body Jesus grew up in. John chapter one says "The Word was with us . . ." Wisdom and Knowledge *Is* the WORD of the Father. "The Word—Jesus—was with us and the world esteemed Him not." The world did not recognize the greatest gift of all, "the Word of God made flesh and dwelt among us."
Mary's body was needed to have *the* very BLOOD of God the Father to flow in the tiny baby Jesus' veins. Why? Because God the Father created women's bodies to impart the father of the babies blood in the baby. DNA of everyone's father born on earth is in their childrens blood. Not the mothers and therefore Joseph

could not, or any other man on earth living at the time of Jesus, because Mary was a Virgin!

When Adam was created his veins were also filled with the Blood of the Father. Adam sinned making him a mortal man now. No longer was the Fathers Blood in Adam. He now had earth—earthy—human—mortal blood. Being mortal, Adam is now carnel minded. And carnality is sin against God the Father. When Cain was born he had the genes of satan for satan was his father, "Not as Cain who was of that wicked one and slew his brother. And why did he slay him? Because his own works were evil, and his brothers righteous." 1 John 3:12.

Just what were the evil works of Cain?
"And in the process of time Cain brought of the field the FIRST FRUIT of the ground an offering unto the Lord. And Abel, he also brought of the firstlings of his flock, and of the fat thereof. And the Lord had respect unto Abel and to his offering: "But unto Cain and to his offering He had no respect."
Gen. 4:3,4

Why was Cains fruit and vegetables not acceptable to our Lord? Because Yeshua, the living WORD of God is THE FIRST FRUIT of everything! And our heavenly Father would not, could not, let satan steal that away from His very own Son. His ONE and ONLY begotten Son. All other "sons and daughters are adopted into the heavenly Fathers fold. 1 Cor. 15:22,23.

Our heavenly Father taught Adam and Eve the power of sacrificial blood, Genesis 3:21, who in turn taught the two sons, how, also. Then, in Exodus 12, God (again) taught the Hebrew people the power of sacrificial blood. 12:22,23, Apply it to the door posts and lentils of their homes and the death angel would pass over them thereby redeeming them and their FIRST BORN? First born fruit of the womb!

Forty years later, they entered into their promised land after their FIRST Passover in hundreds of years. Now God instructs them again. Every Israelite family was to take a special lamb every year, go to Jerusalem and offer the perfect lamb in the Temple. The priest must slaughter it and with the shedding of the lamb's blood, they would keep the annual Passover. Jewish people in Messiah's time still believed that lamb's blood had the power to protect their families. All this was in the perfect planned blueprint of our heavenly Father, since, before the foundation of the world. Again. God's perfect purpose of Jesus' coming to earth had everything to do with the perfect, sacrificial lamb. John Baptist said of Jesus:

"Behold! The Lamb of God who takes away the sins of the world! John 1:29.

We end with this note; a tiny bit of knowledge; I heard a Rabbi's answer to a person in the audience's question. The question was: "Rabbi, why bells? I understand the pomegranates, but why bells?"
The Rabbi answered "Well, would you go up to a house and just walk right in, without ringing the doorbell first.

CHAPTER 21

BLOOD ON THE ALTER

∞

In the Torah there are places God taught the Hebrews the power of sacrificial blood. Genesis 3:21, Face to face God Himself taught Adam and Eve how to make sacrificial blood from the lamb offering killed that day by our Lord Himself, to show them how to make clothing for themselves and to use the blood and meat for HIS ceremony to cleanse themselves. Adam and Eve, in turn, taught their children the same. Else, how would Abel have known to sacrifice one of his perfect little pet baby lambs, born that spring of that year, ". . . And in due time . . ?" Genesis 4:3, the time of Passover.

Then again in Exodus 12:22, 23, Death could not enter into any Hebrew's house that had the blood on their door posts and lentils of their homes. Another way of using the sacrificial blood to keep death away, and purify the people as well. All Israelites knew of the power of the lambs blood.

After wandering in the desert for 40 years, after that Passover, the second one we speak of here, God again instructed each Hebrew family to take a special, perfect in every way, lamb every year, and to go to Jerusalem, offering the lamb in the Temple. Their instructions were to let the priests slaughter the little lamb, and with the shedding of the lamb's blood, they would keep the annual Passover.

Passover was a reminder of the day God overshadowed Israel, passing over, protecting and defending the people. Even in the time of our Savior they still believed that. What they didn't know was that this sacred ceremony was—always was meant to be—actually pointing to God's purpose. Remember God and Jesus' large blue print in heaven?

John Baptist came out of the wilderness preaching they "Must be saved, repent and be baptized. But there's one coming after me of whom I am not worthy to stoop down and lace or unlace his shoes." Then a little further in the same Scripture he looks down the road and yells, "Behold! The Lamb of God who takes away the sins of the world!" John 1:29.

In light of all this, it stands to reason that Passover was and is the first and greatest of all the three—main most important—Feasts; The spring Passover when it is lambing time of the sheep and many other animals as well. We've already explained to you the importance of Sheep to Israel, Israel is Jewish. Jesus was a Jew, the Bible was written for Jews, by Jews and *is* the Jewish Word of God. We Christians did *not* create Christian people *apart* from Jewish tradition. The very name Christian is Christ-the Redeemer—a Jewish name, a Jewish Redeemer "for the Jew first then to the Greeks . . ." which translated means; barbaric, unbelieving dogs. Sinners. The unsaved. The lost. Those held captive by sin and are undone.

Passover is the 14th of the Jewish sacred month, Nisan, which, on our calendar is in March or April. No leaven is allowed in Jewish homes for seven days. Leaven represents sin 1 Corinthians 5:6-8, Galatians 5:9.

Prior to the actual day of Passover, the father in each household, chose a special lamb, he himself carefully inspected for four days. The lamb could not be sick, or blind, crippled or spotted. It must be perfect in every way and solid white as snow, Exodus 12:5, and inbred.

First the lamb must be killed, drained of its blood, then the internal organs removed. A small piece of wood is placed inside (horizontal) to hold the rib-cage open. Then the lamb is stretched across a longer stick. The two hind-legs are stretched and fastened to the bottom of the pole, while its two front legs are stretched and attached to the top of the pole. Since the book of Exodus of the Torah, chapter twelve, this is the ceremony of the preparing of the lamb. The second recorded Passover for the sins of the people. The correct positioning of the lamb on these two poles, forms a wooden cross that at the time of Christ was used only by the Romans. Except for Nero, who set a fire crucified Jews; his "lampposts," leading to his mansion. The cross-beam was much shorter on the Roman cross, and this is what our precious Lord was forced into carrying up the hill of Golgotha; "The Hill of the skull."

A hole was chiseled out of the center of the center piece that was to be placed over the pole already mounted in the ground on top of the hill called Calvary. This, center cut was on the shorter piece of log called the patibulum (see the illustration in the book), which the prisoner was lain on, arms outstretched, then hands nailed or tied to the outer edges of the patibulum. This cross-beam and prisoner were then lifted up, held over the permanent pole and dropped down on it. This was a daily occurrence, it seems, according to Josephus, by the Sanhedrin rulers of the Jewish court of law.

During Passover season, the small children of the Jewish household had—sometimes yes, sometimes no—ample time during those days before the holiday to become very familiar with this little lamb of whom they fell in love with. When it was time to have the priest to slay the lamb, it had to be wrenched out of the hands of the children who would scream and cry for their "pet." My imagination is on the wild side at times, and I can see these little children refusing to eat it. Until, their hunger got the better of them. Still, I can see them weeping even as they partook of the flesh of their baby lamb. Rightly so for who doesn't love a baby, anything. Especially a little lamb. Lamb's love to be cuddled and they are like clay, or a trained pet dog. The difference is; the word "trained."

So for four days the children romped and played with the little lamb. After all the lamb was a baby too.

Yeshua was/is our sacrificial Lamb, ONCE and for all of us. Isaiah saw the horrendous suffering of Him, "He was oppressed, He was afflicted, yet He opened not His mouth. He was led as a lamb to the slaughter, and as a sheep before the shearers in silence, so He opened not His mouth." Isaiah 53:7. Some 700 years later John, the baptizer announced His coming. Matthew 26:63, fulfills Isaiah's prophecy.

So many religions do not preach the "Cross" and yet it is the Gospel of Yeshua, the Christ. Their reason is beyond my imagination. Not want to acknowledge Christ's deity either. Some say He was a good man. A great teacher. A prophet similar to Moses. *None* recognizing Christ had the Blood of the Father of Abraham, Isaac and Jacob flowing in His veins. This alone is deity!

The Cross is a knife in the heart of most "religions", and to others it is a resting place to come to, kneel at, place all their sins there, asking forgiveness, then walking away, FREE. Yeshua said "My peace I leave with you . . ." and how can you get it without recognizing that it is at the cross He left it for us. But no, they seem to want to crush underfoot this precious piece of wood where hung everything the entire world would ever need. It was the Father's *own* Blood being spilt there, caught by angels, taken back to heaven, to purify there the contamination up there satan and his fallen with him, angels.

This great and awesome Blood was a substitution. The innocent for the guilty. God's blueprint in heaven, before the "world began," a second time around, had the Blood substitution written in it. So was Adam's sin included in God's blueprint.

Lets reiterate for a few seconds here:

1 – God came down, killed the first sacrifice's for Adam and Eve.
2 – The Blood of Passover—another Killing of lambs—to apply to the top and two side posts of every Hebrew's home in Egypt.
3 – Rabbi's say the 22nd letter of Hebrew alphabet is TAV and used to be shaped like a cross.
4 – In King Solomon's day—TAV—was similar to our English letter X. In the days of our Savior, the letter changed yet again, and even now looks like the letter n in our English alphabet.
5 – The articles in Moses tabernacle were placed in the shape of a cross.
6 – Ezekile 9:4,6, Righteous men's foreheads were marked by a special angel, with pen and inkhorn, for protection, in the shape of an X (cross) similar—again—like Hebrew letter TAV.
7 – Moses was instructed to take a pole, again like a cross, and call it the "Brazen serpent," And like John 3:14, wrote, "As Moses lifted up the serpent in the wilderness, even so must the Son of Man be lifted up."
8 – A serpent represents sin. Remember Eve being tempted in the garden of Eden by a serpent?
9 – Christ Himself compared His death on the cross to the serpent on the pole. Christ our Lamb of God, likened His redemption, His healing, and His deliverance to the deliverance of Israel in the wilderness, 2 Corinthians 5:21.

10 – People looked to the serpent AFTER they'd been bitten by the poisonous vipers. Those who looked upon the serpent were healed, Jesus said those who looked upon the suffering of Christ and believed on Him would be cured of the plague of sin and death.

No other man's death, in the history of the world since time began, has been more publicized then that of our Savior. Josephus wrote quite a few horror stories of crucifixions in the middle-east, namely, Jerusalem. Jewish wars; 2:241, Felix was known to crucify, without much provocation, I might add, both zealots and rebels. He would even crucify anyone he had the slightest suspicion of collaborating with his enemies. Guilty or not you were crucified.

Titus besieged Jerusalem. A most famous affair in his day (Jewish Wars 5:449-452). He had all the Jewish prisoners crucified on the walls of the city at a rate of 500 a day. In one instance there were 800 Pharisees crucified while their wives and children looked on. Jewish wars 13:380,381. History is swimming in the blood of victims crucified in the era of Roman occupation of Jerusalem, Israel. But only ONE received worldwide "fame?" that still lives on here in the 21st century. THE most talked about in the free-world, aloud, and hushed-speech in places where communication rules. And that includes the Arabic world of "Ali, and Mohamed is his messenger."

During Passover in the era of our Lord Messiah, people coming into Jerusalem with their sacrificial little beloved lamb, would bring with them, or purchase a bronze name tag. With the family's name on it. They hung it around the lamb's neck. Every father wanted the Lord God to know that that little pet lamb, with their name on the bronze name tag was theirs being sacrificed for them, as God's law recommended they do.

So when Pilate wrote what he did and had the audacity to NAIL it to the Cross, was it any wonder the Pharisees were lived with anger!
Pilate wrote: "Yeshua of Nazareth, The King of The Jews," written in Hebrew, Greek and Latin John 19:19,20.

Deuteronomy 21:3-7, gives instructions for all those seeing the dead body an presumed it innocent. The elders of the city would take a heifer to a place of running water to the nearest city. They would wash their hands then cut off the heifer's head. Or cut the throat of it, to "shed innocent blood" reprehensive of all the people in the city were innocent of this dead persons killing. When Pilate washed his hands, proving to all around him, he was innocent of the shedding of "this innocent Man's blood," our Savior's blood. All the Jews there knew exactly the meaning of what Pilate had just did.

When Pilate wrote what he did, it was like God had put His Name on His Lamb for the whole world to see. "This Lamb is for our Family," in heaven.

CHAPTER 22

BLOOD—MOURNING

Everything that happened at the crucifixion and in the temple were planned, since God's precious Lamb was slain from the foundation of the world, Revelation 5:8, 9, 13:8. Lest we forget, remember God and His one and only Son's blueprint from the foundation of the world.

YOM KIPPUR or The Day Of Atonement was observed every year. A day of fasting and praying for all Israel.
To prepare for this day the high priest was to set himself apart from people and his family, in the temple in a chamber there especially for this purpose. When this very special day came he appeared; Leviticus 16:4, wearing four things. Different from his priestly garments:—A linen robe to the ankles and had long sleeves. 2 – A linen belt tied at the waist. 3 – A pair of linen breaches, Scripture reads—Breaches—. 4 – A linen turban that fit around the head, covering all his hair.

Since Israel sinned with the golden calf, God would not let the high priest to enter the holy of holies carrying gold upon himself. During this time the high priest offered special animal sacrifices for himself, the other priests, the Levites his family, as well as the whole population of Israel. On this day God would decide whether He would forgive the sins of the nation. Or not.

Jewish tradition (oral law), holds that when the priest entered into the temple, the sound of cherubim's wings (holy angels) could be heard beating against each other.

When he entered the holy of holies the sound ceased. They were waiting on God's approval whether the priest was pure—he would live—impure—the priest would die. When God forgave Israel the angel wings would start beating again.

Ezekiel 10:5 explained this beating of wings, as the voice of Almighty God when He speaks. This prophet also saw the "Glory of the Lord depart from the threshold of the temple," 10:18.

Cherubim guarded the entrance of the Garden of Eden after Adam sinned, Genesis 3:24. Two of these cherubim sat on the lid of the Ark of the Covenant, and two large gold cherubim were in the holy place of Solomons temple, 2 Chronicles 3:10-12.

Peter, of the New Testament said the angels desired to look into these things, 1 Pet. 1:12.

The priest would enter into the holy of holies with the blood of a bull and sprinkle the east side of the Ark of the Covenant seven times, Leviticus 16:14. Without the shedding of blood there is no remission of sins.

During this important moment, the high priest would bring two goats with him. The goats had to be identical in size, color, age, spotless, no blemish of any sort, etc. The priest would cast lots (of three red threads), with the other priests? We don't know. We just know Scripture reads "high priest would cast lots to see which goat would be burned on the alter and which goat would be the scapegoat." Reaching inside a little wooden box, the high priest brought out a gold-engraved marker that read "For the Lord." Then this goat was marked immediately with a long piece of red thread, tied between the horns. This meant this goat would be sacrificed!

"AZAZEL" was marked on the other goat Leviticus 16:6-8. This meant "scapegoat." Josephus, secular history, the Scripture all use the term "magical purposes." Almighty God instructed all Israel to tie a scarlet thread around the scapegoats neck, the Azazel goat. The high priest then laid his hands on this goat. The purpose being; to transfer the sins of all Israel onto the goat. A man was selected to led the goat outside the east gate, across a ramp and toward the Judean wilderness, in the days of the temple. It was still practiced in the days of our Savior.

Since it was believed demons hung out in the dry places such as a desert-Luke 11:24—, therefore the person leading the goat out into the wilderness, would push it off a cliff, or kill it in some other way, because, God did not want the sins of Israel to come back into Jerusalem.

Read your dictionary (unabridged) or your set of encyclopedias, to learn AZAZEL is another word for satan.

The third scarlet thread was tied to the door of the gate to the temple. When the goat died in the wilderness, this red thread on the door was said to turn white. While looking upon this now white thread, all Israel could breath a sigh of relief, their sins were forgiven. Three red threads. Could this possibly mean three crosses as well? Maybe this is what Isaiah meant when he wrote "Though your sins be as scarlet they shall be as white as snow. Though they are red like Crimson they shall be white like wool," Isaiah 1:18.

Our blessed and wonderful Savior, died on the Cross, representing the goat that died on the brass alter on the Day Of Atonement.

Barabbas is an Aramaic word—two syllable word meaning "son of Abba. Romans 8:15, Galatians 4:6, in the King James means "father." Barabbas means "the son of the father." Therefore

Barabbas was the "scapegoat" led into the wilderness and killed for the sins of Israel.

Luke 23:19, explains Barabbas had caused a sedition in the city and was guilty of murder. Rabbis believe the other thief was part of a gang of bad people in Jerusalem and Barabbas was their leader. Except the other thief represents the red thread wrapped on the handle of the outer gate to the temple, that turned white when the scapegoat died. Remember? He spoke to Yeshua and asked, "Lord, remember me when you come into Your Kingdom." Messiah said, "Today you shall be with me in Paradise." Messiah went to Abraham's Bosom that looked into hell where the rich man was. Messiah took away those keys of hell and death from satan who chained people's spirits, good and bad to hell—grave—and they could not go to Paradise, a "type of heaven" one "floor" removed from THE HEAVEN where Almighty God lives. As of yet, we—the bride of Christ have not been invited to heaven. YET! Only when we are "Caught up to meet the dead and the Lord in the Air . . ." 1 Thess. 4:17, Rev. 1:17, 18. The very first mortal human to be redeemed by our Saviors shed Blood.
Three worlds were disturbed, or had a reaction when our Savior cried "It is finished!"

A large curtain, Scripture calls it a veil in the temple was split into two, we feel certain it was that large crash of lightening accompanied by the earthquake. The "Finger of God" split that thing in two pieces. It was supposedly 80 feet high, 20 feet wide and 18 inches (1½ feet) thick. The whole universe went into total revolt. The day became night.

Tough "Manly" Roman soldiers made their confessions to God that this "truly was the Son of God," Matthew 27:54. All the fearfully petrified followers of our Savior, scattered themselves. John the beloved stayed and took Mary, the mother of Yeshua home with him. Nothing, or anyone would ever be the same, in their world that seemed to be turned upside down.

Revelation 8; gives a small glimpse of what went on in heaven at that moment. Matthew 4:11, Angels ministered to Him in the garden of Gethsemane, and at the cross capturing every drop of our Saviors Blood in each and every place it it would have spilt on the ground. Angels were present at His Resurrection John 20:12.

Hebrews 12:2, "Who, for the joy that was set before Him, He endured the cross, despising the shame."
The righteous waited for thousands of years to be taken out of that place "Abrahams Bosom," to take them to Paradise. "When He ascended on high, He led captivity captive, giving gifts to men. What say we then, He ascended, and what does it mean but that He also descended into the lower parts of the earth."
Ephesians 4:8,9

Talk about preaching evangelistic style! Our Savior held a week-end revival at the gates of hell!

Almighty God, in the book of Job, covered His throne in heaven so the spirits on earth (good and bad) could no longer look directly into God's heaven anymore, Job 26:7-11.
Job 1:6,7, is the exact reason Almighty God covered His throne. So satan does *not* know everything. 1 Corinthians 2:6-8, "We speak wisdom unto all those who are mature (in His Word), yet not the wisdom of this world, nor of the rulers of this world who are coming to nothing. But we speak the wisdom of God in a mystery. The hidden wisdom which God ordained before the ages for our glory, which *NONE* of the rulers of this world knew, for had they known, they would not have crucified the Lord of glory."
The fullness of this mystery was revealed to Paul—Romans 16:25,26—, but the powers of darkness were caught totally off guard! Wonderful! Praises to You Almighty God. Just let me revert back to childhood for a second: with tongue hanging out, Nah—Nah—Nah—Nah—Nah—Nah—satan!! Ahhhhh, that felt so good.

A Greek word for Bulls is ABBIYR and its meaning is quite clear, meaning "angel. Mighty one. Stout," implying a strong unseen world spirit.
Psalms 22:12,13, "Many bulls have surrounded me; strong bulls of Bashan have encircled me. They gape at me, with their mouths like a raging and roaring lion."

Many learned, expert scholars believe these bulls apply to the wicked and cruel people; soldiers and especially the ignorant cruel people passing by or just standing around—as my friend's at Namaste' Alzheimers nursing home, say to me when I explain how a horrible accident, or one not so bad, happened on the freeway on the way down there to visit my much—beloved husband who lives there—"people just rubber-necking on both sides of the freeway." Which, to me was quite funny, seeing as how it was an entirely new statement to me concerning accidents on a freeway.
These Scripture speaks of, are not these cruel "bulls" although one can call them that. These bulls go much deeper than that.
When we read about Moses we find there a land actually called Bashan, and was a land of giants—satans children. A race of people mentioned, Deuteronomy 3:1-8, and their leader or "father," or "King" also a giant named, OG. A very fertile land with many cattle herds. There were no cattle in Jerusalem, therefore no bulls. Our Savior knew the evils of darkness would come and heckle Him from the garden to the cross, John 14:30. Praise our Father in heaven Christ also knew they had no control over Him.
Talk about pressure! Our Savior's spirit, soul and heart were so tied in knots that He "sweat great drops of blood." Mental torment, Luke 22:44. Agony does not even begin to explain the torment He had to endure "And He despised the SHAME" of it all.

CHAPTER 23

BLOOD—TOO MUCH VAMPIRISM FOR SATAN

Joseph of Arimathea was a trader in tin. A few hundred to a thousand or more years earlier, tin had been discovered in England; the United Kingdom. This Joseph was also a member of the Sanhedrin, a wealthy man. One of the wealthiest in Jerusalem. He was also honorable and a counselor, Mark 15:43.
Ephesians 4:8-10, records the righteous saints of old as well as the unbelieving were listening to our Savior's sermon in the nether-world. satan was afraid that his time had truly come, but no, not just yet. Our Savior, we feel sure, had to wrestle those keys away from satan.

Joseph had more influential-political-power to ask—not "I beg my Lord for possession of the body of the one they called Yeshua—" No, Joseph asked Pilate for the body of Yeshua. Josheph and Nicodemus were secret disciples, followers, if you will, of Yeshua, but Pilate had not the slightest idea of this fact. If you—the reader—will remember Nicodemus came by night—secretly—to speak to Yeshua John chapter three. Scholars believe Nicodemus owned the Garden of Gethsemane where our Savior often would go for prayer, Matthew 26:36.

If these two men had not taken possession of our Savior's body, the Roman soldiers would have taken the body along with the other two dead bodys and cast them into the valley of Hinnom.

There was a deep canyon there on the west side of the city where garbage was dumped, manure from animals, the waste from the temple, dead animals and etc., everyday trash was dumped there.

The King James was taken from the Greek language which—stands to reason—when our Savior used the word "hell" He used the Greek word GEHENNAH, which means "Valley of Hinnom." A fire was continual in that valley year after year after year. The fire was never quenched, it just kept burning, for fuel was added each day. Judas hanged himself over the edge of this foul smelling, awful place.

King David was well aware of this foul place where the body of a criminal would catch fire almost immediately. We feel certain this is why David wrote in the book of Psalms "Thou will not leave my soul in hell, nor did His flesh see corruption," Acts 2:31, also.

Scripture and Josephus records there were over a hundred pounds of spices and linen cloth were need to cover the body with. These were purchased by these two "secret disciples" Mark 15:46. Joseph himself offering up his newly hewn—out of stone, burial place. A giant stone Limestone is believed to have been the stone of preference during the times Romans were in rule of the world. John 19:30, records when the last little lamb had been offered, the priest would yell out "it is finished!" At the exact same time Yeshua said "It is finished!" John 19:30, while on the cross.

We receive B.A.R. on a bi-monthly basis. The letters stand for Biblical Archeology Report. An article in one of them years ago informed the public: "In the late 1800's, large scrolls were found in Istanbul, now Constantinople, Turkey at the Saint Sophia monastery and translated immediately into English. One section of particular interest to the church read something like this:
"I sent Him to the captain of the royal guard, Malkus, to tell them to take as many Jewish soldiers as he needed to place them around the sepulchre. Then, if anything should happen they could??? themselves and not the Romans.

When the great excitement arose about the sepulchre being found empty, I felt a deeper concern than ever. I sent for Malkus, who told me he placed his lieutenant Ben Isham, with a hundred soldiers around the tomb. He told me that Isham and the soldiers were very much ashamed at what had occurred there that morning. I sent for this man Isham, and he related to me as near as I can remember the following circumstances:

He related about the beginning of the fourth watch of the night, they saw a soft and beautiful light over the sepulchre. At first he thought the women had came to embalm the body of Jesus, as was their custom, but he could not see how they could have gotten past the guards. While these thoughts were passing through his mind, surprise!? The whole place was lighted up. There seemed to be crowds of the dead in their grave clothes. All seemed to be shouting and filled with ecstasy. While all around and above was the most beautiful music he had ever heard; and the whole air seemed to be voices praising God.

"At this time there seemed to be a recling and a swinging of the earth so that he turned sick and fainted and could not remain standing. He said the earth seemed to leave from under him and his senses left him so he knew not what occurred. I asked him what position he was in when he came to himself and he said he was lying on the ground with his face earthward." End quote

The fourth watch begins at three am in the morning, and was the time our Savior often went to pray in the garden, Mark 6:48. Matthew 28:4, confirms this mans words written on the large scroll. The guards fell down as dead men. Many of the saints were seen alive, walking through the streets of Jerusalem after our Savior arose from the dead, Matthew 27:52.

Several women, close to the Savior, came to minister to his body that same morning unaware that He had risen, Mark 16:1. They were worried how they would move the stone aside to be able to go in and do their "last rites." When they arrived, they found the stone had been rolled away and the tomb was empty, and angels awaiting their arrival. Line upon line, precept upon precept.

Mary stood outside, weeping. She saw a man nearby. The man was dressed in garden-keepers clothing. John and Peter came and saw the grave clothes neatly folded inside the tomb; John 20:5-7.

John 20:17, After Mary knew He was not the gardener she took hold of him and would not have let go, except, for the words of the Savior. "Don't touch Me for I have not yet ascended to my Father and to your father; to My God and to your God."

Genesis 2:2-7, and Hebrews 4:4, Mary mistook our Savior for the gardener. God was about to create a garden and place the first Jew in it. Almighty God created Adam OUTSIDE the garden. Then He created the Garden of Eden v-8 ". . . And there He put the man." Our Almighty God, our Father finally had gotten His eternal—living—gardener—High Priest ". . . Unto us a Son is given and the government shall be upon His shoulder and His Name shall be called Wonderful, Counselor, THE Mighty God, THE Everlasting Father, THE Prince of peace," Isaiah 9:6.

Jesus was about to ascend to the Father. As the priest on The Day of Atonement put on four pieces of clothing (linen). He had to fulfill all the priestly patterns in the Law Almighty God gave to Moses. Our Savior was to "ascend to the Father" to complete the entire mission of purging the heavenly vessels in the one true life size temple in God's heaven.

Heavenly angels and or the Holy Spirit collected the Blood our Savior shed that day to keep it from touching anything earthly. The pure Blood of the heavenly Father. It was pure uncontaminated Blood when it went into our Saviors veins. And it was Pure uncontaminated when He bled so profusely all that day into the early evening-time. Our heavenly Father provided our Savior's clothing when the angels came to administer to Christ on His resurrection. Such as: As the high priest on the Day of Atonement put on four pieces of linen clothes, Jesus, the newly appointed High Priest was given linen breaches, a linen belt, line robe, and a linen head dress, fulfilling all the commandments and patterns of the Law. Line upon line . . .

Our Saviors Blood still contains the resurrection power. Life giving power. For all those who put their lives, their very souls in Him, trusting. When satan goes before God now to accuse the saints, Revelation 12:10, his case is null and void and the Father dismisses satan for a lack of evidence, Heb. 9:22.

"Now, this is the main issue of the things we are saying; We have such a High Priest, who is seated at the right hand of the throne of the Majesty in the heavens, a Minister of the sanctuary and of the True Tabernacle which the Lord in heaven designed and built and not man," Hebrews 8:1,2.

Yeshua has entered into the heavenly Temple, and by His Blood has given you and I the right to approach God Himself! We do not need to pray to saints who have died or rely on the prayers of an earthy mediator, who is every bit as human as we are:
"For there is One God and One Mediator between God and man, THE MAN Yeshua the Christ," 1 Tim. 2:5.

There is only one Priest! The High Priest Yeshua! We can pray anywhere, any time we need to. We do not need another human to pray for us. *We* have our Blessed Savior THE ONE—THE ONLY—living forever High Priest Jesus! Who will hear us each and every time we pray in His Name. This was the whole purpose of His living, dying, and being resurrected.

CHAPTER 24

CONTROL YOUR TONGUE?

There is a part of our bodies that, for some, is impossible to keep it from sinning. That is—a small thing—our tongue. David had trouble with his, at times it has been hard for us to control that little organ that is so necessary for life itself, "Keep your tongue from evil . . ." Psalms 34:13, 1 Peter 3:10.

Job experienced "the Power of the Tongue; from Eliphaz the Temanite, Job chapter four. In chapter five he has these words for Job: "God makes sore and bind's it up, He wounds and His hands make whole. He shall deliver you in six troubles, yea, in seven there shall no evil touch you:

1 – in famine, He shall redeem you from death.
2 – in war, from the power of the sword.
3 – You shall be hid from the scourge of the tongue neither shall you be afraid of destruction when it comes.
4 – At destruction and famine you shall laugh
5 – Neither shall you be afraid of the beasts of the earth, for you shall be in league with the stones of the field; and the beasts of the field shall be at peace with you. Then you shall know your tabernacle shall be in peace, and you shall visit your habitation and shall not sin.
6 – You shall know also that your seed shall be great, and your offspring as the grass of the earth.

7 – You shall come to your grave in a full age, like as a shock of corn comes into his season.

"Lo, this we have searched it, so it is. Hear it, and know thou it for your good." 5:18-27.

Eliphaz spoke words of life with his tongue. Poor Job! God knows this man needed it for the torment he was in. In his body as well as his spirit, having lost all his wealth his children, and a nagging wife telling him to curse God and die. He had every right to feel sorry for himself but he didn't. Job's history doesn't record him feeling sorry for himself. Greatly disappointed but no "woe is me."

James 3 records "The tongue is unruly."

"The tongue of the just is as choice silver. The tongue of the wise is healthy. A wholesome tongue is as a tree of life" Proverbs 10:20, 12:18, 15:4.
Proverbs 18:21, "Death and life are in the power of the tongue."
"Whosoever keeps his tongue, keeps his soul."
Prov. 21:23

Isaiah 30:27, "His tongue as a devouring fire."
This speaks of our precious Father "Behold, the Name of the Lord comes from afar burning with His anger and the burden of it is heavy. His lips are full of indignation, and His tongue as a devouring fire." Which brings us to the Words our blessed Savior gives to His people, the Jews on His second coming to touch His feet to the earth:

"And one shall say to Him," What are these wounds in Your hands?" Then He shall answer, "Those with which I was wounded in the house of my friends." Line upon line, precept upon . . . Zechariah 13:6.

And really, the worse type's of wounds are the scars left by those we once called "friends". Emotional wounds are not physical wounds, as was—both—heaped up—packed down—full—and running over, with these perverse injuries of our Savior. Even now, in our day "Christians" are guilty of wounding our heart—their fellow—believers, with their words. Not only that, their actions alone are wounds to our soul.

Yeshua suffered intense cruelty of every sort; verbal mental and physical, not to mention the shame of it all, plus being hanged naked. You yourselves know that type of shame. Remember? Your wedding night? Need I say more.
Our Father in heaven allowed all this to happen to His only Son; because He is all-knowing in each and everything we—ourselves—have to forgive: "Forgive us our trespasses as we forgive those who trespass against us."

Christ was our substitute. He took our place. He, who knew no sin, took on the sin's—plural—of the entire world! We, who are guilty, must beg, and if necessary, plead! For *Him*! This sinless—perfect—human/God figure, to forgive *US*! Yes us, "For *all* have sinned and come short of the glory of God. And *WHO* is GLORY? Yeshua! "He is the LIGHT of the world." What is glory? Glory is Light! When Hollywood shines lights—they call—the limelight—on a lone movie star, what do they say about that star in the tabloids the next day? "There she is, in all her glory!" Under the "limelight." Or "There he is, in all his glory!" Even the narrators who were there at the moment the limelight was shown on them and the photographers camera's flashing everywhere say "Okay. A moment of silence here, for here they come."

What is TRUE light? True light is Wisdom and Knowledge that comes only from one source; THE Father who is in heaven, giving *all* EVERYTHING to His One, His Only Son (all others we adopted!) Read all of Isaiah 53, to understand, fully, that there was nothing left undone by our Savior, from the Garden to the Cross.

When soldiers came home from Viet Nam, whether they walked upright or were arriving in wheelchairs, all were spat upon. Our Savior also was spit upon, "I gave My back to the smitters . . . I did not hide my face from shame and spitting." Isaiah 50:6. This is the worse type of insult, people, and scholars say.

To be spit upon is disgusting, degrading and any English word that is horrible as well, you can think of.

When the Israelites were wandering in the desert and Moses was leading them. Miriam, Moses' sister was busy mocking Moses' wife and God caused leprosy to come upon Miriam. Moses begged God to heal her and the Lord answered: "If her father had spit in her face would she not be shamed seven days? Let her be shut out of the camp seven days, and afterward she shall be received again." Numbers 12:14.

The law given to Moses, by Almighty God, meant spitting was an act of condemnation. If we are condemned—spiritually—we must repent and turn to God. For a Christian to feel condemned they too must repent, but for some time afterward we still feel as though we—still—are under condemnation, others have said.

The book of Ruth records when Naomi's brother-in-law refused to marry Ruth, he took his shoe off and she spit in his face and slapped him. A good thing too, else Boaz could not have paid for Ruth and was then able to marry her. A Jew marrying a Gentile. Jesus, a Jew, called us and we are Gentiles, His bride. John 1:11, "Christ came to His own and His own did not receive Him." Oppressed—rejected—despised—Afflicted—wounded—smitten—experienced sorrow and grief as well.

"If we confess . . ." say aloud! For even the walls have ears. ". . . Our sins He is faithful and just to forgive us our sins and to cleanse us from all unrighteousness," 1 John 1:9.

183

Our confessing unto salvation means to agree with the covenant. The New Testament *is* the covenant, and to acknowledge the covenant! The Blood of Jesus—which is God the Fathers BLOOD—must be applied and confessing does that. The BLOOD of Jesus is the most powerful substance on earth! In the whole universe!

Isn't it strange that when people speak the name of our Savior—Jesus—or even bow our heads in silent prayer in public, suddenly the whole community is outraged. Yet, if you mention the name ALLAH, Buddha or Mohammed, not one single person is offended. Here in America, I speak of. That solid fact alone ought to explain "There's just something about that name. Jesus, Jesus." Its because they are "As Cain, who was of that wicked one," satan!! 1 Jn 3:12
Our Savior's Blood deals with sin and His very Name—Yeshua—is one powerful weapon. It can attack sickness', defeat sin and put *any type* of demonic activity back where it belongs.

"The first covenant had also ordinances of divine service and was a worldly sanctuary. For there was a tabernacle made. The first wherein was the Menorah, the table, the show bread, which is called the sanctuary. After the second vail, the tabernacle which is the Holiest of all; Which had the golden censer, the ark of the covenant overlaid—all over—with gold which held the golden pot of Manna, Aaron's rod that budded and the stone tablets of the covenant. On top of its lid were Cherubims of glory overshadowing the mercy set of which we now speak of particularly.
When these things were first ordained, the priests went always into the first tabernacle accomplishing the services of God. But in the second, went the High Priest alone once every year and not without blood, for which he offered for himself and for the sins of the people: The Holy Spirit now signifies that the way into the Holiest of Holies was not yet made manifest, while as yet the first

tabernacle was yet standing, which was a figure for that time—then present—in which were offered both gifts and sacrifices that could not make him that did these services, perfect, as pertaining to our conscience brain. Which stood only in meat and drink and diverse washings and carnal ordinances imposed upon them *until* the time of reformation. NOW! Christ has come—with His death/ resurrection—A High Priest of good things to come by a greater and more perfect tabernacle not made with hands, that is to say, not of this—Solomon or Herod's—building, neither by the blood of goats and calves, but by His Own Blood He entered in Once into the Holy of Holies, having obtained eternal redemption for us. Because the blood of bulls and of goats, and the ashes of a heifer sprinkling the unclean, sanctifies to the purifying of the flesh: How much more shall the Blood of Christ, who through His eternal spirit offer Himself without spot to God, purge your conscience from dead works to serve the Living God? And for this cause He is the mediator—the lawyer—of the New Covenant (testament), that by means of death for the redemption of the transgressions that were under the first covenant (testament), they which are called might receive the promise of eternal inheritance. For where a testament is, there must also of necessity be the death of the testator. For a testament is of force ONLY after the testator is dead and has no strength while the testator lives."
The first testament was not without blood. It was dedicated with blood, so must the second testament be bought with Blood.

Hebrews 9:1-18

Hebrews 9:14-22, Christ, the testator of the second testament was taken back to heaven and His flesh burnt on the Brazen Alter there. Revelation 8:1, The Brazen Alter in the Holy of Holies in heaven there—thus—the one half hour of silence in heaven during that time.

Hebrews 9:23,24, Proof that the Holy of Holies is in heaven.

Hebrews 9:5, Two angels sat, facing one another wings outspread in a protective mode. One at the foot and one at the head—or top or bottom—of the mercy seat.

Mary Magdalene saw these two angels at the top and bottom, in the tomb, where they had lain the Christ. Thus, again, "The Mercy Seat."

When Christ hung on the cross, the Romans had nailed his feet to the extra little board they had attached to all crosses, calling it "the mercy seat." It was used by the victims hanging on these crosses to stabilize their feet while lifting their bodies up to catch a full breath while hanging there. None of them ever realizing they were prolonging their life by doing that, thereby feeding the sadistic nature of the soldiers assigned to these gruesome tasks of theirs. These soldiers had nothing to do all day. They weren't at war. So they sat around devising grotesque ways of causing slow deaths of those doomed to hang on a tree.

CHAPTER 25

GENERATION X' ERS

Is a generation whose names once served as marketing shorthand for "restless youth," ready to assume the reins of power? I don't think so.

Matthew 24:13, Mark 13:13, "He that shall endure shall be saved." Endure what? The verse before it which reads, "Many false prophets shall arise and shall deceive many. Many shall be offended and shall betray one another, they even shall hate one another." Verses 12, 11.

Mark puts it this way, "Now the brother shall betray the brother to death, and the father the son, and the children shall rise up against their parents and shall cause them to be put to death. You shall be hated of all men for My Name's (YAH) sake, but they that endure to the end shall be saved."

"Then there came unto Job all his brothers and sisters and all they that had been of his acquaintance before, and all did eat bread with him in his house. And they bemoaned him . . ."

Bemoaned means together they relived all the awful things that had came upon Job agreeing with him, and complaining with him of the evil that can enter into people to cause them to feel they have been totally abandoned by God Himself.

". . . Bemoaned him and comforted him over all the evil that the Lord had brought upon him. Every man also gave him a piece of money, and everyone an earring of gold. So the Lord blessed the LATTER END of Job more than his beginnings . . ." Job 42:11,12.

Why? Because Job *made* himself an overcomer as is spoken of in Revelation chapter three. Job lifted up his head and, as Jesus said ". . . for your redemption draws nigh."

"*Blessed* are you when men hate you and when they separate themselves from you, not wanting to be around you anymore, and shall *reproach* you and *cast out your name as evil*, for the Son of man's sake. You *Rejoice* in that day and leap for joy, for Behold, your reward is great in heaven, for in this like manned their fathers did to the prophets.
"But WOE! Unto you that are rich for you have received your consolation. WOE! to you that are full for *you* shall be hungry. WOE! to you that laugh now! For you shall mourn and weep. *KEY!!* WOE! Unto you when all men speak well of you! For so did their fathers to the false prophets. (Redemption?) But I say unto you which hear, *LOVE* your enemies! Do good to those that hate you. Bless them that curse you. Pray for them that despitefully use you. Unto him that slaps you on one cheek, offer also the other cheek. To him that takes your cloak give them your coat also.
"Gives to every man that asks of you, and of him that takes away your goods, don't ask for them back . . ."

KEY! The golden rule I was taught in school! "And as you would that men should do to you? You also do to them likewise!" Luke 6:22-31.

Wow! The Word of God truly is powerful! And sharper than any double—edged sword. Able to cut into two any persons soul from their spirit. Wonderful.

"Yea though I walk through the valley of death I will fear no evil for thou art with me."

Psalms 23:4

The "Valley of the shadow of death" is the valley of Armageddon "The mountains of Megiddo (reference Rev. 16:16) and is the Plain of Esdraelon "the classic battleground of Scripture," Ezekiel 38:8,21, 39:2,4, Isaiah 14:25, 2 Ki. 23:29, Zech. 12:11.
"Evil shall slay the wicked, and they that hate the righteous shall be desolate." Ps. 34:21.

"My enemies speak evil of me, When shall he die, and his name perish?" Ps. 41:5.

"You give your mouth to evil and your tongue frames deceit." Ps. 50:19.

"He (God) shall reward evil to my enemies, cut them off in Your truth." Ps. 54:5.

"You that love the Lord? Hate evil. He preserves the souls of His saints. He delivers them out of the hand of the wicked." Ps. 97:10.

"Let this be the reward . . ?" This? The garment that the enemy and his girdle (wide belt) wherewith he is girded continually. "One set of clothing. One belt that girds him continually means" dressed for WAR.
"Be the reward of my adversaries from the Lord, and of them that speak evil against my soul (body)." Ps. 109:19,20.

"For their feet run to evil, and make haste to shed (innocent) blood." Prov. 1:16.

"But whosoever listens to me shall dwell safely and shall be quiet from fear of evil." Prov. 1:33.

"Our Lord has made all things for Himself. Yes, even the wicked for the day of evil." Prov. 16:4. WOW.

"An ungodly man digs up evil, and in his lips there is a burning fire Prov. 16:27.

It used to be only journalists were the ones digging up "trash" on people. This was called Yellow journalism. Other journalists reported the words given to them. Now days, it is not just yellow journalists digging up trash on prominent people in the news. Its people we know! And hold dear to our hearts! It might even be your neighbor or family member! God help us. Please deliver Your children from any and all of this degradation of evil in Jesus Name.

"Devise not evil to your neighbor seeing as how he lives securely beside you." Prov. 3:29.

"Say not thou, I will recompense evil, but wait upon the Lord and He shall save you." Prov. 20:22.

"The soul of the wicked desires evil, his neighbor finds no favor in his eyes." Prov. 21:10.

"A prudent man foresees the evil and hides himself . . ." Prov. 22:3. Oh how I want to be a prudent person.

"A prudent man foresees the evil and hides himself . . ." Prov. 27:12. Solomon must have forgotten he'd wrote this earlier? No. He knew exactly what he was doing. Scholars have always said when God repeats Himself, He is doing so to get our attention.

"Hey! Are you listening to Me?!" (God)

"Their feet run to evil and they make haste to shed innocent blood. Their thoughts are thoughts of iniquity. Wasting and destruction are in their paths." Isa. 59:7.

"The righteous perish and no one lays it to heart. And merciful men are taken away none considering that the righteous is taken away from the evil to come. He shall enter into peace, they shall rest in their beds, each one walking in his uprightness." Isaiah 57:1,2.

"Woe to him that covers an evil covetousness to his house that he may set his nest on high that he may be delivered from the power of evil! You have consulted shame to your house by cutting off many people and have sinned against your own soul." Habakkuk 2:9,10.

"Rejoice with them that do rejoice and weep with them that weep. Be of the same mind one toward another. Mind not high things but condescend to men of low estate. Be not wise in your own conceits. Recompense to no man evil for evil. Provides things honest in the sight of all men. If it be possible as much as lie's within you, live peaceable with all men.
"Dearly beloved, avenge not yourselves. But rather give place to wrath, for it is written, Vengeance is Mine, I will repay, saith the Lord."

Romans 12:15-19

It would be to everyones interest to read 1 Corinthians 13:1-13. What a wonderful insight on one word. That word is CHARITY.

"Speak evil of no man . . ." Titus 3:2.

"But the tongue can no man tame. It is an unruly evil, full of deadly poison." James 3:8

"Beloved, don't follow that which is evil but that which is good. He that does good is of God. He that does evil has not seen God." 3 John 11.

CHAPTER 26

AMOS DECLARED, "A LION HAS ROARED

In recent history there have been various great turning points. For instance, we read about the turning point in 1968, sort of a culture revolution. In the 1990's, there was a turning point in the communist world. Which brings us to this moment in time. We have seen the Arab world, "An Arabellion" or Arab Spring, as it is called. Also, now, we are in the midst of an economic turning point, taking place all over the world ("New World Order," Lisbon Treaty). Scripture speaks of a turning point which will characterize society in these last days. People are always saying that TIMES are getting worse. Times are still the same, its the people who are getting worse. There have always been people whose behavior is as we will describe.

"This know also that in the last days perilous times shall come. For men shall be lovers of their own selves, covetous, boasters, proud, blasphemers, disobedient to parents, unthankful, unholy, without natural affection, trucebreakers, false accusers, incontinent, fierce, despisers of those that are good, traitors, heady, highminded, lovers of pleasures more than lovers of God (our Creator); having a form of godliness but denying the power thereof: from such—turnaway." Don't have any more to do with them. 2 Timothy 3:1-5, Romans 1:29, 32.

"This know also . . ." shows the urgency of heeding the prophetic statements of the Bible. We should not close our eyes to them and simply just pass over them. No. Neither should we leave them unmentioned and unheeded just because they do not suit us, seem to be too negative, not evangelistic enough, or because other matters seem to appear to be more important to us. The Church, the body of Christ should not suppress the truths concerning the end times.

1 – IN THE FUTURE. The "last days", in verse one in Greek is ESCHATOS, from which we get our word eschatology—the doctrine of the last times. Describing something that comes last, the time when God's spiritual history will come to its climax. Paul writes "in the last days perilous times shall come." He is not describing his time although there were people with such characteristics even then, from whom Timothy was to turn away from, verse 5. He was concerned rather with a time which lay in the future, the "last days."

2 – WORLD EMBRACING. Paul writes, "For men shall be . . ." In the end times there will be a world—embracing, global attitude of mankind which has all the characteristics described in 2 Timothy 3:1-5.

3 – CHRISTIANIZED WORLD. The apostle says concerning this . . . "having a form of godliness . . ." This means that Christianity must be widespread before the people later develope from Christianity to this negative anti-Christian characteristic. At the time of the apostle Paul, this was not possible in such a form. This does however, to our Christian West of the 21st Century as to no other time before it.

Some years ago the former German President, Gustav Heinemann said of "Christian" Europe, "Europe has the gospel of Jesus Christ to thank for the position in the world which it has led in the past." But, today the world is turning away from Christianity increasingly. This is why Alexander Solzhenitsyn once said, fittingly, "If I were asked to determine the main thing about the whole of the 20th century, and to put it in a few words, I would be incapable of finding anything more exact and more striking than to repeat, 'Mankind has forgotten God.'"

PERILOUS TIMES—PLURAL, not perilous time, point to the fact that chaotic social circumstances are increasing in intensity—like waves in the end times. Its an "up and down," a "to and fro" movement. This should remind us of the interval "between birth-pangs," Matt. 24:8, and Revelation 12, for Israel. The youth and student movement of the 1968 revolution we've read and heard so much about, which practically coincided with the conquest of Jerusalem by the Israelis are such a wave. The end times are connected in an absolute sense with the restoration of Israel, Luke 21:29, the fig tree and all the trees; Ezekiel 36:33, and Romans 11:25, 27, Jeremiah 30:24-31, 32, 33:7, 8, Psalms 102:13-18, Deut. 4:30, 31:29. Did these "perilous times" of the last days begin here? Just sayin'. Of this time it is written: "1968—What a year! A liberated unleashed youth overthrew the rotten moral of the German postwar society, stormed across the broken idols, and with much laughter trod into the dust what had been reputed to be the highest virtues for centuries: chaste abstinence, modern contentment, piously devoted obedience, and submissive respect of law and authorities—and cheeky and cheery these youth began to build their new world, to live their own lives, to find their own moral. Like every true revolution, it was a revolt of the youth; it was directed against the old order and the old ones; against the proven and the wrong traditions, against the existing establishment . . . '68 has become a myth! It was the onset of a totally new age:" "This know also that in the last days perilous times shall come." With a new conception of how people should be "For men shall be . . ." This movement feels they should be free and self-determined, not to be governed by the authorities from above, but able to create for themselves a new free and democratic world where they would find room enough to develope their own personality all around," END. And they did it—all without God our creator. THE ONE without whom nothing would exist. In this era Sherily McLaine emerged with her "New Age" movement, that, today is a massive cult with many, many followers. Also Mr. Armstrongs Scientology movement. Someone I am personally acquainted with, by no means "friend" belongs strongly with Tom Cruise's revolutionary movement. There are times when a Christian gets "a toe in the door" of these people on a one to one basis, can—at times—persuade this person on just how that our Savior has no part-at-all in these cult movements lives not to mention their By-Laws. Messiah should be the very heart of their movement. Just as He is with all Christians. But, these are no where near a Christian as a true Christian knows. Like Paul said, "If any one—whether a person or angel from heaven—come's preaching to you any other gospel, other than the one we've preached to you, the gospel of Jesus Christ and Him crucified, don't listen to them." They are already damned, and don't bid them Shalom.

For "perilous times," again, we can say "hard times," "evil times." It is a time of change, a great turning point in all places for all peoples. With these statements, the Holy Spirit does not give us any hope of better times to come. He states quite simply times will get worse. Concerning our time, a society with no values is openly spoken of today, a state of terror and of a lobby which is changing our society. Our world is characterized by change, violence, terror, revolutions, demonstrations, rebellions and liberality. In the following we will consider the 18 references in 2 Timothy 3:1-5, which describes the society of the end times.

MEN WILL BE:

1 – SELFISH. This has been translated as "lovers of their own selves" such as in the two cities, one of which was Sodom. KJV, says "egotistical, egocentric." Man is in the center. Man takes the place of God. A psychoanalyst explained, "The supreme maxim in psychoanalysis is self-realization and autonomy."

Another example of this are the ubiquitous casting shows. Go on line to WELT ONLINE, and read: "Castings produce a cult of permanent self-production, self portrayal and publicity—seeking—the casting society is no longer restricted to television. In the business world, on social networks, and in their private lives many people are according to experts, indulging in self-production . . . casting shows such as "American Idol" and "The X Factor" are, according to experts, such as Bernhard Porksen in Tubingen, Germany, an important sign of a social change. Casting has become a lifestyle in which the individual continually has to be in the limelight. The battle for publicity is no longer restricted to celebrities and media professionals, continued Porksen. Even a Bavarian building industry union used a "building camp" on a German TV show, "Your chance," in which three candidates were competing for a job. America has one too run by Donald Trump. A sort of "cult of permanent self-production" has come about which is promoted by television and and the internet. Thousands of people have put their photographs and video clips on social networks and their own homepages. Porksen sees a development in which everyone is suspected of only wanting to portray themselves.

2 – GREEDY and COVETOUS:
"The rich answers roughly," Proverbs 18:23. This is not a principle, but suggests that money can ruin the character. Do not the EURO/bank and debt crisis—and everything connected with them—illustrate this Biblical truth? Business without moral foundations as spoken of, where there are allegedly no guilty people but many victims. A material way of thinking is replacing spiritual values.

We're not talking just about a financial crisis but a crisis of moral values. The states incur horrendous debts in order to finance consumer greed, because no one is prepared to go without anything. Which leads us to wonder and fittingly ask, "Are we too satisfied for God . . ? A German Finance Minister Wolfgang

Schaeuble, "As successful as the market economic model is, the more it depends on mechanisms which—if they are not controlled and limited—will result in inhuman consequences. The infinite striving for profit for which there is no automatic halt, the production of ever newer needs of the consumer society, and the depletion of all our natural resources of the earth, all lead to conditions which are a threat to human survival . . . If the European Union, in particular the Eurozone, come under pressure of financial markets to the limits of their tolerance, this also has to do with human extravagance . . ."

3 – BOASTERS:
This means boastful, arrogant, self-importance, conceited. Think—present day politicians, the newly rich, etc.

4 – PROUD:
This means exactly what it says; exalting oneselves over all moral, ethical and social limits.

5 – BLASPHEMERS: The Lord GOD has spoken!
"Abusive." It is about people's self-made importance. Exalting themselves by putting other people down. Their abuse is directed at God and at man. Its against politicians, governments and Christian; Christianity in general. Television comedy shows ridicule politicians, for instance SLANDER is their norm, made fun of, and Christian values are dragged in the mud.

6 – DISOBEDIENT to PARENTS:
This is not merely about children not obeying parents and rebelling against them, but its a widespread end-times system. The family, the smallest unit of the state is attacked and parents are robbed of their power. Values which demand living in families and society are abandoned or devalued. God, the family and the neighbor are despised.

Who will not fear?

7 – UNTHANKFUL:
People regard everything as their very own achievement. They look back on previous times with deep and utter contempt. Young managers unscrupulously fire older coworkers. Employees, who in the past would have earned a bonus for their faithfulness and loyalty, instead lose their jobs.

8 – UNHOLY REVERENCE:
Absolutely nothing is sacred and holy to man any more. People have no respect for godly principles, state laws, social guidelines, the family, unborn children or the aged person. They don't shrink back from anything *un*holy, neither abortion nor euthanasia.

9 – WITHOUT NATURAL AFFECTION, HEARTLESS, COLD:
This is the fulfillment of Matthew 24:12, "Because iniquity shall abound, the love of many shall wax cold."

10 – TRUCE-BREAKERS:
People don't want to commit themselves to anything; therefore, we have relationships without a marriage certificate. This has an effect on greater or smaller matters and results in family—neighbors—others—feuds, divorces, disputes, demonstrations, in irreconcilable differences between social classes. Love for our neighbor, the will to change and integration are lacking.

Who will not fear?

11 – FALSE ACCUSERS:
In Greek its diaboloi. You know, folks from Mexico call satan, diabolo. The devil is on the one hand diabolus, that is, the bringer of confusion, and on the other hand the accuser, Revelation 12:10. These last times are truly diabolic times, full of false accusations in which the truth is distorted and values changed. Truth is declared to be a lie, and injustice and lies are called truth. God is said to be nonexistent, for instance, and creation is made

to be God. What the Word of God says about sin is despised, but sin against the environment is observed and condemned.

London England. Islamists and their sympathizers have been able to force the main—branch of the Israeli firm AHAVA (Love), which produces health and cosmetic products to close down. The police will not be able to protect the shops.

Whoever believes in the Bible, confesses it and wants to live in accordance with it, can be legally prosecuted and quickly becomes a persecuted person who is a nuisance to society. Apparently this is not the case if you adhere to the Koran. At the end of 2006, a German woman from Morocco accused her Moroccan husband of beating her. The charge was overturned on grounds she should have known before that Muslims beat their wives—that is contained in the Koran!

The Lord GOD has spoken!

12 – INCONTINENT
Doctors call a person unable to control their bodily functions, incontinent. The NIV translates this word "Without—self-control," which adds up to the same thing. People on drugs are unable to control themselves. They kill, steal, rob, beat up people simply for what little bit of money they obtain to buy *more* of the same drug that made them incontinent in the first place. And yet they have the absolute nerve, the audacity to say, "I'm not hooked on any drug."
Incontinent means acting on impulse, unprincipled. It's a total and complete walk without the Holy Spirit, Galatians 5:16-21.

13 – FIERCE, BRUTAL, CRUEL: Who will not fear?
This means impulsive, showing no mercy, uncontrolled anger, inclined to violence. Mobbing at school, place of work, churches, falls into this category. As long as it serves one's own interests, the right to demonstrate is taken advantage of. Police are attacked and

become targets. If people think differently demonstrate peacefully for their convictions, i.e. protest marches against abortion, these are often hindered by violence. Far-right extremists are rightfully restrained by the state, but left-wing extremists are tolerated. If victims of communist regimes take to the streets and protest against left-wing elements, they are attacked.

The Lord GOD has spoken!

14 – DESPISERS of THOSE THAT ARE GOOD:
This is about despisers of virtue, who reject those who love to do good. There is active resistance to what is good, to all morality. Civil disobedience is propagated, gender mainstreaming promoted, marital infidelity furthered, etc. The homosexual lobby for instance, influences the media and the legal system in their favor increasingly and so it seems, permanently.

Who will not fear?

15 – TRAITORS:
This reminds us of Judas who became a traitor to our messiah. There is a parallel to this in the end times, in which an apostate Christianity betrays the doctrine of Messiah and aids anti-Christianity. Doctrines other than the Bible are promoted, while the Biblical doctrine is despised. Thus, a theology professor has been quoted as saying, "Whoever takes the Bible literally does not take it seriously."

The evangelist and journalist, a German, Helmut Matthies, pointed out that more people in churches believe in the dogma concerning the environment than the virgin birth of our Savior Jesus. Many church people are far better known to the public for their warnings concerning climate change than through their witness for Christ. According to Franklin Graham, son of Billy Graham the name of Jesus Christ is being suppressed in public life increasingly. It is allowed to pray publicly to "a god," but not to our Lord Jesus Christ.

16 – HEADY:

Some translators say "RASH." This means behavior based on emotions or passions. Meaning they are adventurers who are prepared to risk everything, and do. I have a "for instance" of my own to share with you,

Having just met a lady for the very first time I felt I knew her from somewhere and I said as much to her. She assured me "no, we've never met as far as I know." I was convinced it was the Holy Spirit within us identifying Himself. Am so sorry to report to you I could not have been so wrong!

Having worked at a news agency for 17 years I felt I'd been subjected to any and everything—snide—in this whole wide world. Every holiday the people who worked in the warehouse of the News Agency would get drunk on the job. No one was ever fired over it for in the bosses office, he and his secretary did the same. In our office—of three individuals—nothing like that went on, at all, that I could tell. I was not the only Christian working there, but rest assured I was the only one the brunt of drunken jokes. Being a child of God Christian—they didn't like. My obstaining from everything worldly—they didn't like. I knew not what actually went on outside of home—work—church so my own ignorance of the world was the brunt of their jokes. These were not bad people at all, and they were careful not to hurt my feelings even though drunk. So I didn't mind at all. We loved one another. Then, the lady I'd just met not even a year ago of whom I was so sure the Holy Spirit had revealed Himself to me through her? She and her husband invited me for an overnight at their house. I felt they were good Christian folk so I readily accepted. Talk about a drill sergeant. One was enough in the Air Force. I thought. But two at once, and finding out I knew not the things they knew was absolute fodder for them. After finding out all they wanted to know about me, from me, who still remained in the dark about what was going on, went to bed without a glass for water for moisture for my mouth and to take my medicines so my night was miserable, although the bed itself was an absolute dream it was so comfortable.

The next morning everything had changed and each of them were tripping over each other. They could not get me out of their house quick enough. After a day or two, even a night of wondering what went wrong, searching every nook and cranny of my brain to remember what I'd done so awfully wrong to be thrown out like something the cat had dragged in the night before. Could not think of a thing but their answer arrived in my mail two days later. Was called a liar and a coward by these two supposedly "Christian" people. Talk about a Daniel in the lions den! The whole armor of God is an absolute necessity even in and around so-called—Christians. I did learn from the drill sergeant the enemy infiltrates the camp of Gods people. And sometimes they come in as a "double spy," working for both sides. That is what this man and woman were. Double spy's. Jesus said "A double-minded-person is unstable in all their ways," James 1:8, and God hates it. From the first phone call I was sabotaged. Entering their home? Worse!

17 – HIGHMINDED:
Or conceited. People only thinking of themselves as being important and have only their own goals in view.

18 – LOVERS OF PLEASURES MORE THAN LOVERS OF GOD:
This describes a lifestyle from which God is completely excluded. They are open to everything that is fun but closed to everything divine. Fun has become the substance of their life, and we are subjected to living in their fun society.
Our Bible even speaks of people whose belly is their God, Philippians 3:19. In keeping with what we have spoken of here and summarizing it, is a book that has already become a bestseller. Its called "The Coming Insurrection." It is an anonymous book whose authors hide behind the name, "The Invisible Committee."

According to the German Magazine "Factum," the book is an anarchist manifesto, a provocative essay producing violence and lawlessness.

The above 18 end-times characteristics are summarized into a 19th century . . ." . . . Having a form of godliness but denying the power thereof. . ." These unspiritual and brutal changes which the people of the last times are bringing about do not stop at the gates of the church. Verse 13 says that these are deceived deceivers, "But evil men and seducers shall wax worse and worse, deceiving and being deceived."
Things are not getting better; they are getting worse. They cling to certain forms and certain religiosity, church traditions, garments, titles, ceremonies and rituals, but totally deny the power of the sweet Holy Spirit, "From such turn away." Even Timothy was instructed to keep himself from people with such characteristics.

2 Timothy 3, "Finally brothers and sisters, whatsoever things are true, whatsoever things are honest, whatsoever things are just, whatsoever things are pure, things that are lovely, things that are of good report; if there beany virtue and if there beany praise, think on these things" Philippians 4:8.

The great turning point will come with the return of Yeshua. Yeshua Himself will have the last Word, "And He that sat upon the throne said, Behold, I make all things new. And He said unto me, write: for these words are true and faithful," Rev. 21:5. Let us live our lives as True Christians! Our Savior instructed me when I was a young girl of 11 or 12, that He would avenge my enemies before my eyes. I will not die until He has avenged me of each and every enemy of myself.

CHAPTER 27

BLIND LEADING THE BLIND SABOTAGES THE INNOCENT

Lately it seems satan has done way more outside the church, than under the cover of the four walls of the church. Assassians, murderers, treacherous as these two are, and I might add, these two embodiments are premeditated you can rest assured of that, have filled church members hearts with these ugly deceitful horrible things. Whether the church member is in or out of the Church, they've a mind-set to destroy true Christians character and fill them with shame.

Luke 6:42, Matthew 7:1 "Judge not lest you be judged by the same judgment . . . You hypocrite . . !" You hypocrite!" Matt. 15:7, 16:3, Mk. 7:6, Lk. 12:56, Matt 22:18, 24:51.

And now that I've told you the truth, "Will you also go away? John 6:67.

"Lord, who shall live in Your tabernacle? Who shall dwell in Your holy hill?" Answer; "He that walks uprightly and works righteousness and speaks the truth in his heart." Psalms 15:1, 2.

"The meek will He guide in judgment: and the meek will He teach His ways. All the pathes of the Lord are mercy and truth unto such as keep His covenant and His testimonies, For Your Names sake. O Lord, pardon my iniquity for it is great."

Psalms 25:9-11

"Pull me out of the net that they have laid for me privately, for You are My strength. Into Your hand I commit My Spirit, You have redeemed me O Lord God of truth, I have hated them that regard lying vanities, but I trust in You Lord."

Psalms 31:4-6

"He shall send from heaven and save me from the reproach of him that would swallow me up. God shall send forth His mercy and His truth. My soul is among lions: and I lie even among them that are set on fire, even the sons of men whose teeth are spears and arrows, and their tongue is a sharp sword." Psalms 57:3-5.

When horrible things like these happen we are reminded of the Words our Savior spoke, "When you see all these things happening, lift up your head for your redemption draws nigh." The people ostracized our Savior too. We are not alone.

"You have shown your people hard things, You have made us to drink the wine of astonishment. You have given a banner to them that fear You that it may be displayed because of the truth." Psalms 60:3, 4.

"Mercy and truth have met, together. Righteousness and peace have kissed each other." Ps. 85:10.

"You Oh Lord are a God full of compassion and graciousness, longsuffering and plenteous in mercy and truth." Ps. 86:15.

"Justice and judgment are the habitation of Your throne, mercy and truth shall go before Your face. Blessed is the people that know the joyful sound: they shall walk O Lord in the light of Your countenance. In Your Names shall they rejoice all the day, and in Your righteousness shall *they* be exalted." Ps. 89:14-16.

"They that dwell in the secret place of the Most High shall abide under the shadow of the Almighty. I will say of the Lord, He is my refuge and my fortress, My God, in Him will I trust. Surely He shall deliver you from the snare of the enemy, and from the noisome pestilence. He shall cover you with His feathers and under His wings shall you trust, His truth shall be your shield and buckler. You shall not be afraid of the terror by night, nor for the arrow that flies by day, nor for the pestilence that walks in darkness nor for the destruction that waste's at noon day."

Ps. 91:1-6

"With trumpets and sound of cornet make a joyful noise before the Lord, the King." Ps. 98:6.
"For the Lord is good, His Mercy is everlasting, and His Truth endures to all generations." Ps. 100:5.
"For His merciful kindness is great toward us, and the truth of the Lord endures for ever. Praise you the Lord." 117:2.
"I have chosen THE WAY of truth: Your judgments have I laid before myself. I have stuck to Your testimonies O Lord please don't put me to shame." 119:30, 31. Jesus said to His disciples "Now that you know the truth, will you also go away?"

Psalms 142: "I cried unto the Lord with my voice, with my voice to the Lord I did make my supplication. I poured out my complaint before Him, I showed before Him my trouble. When my spirit was overwhelmed within me, then You knew my path. In the way wherein I walked have they privately laid a snare for me. I looked on my right hand—and behold—there was no man that would know me, refuge failed me. No man cared for my soul.
"I cried to You O Lord, I said, YOU are my refuge and my portion in the land of the living. Attend unto my cry, for I am brought very low, deliver me from my persecutors, for they are stronger than I. Bring my soul out of prison that I may praise Your Name. The righteous shall compass me about, for You shall deal boundifully with me." Psalm 142.

Our God made, "Heaven and earth, the sea and all that therein is, which keeps truth for ever."

Ps. 146:6.

From all the above Scripture's we have learned: That God is truth. All truth knowledge and wisdom comes solely from Him, without Him and His attributes we, all of us, would most definately be, "the blind leading the blind," as our Savior Himself said.
Messiah also said "And when these things begin to come to pass—then LOOK UP—and lift up your heads, for your redemption draws near." Luke 21:28.

We need not be ashamed. Of any thing, and especially with the "sly as a fox," blindsiding us with their "terrors by day and their flaming arrows by night." Yes, we agree, the forked tongue of the enemy spews out venomous poison, that shames us whether their accusations are true or an out and out lie, which in the case of two such people I've known who have received similar accusations from the exact same person! Go figure. And none of it true. These people are out to strip us of our character, confuse us, hurt us, shame us and God only knows what else they had in mind when they judged us. Our Savior said "judge not lest you be judged by the same judgement." While this is happening our Savior said ". . . Look up for your redemption draws nigh." We don't have to be bent-over with shame. No! We haven't done anything wrong. Look up! Redemption is now!

Hebrews 12:2, Our blessed and wonderful Savior "Endured the cross despising the shame of it." If our Savior despises shame and how it makes us feel, bowing our soul completely to the ground, than who are we to proclaim we like it? No, no, no. As for myself? I too will despise the shame that false accusations causes. People in general, put our precious Messiah "to open shame," Heb. 6:6. Some do this on a daily bases. Some, though very few do not know they are doing it. Is why David said "O Lord forgive me of secret sins." Myself? Regularly. On an almost daily bases.

Redemption? We feel this needs a bit of looking into. Redemption means to redeem something. In our house we drink a lot of milk, so when we run out, someone goes to the grocery store to exchange silver coins, currency or a paper check. Who ever buys the milk must go to the back of the store where it is kept in giant coolers. Select a couple of bottles of milk, a gallon each. Some hand carry their milk up front, others, like myself, put them in a four wheel cart and push that up front. We have our milk, we have paid for it, now we are on our way home to put the milk in our refrigerator to keep it cool for ourselves.

What just happened here? We needed milk to complete what we needed in our own cubbard. Our own stock of food. We redeemed milk from a grocery—store by the exchange of something valuable. Equal in value. We "have paid the price." We live in earthen vessels, our bodies of clay most people call a "soul." A spirit and a soul God made to live forever. Somewhere. In the New Earth or in hell created for satan and his demon-devils. Our Father God does not send any of us in either of these places. *We* send *ourselves* to either place. Jesus calls our bodies, worms. Websters calls worms a body without arms and legs. Just a long sausage with a head. This "worm" and head is exactly what our Savior suffered and died, resurrected to redeem us from. satan is in charge of *"dirt."*

Our God is an awesome God and He sat down in heaven, where He lives, with all His Corporate Members, to discuss how best to go about redeeming this giant patch of dirt to build His house on. His planned blue-print was made long ago. Now all they have to do is wait until all the seeds they've planted—together—grows up and become perennials. Why perennials? So He doesn't have to keep scattering seed around, year after year after year. "Now that you know the truth, will you also go away?"

Psalms 49; is a chapter about redemption. "Listen all you inhabitants of the world: Both low and high, rich and poor together:

"My mouth shall speak of wisdom, and the meditation of my heart shall be of understanding . . . Wherefore should I fear in the days of evil when the iniquity of my heels shall compass me about? They that trust in their wealth and boast themselves in the multitude of their riches. None of them can by any means redeem his brother or his sister, nor give God a ransom for them. For the redemption of their soul is precious and it ceases for ever. That they should live forever and not see corruption. For He sees that wise men die, likewise the fool and the brutish person perishes and leave their wealth to others.

"Their inward thoughts are that their houses shall continue for ever, and their dwelling places to all their generations, they call their lands after their own names.

"Nevertheless man being in honor abides not, he is like the beasts that perish. Like sheep they are laid in the grave, death (corruption) shall feed on them, and the upright shall have dominion over them in the morning and their beauty shall consume in the grave from their dwelling.

"But God! (Shall) will redeem my soul from the power of the grave. He shall receive me." 49:1-15

"The fear of the Lord is the beginning of wisdom." A good understanding have all they that do His commandments. His praises endures for ever 111:10.

". . . With the Lord there is mercy and with Him is plenty of redemption." 130:7.

"For all have sinned and come short of the glory of God; being justified freely by His grace through the redemption that is in Christ Jesus."

Ex. 30:10, Rom. 3:24

One will never be redeemed unless one asks our Father in Jesus Name to forgive us our trespasses (sins). Jesus Himself said "if we ask something of our Father He will give it to us; "For we know the whole creation groans and travails in pain together until now.

And not only they but ourselves also which have the first fruits of the (Holy) Spirit, even we, ourselves, groan within ourselves, waiting for the adoption, or shall we say, the redemption of our body." Romans 8:22, 23.

"But of Him we are in Christ Jesus who of God is made to us—wisdom, righteousness and sanctification and redemption." 1 Cor. 1:30.

Let us return to Luke 21:28, ". . . Lift up your head for your redemption draws nigh." When all these bad things—through people—begin to happen to us, stand tall, our redemption draws near."

Make no mistake dear reader, when we are attacked by satan, through people, we suffer "battle-scars." Some run deep. Which reminds me of a song someone wrote "The first cut is the deepest." Of course they were speaking of when a loved-one had cheated on them. Of course this causes great shame to you, as well as a giant stab to the heart from your partner, thus; "The first cut is the deepest."

Hebrews 12:2, "Looking unto Jesus the author and finisher of our faith: Who—for the joy that was set before Him; endured The CROSS despising the SHAME of it, and is set down at the right hand of the Throne of God."

He was:

    1 – Lied on—spit upon
    2 – Stripped of His character causes shame
    3 – Beaten in an open court-yard to be laughed at by others
    4 – Mocked—cruelly
    5 – False crown of thorns
    6 – False draping of Kingly clothing
    7 – Beard—literally pulled out with the flesh
    8 – Hung naked on a cruel cross, causing more shame

Christ bled in several places as well:

JESUS HIT BY A ROADSIDE BOMB

1 – in the garden Sweat great drops of BLOOD.
2 – Beaten publicly. Job 33; explains there was not one piece of flesh left on His back "All my bones are exposed." BLOOD.
3 – crown of thorns. BLOOD.
4 – 5 – Hands nailed with railroad spikes. BLOOD.
6 – 7 – Both feet nailed-same way-to the cross. BLOOD.
8– While on the cross they pierced His side. BLOOD/water.

Adam created on the 8th day. Do you see the parallel here?

Put to an open shame . . ." Hebrew 6:6.

Key Scripture—Hebrews 12:2 "...Endured the cross—DESPISING the SHAME," of it.
His character was completely assassinated. What is an *assassin?*:
"A murderer, killer, especially one who kills for fanatical or monetary reasons often restricted in usage to the murderer murdering a prominent person. Mustims from Persia (Iran—Iraq) and Syria around 1090-1272 whose chief object was to assassinate crusaders."
Assassinate: "To kill suddenly or secretly, murder premeditatedly and treacherously to destroy or denigrate treacherously and viciously; to assassinate a persons character, or them. Literally!" heading to war
"When you see these things happening to yourself. the shame!
". . . Lift up your head for your redemption draws near." Luke 21:28.
Isaiah said to those who cause shame on others ". . . Your reward shall be double." 61:7.

Jesus was teaching in the synagogue as He had taught in Capernaum, "Therefore many of His disciples . . . said This is a hard saying, Who can hear it? When Jesus knew within Himself that His disciples murmured at His saying, said to them, Does this offend you?

"What and if you shall see the Son of man ascend up where He was before? It is the Spirit that quickens, the flesh profits nothing: The Words I speak to you, they are spirit and they are life. But there are some of you that do not believe."

"For Jesus knew from the beginning who they were that believed not and who should betray Him. And He said, Therefore said I to you that no man can come to me except it were given unto him of My Father.

"From that time many of His disciples went back and walked no more with Him. Then Jesus said to the twelve:

"WILL YOU ALSO GO AWAY?"

John 6:59-67

And now, that I have told you the truth, "will you also go away?" from Me?

The
BLOOD

Rev. 12:11, "And they overcame him (satan) by the word of their testimony and the blood of the Lamb and they loved not their lives unto the end."

STAYIN' ALIVE "You mighty warrior of valor."

CHAPTER 28

DESTRUCTION OF THE UNDERCLASS

There are people, as well as nations . . . void of counsel, neither is there any understanding in them . . . Their rock is not as our Rock (Messiah), even our enemies themselves are our judges. For their vine is of the vine of Sodom, and as for their fields are of Gomorrah, their grapes are grapes of gall, their clusters are bitter. Their wine is the poison of dragons (devils), and the cruel venom of asps . . . To me belongs vengeance and recompense; their feet shall slide in due time, for the day of their calamity is at hand, and the things that shall come upon them makes haste" to do so. "Oh that they were wise. That they understood this. That they would consider their latter end."

Deut. 32:28, 30-35, 29

Oh Father, "Look upon my affliction and my pain and forgive all my sins. Consider my enemies for they are many and they hate me with cruel hatred. Oh, keep my soul and deliver me. Let ME not be ashamed because I put my trust in You. Let integrity and uprightness preserve me for I wait on You." Psalms 25:18-22.

"You be my strong habitation where unto I may continually resort; You have given commandment to save me for You are my Rock and my fortress. Deliver Me Oh My God, out of the hand of the wicked, of the unrighteous and cruel man. For You are my hope, O Lord God, You are my trust from my youth up." Psalms 71:3-5.

"Let them be ashamed and confounded . . ." This word means confused. ". . . that seek after my soul. Let them be turned backward, and put to confusion that desire my hurt. Let them be turned back for a reward of their shame that say Aha aha." Psalms 70:2, 3.

Psalms 25:22, speaks of one's integrity. Well, what does integrity mean? You may ask:
INTEGRITY: "A sound personality. An adherence to moral principles and character, uprightness and honesty."
Now we have another word that may be foreign to some of us:
CHARACTER: "The aggregate of features and traits that form a person's individual nature. A feature or trait such as honesty, courage or both. Reputation of good repute."

If we continue just one word more and we arrive at TRAITOR! Wow! Who would have thought that! "One who betrays a person." Notice a human being, a person, is top of the list for traitor.

A person betraying another person. "A person who betrays a person, a cause, or any other trust. One who betrays their country. One who is guilty of treason. A dangerous person."

"The merciful person does good to their own soul. But they that are cruel troubles their own flesh."
Proverbs 11:17

"A talebearer reveals secrets. But they that are of a faithful spirit conceals the matter." Prov. 11:13.

"The mouth of the just brings forth wisdom. But the forward tongue shall be cut out. The lips of the righteous know what is acceptable. But the mouth of the wicked speaks forwardness." Prov. 10:31, 32.

214

All of the above I have come across during my very long life. But this next one lets all of us know exactly what a poison tongue will do; although *all* of the above is exactly what the people in these last days have multiplied upon themselves: "They will say to you 'Come! Let us lay wait for blood, let us lurk privily for the innocent without cause. Proverbs 1:11.

I had the misfortune to spend an overnight with just such a couple. From the beginning of our short "friendship" I had not one clue as to their character until that day and night that they were so blood thirsty hungry for the soul of others, least of all my own! Praise God He delivered me just as He did Daniel in the lions den. But just as soon as I was home a day or two these two "out for the blood of the innocent" came pouring in. Oh wow! Am so thankful and most certainly grateful our Father protected and delivered me in Yeshua's wonderful name.

"Wrath is cruel and anger is outrageous. But, who is able to stand against envy?.? Faithful are the wounds of a friend, but the kisses of an enemy are deceitful." Proverbs 27:4, 6.

Oh Lord "Deliver me not over to the will of my enemies: for false witnesses are risen up against me and such as breathes out cruelty." Ps. 27:12.

In churches all over the United States, are people such as these we've just described. Way more so now in these last days than there ever was when I was growing up. Or, so it seemed. These people are frighteningly evil and Paul the apostle has these words to say of them:
"For it is impossible for those who were once enlightened and have tasted of the heavenly gift and were partakers of the Holy Spirit, And have tasted the good Word of God and the powers of the world to come, If they should fall away, to renew them again to repentance; seeing as how they crucify to themselves the Son of God afresh and put Him to open shame . . . But that which

215

bears thorns and briers is rejected and is nigh unto cursing whose end is to be burned." Hebrews 6:4-6, 8.

These people that have sat rated our churches in these last days are like the ACLU, Obama and Polocy when Obama first took office. These two people set out on a public campaign each time they were on television, which seemed daily, of a character assignation of each and every American. For the first year it seemed they couldn't get enough of saying how "ignorant American's are." "How illiterate Americans are." "They're nothing but peasants beneath all of us." Of course the ACLU have been doing this for years and Americans have gotten used to their American character assignation and way of doing things. Hitler always said "if you assassinate the character of a people long enough, they'll soon act the part. Act the part so long they'll really believe they are the scum of the earth we make them out to be." From the book Marxism.

These people are pawns of satan who are so deceived by him they feel they are honest Christians and doing the work of our true Lord by doing the "work" they are doing. They are like wolves deceiving their prey into thinking they mean the Christian they've lured into their home's no harm. They are satans assailant'ssatan who hide their hostile hatred for them by big smiles and endless compliments. When all the while they have one thing on their mind, to assassinate the character of the unsuspecting true to our Savior Christian. We should not cast this warning aside for Jesus said people such as these "will wax (grow) worse and worse as satans time draws near, and these "workers" in the church for him will think they are 'doing the will of God' by actually killing you." Not just our character.
"These things I have told you that you should not be offended. They shall chase you out of the synagogues. Yes. The time comes that whosoever kills you will think he does God's service. These things they will do to you because they have not known the Father or Me." John 16:1-3. "If I (Jesus) had not come and spoken to

them they would not have sinned, but now they have no cloak to hide behind and it is out and out sin."

John 15:22

My my my my my! Talk about Jekyll's and Hyde's! The whole world will be full of these assassins.

CHAPTER 29

BEAMS AND BOULDERS

We feel certain everyone knows what a railroad beam is, so we won't elaborate except to say, it is a 6x6, or and 8x8 beam shaped in a square from a log. A railroad worker would call these "railroad ties."

Scripture is very clear, and simple enough when speaking about the railroad "BEAM", although it must be added here; trains and railroads would not come into existence until nearly 2,000 years later, AFTER Yeshua even mentioned for us to get the "BEAM" out of our own eye before we can accuse another of the smallest of things.

Matthew 5:&6; begins with just such a lesson every Christian ought to have branded into their memory file, "Sufficient unto the day is the evil thereof." (5:34). "Do not judge others so that you be not judged with the same judgement, for with what judgement you judge, you shall be judged: and with what measure (amount) you hand out judgement to others it shall be measured back to you again. And why do you behold the mote . . ." A mote was a body of water around a castle in medieval times when the K.J. Bible was written. In the "mote"—body of water—the people living in the castle used it for a toilet, a garbage dump and what ever else they felt like discarding into it. Archeologists in digging up one such mote in England, found they had buried their dead in the mote as well. So, a mote is not a pretty sight, plus the odor had to be unbearable. Motes were muddy as well.

". . . The mote in your brothers/sisters eye, and don't consider the BEAM that is in your own eye? Or, how will you say to your brother/sister "here! Let me pull the mote out of your eye when, look! A beam is in your own eye?

You hypocrite! First, take the beam out of your own eye. Then you shall see clearly to take out the mote out of your brother/sister's eye. Don't give that which is holy to the dogs . . ." Father forgive me if I have done such evils, in Jesus Name. ". . . Neither cast your pearls before swine for they will trample them underfoot, turn around (for food, seeing you have none) and attack you." 6:1-6, Luke 6:41, 42.

Someone once said, if a person does wrong or harm to you, you were completely innocent of all their charges, leave immediately, forgive them no matter how hard it is to say, and never be around that person again. Our Father will take care of and settle the rift His way.

Being in a house of people who I felt were my friends, and having to spend the next 24 hours with them, I had not one clue the sharp flaming arrow's each were flinging my way. For instance; a worldly question was asked of me. I did not know the answer. The lady of the house had asked this, was upset of my not knowing the answer.

In fact I would say expertly hid her displeasure and asked her husband if we could all pray together. He immediately pulled up a chair between us and began praying. He never asked anything for God to grant to me. She began praying. Her whole pray was long, drawn-out and all about "and Father I just ask you to give Belva wisdom, so she will have more." Then I prayed for our Father, "to bless these two people, their home and, thanked Him for their letting me have an "overnight" with them in Jesus Name."

All day this went on. At dinner time each of them fixed their own. Asking if I could help. "No. no, I've got it." She said, as she brought over a plate with two slices of bread and a slice of smoked turkey. Not put together! And a glass of ice water. First food I'd had all day and it was seven pm evening. They ate much and heartily, and I praised God silently for what I had, and ate. They had dessert. No offer. I excused myself to go take a shower and to bed. The house absolutely immaculate, the bed could not have been more wonderful and yet it was. P.T.L. I could not sleep. Wondering what in the world had happened between a loving phone call and my arrival. Four phone calls to be exact, and two from another friend of mine very dear to my heart who I've been a dear friend to (vice-versa) for 30 years. These two I chose to spend the rest of that day, that night with, were new friends? I truly believed they were friends.

Next morning I came downstairs around 9, they'd been up since 6:30 they said. They busied themselves almost immediately, offered me something to drink, I chose ice-water. The man tried to offer me food several times, each time, before he could finish his sentence, "Belva doesn't eat breakfast." About three times this happened, he gave up. I was glad. He—again fixed his own. She too. She drew her breakfast out-long-as if to tease me with her fruit, and especially her blueberries. At each blueberry, she held it on the fork, looked at it and slowly said "Blueberries are brainfood. Did you know that Belva?" About 10-12 blueberries later they were gone. But she was not through. She brought something out of the microwave, hot, and began picking pieces off of it and said, "This is called a Blueberry Round, Belva." I answered "really? It smells good." Not all her bites had a blueberry, but rest assured, when one was found the same thing—again—over and over. The both of them acted as though I didn't know what was going on and I let them. I was not mad or angry, but I did feel as though they themselves did not know they were driving that blueberry knife deeper and deeper into my heart. Sorrowful heart. After their breakfast and they were satisfied. The gentleman could not work fast enough to get my things out of their house and into my car.

I had brought two mountain-dew for each of us, total of six. I'd forgotten about them. She remembered. Ran back into their house retrieved them, handing them to me through my car window, each saying with one voice, "Heres your mountain dew. Don't know why you even brought us some. I—we don't even like mountain dew anyway." Their last dig.

This is just one trial in my life I need to overcome, and get on with my life. When people fill us with shame, a preacher once said "shame is satan's sadistic laugh. A cruel-evil-laugh, at us."

Since the age of eight and I was aware of our Almighty God, through God's mentor He provided, I was taught by this one verse, ". . . Come out from among them, and YOU be separate saith the Lord. Touch not the unclean thing and I will receive you." 2 Corinthians 6:17. Have lived by it ever since.
satan started shame in the Garden of Eden when Adam and Eves eyes were opened, they realized they were naked and tried to cover their nakedness up with fig leaves. God came down in the cool of the evening to walk and talk with Adam, but this day God couldn't find Adam. Oh, He knew all along where Adam was and what had happened. He just wanted Adam to admit it, aloud, to Him. Yeshua said if we admit our sins, He is faithful and just to forgive us.

Genesis 3

Psalms chapter four is all about a prayer of our Messiah and not David's alone: "O you sons of men how long will you turn my (God's) glory into shame? How long will you love vanity and seek after leasing? Selah. But know this, that the Lord has set apart them that are godly for HImself: The Lord will hear when I call to Him."

Verses 2, 3

"Have any of the workers of iniquity no knowledge? Who eat up my people as they eat bread, and call not on the Lord. There were they in great fear: for God is in the generation of the righteous. *YOU* have shamed the counsel of the poor, because the Lord is his refuge." Psalms 14:3-6.

"Let them be confounded and put to shame that seek after my soul: let them be turned back and brought to confusion that devise my hurt . . . Let them be ashamed and brought to confusion together that rejoice at my hurt: Let them be clothed with shame and dishonor that magnify themselves against me." Psalms 35:4, 26. This is a Psalm that Jesus prayed. The human part of Him. This Psalm 40, as well, speaks of His death-ascension-resurrection and ascension again.

"But You have saved us from our enemies, and have put them to shame that hate us." Ps. 44:7. Praise the Lord.

"Fill their faces with shame that they may seek Your Name Lord. Let them be confounded and troubled for ever, yea, let them be put to shame and perish." Psalms 83:16, 17.

Our Savior and David suffered shame as well. Yeshua, meek, humble, a man of sorrows. David, for a time, also meek, but bold in the Lord, fearless and a man of war. Yet our God had chosen him—David—a mighty warrior to sit on a throne in the New Earth, while Yeshua sits on a throne in the New Jerusalem. Both will judge. "Help Me O Lord my God: O save me according to Your mercy, that they may know that this is Your hand, that You Lord, have done it.

Let them curse, but You bless. When they arise let them be ashamed but let Your servant rejoice. Let my enemies be clothed with shame and let them cover themselves with their own confusion as with a mantle. But I will greatly praise You Lord with my mouth; yea, I will praise You among the multitude. For You shall stand at the right hand of the poor, to save them from them that condemn their soul." Psalms 109:26-31.

"His enemies will I cloth with shame, but upon himself shall his crown flourish."

Ps. 132:18

Our Messiah did all this for David who spoke-spiritually—Words of our Savior's human side, we, Christ's followers, will be given the same immunities beyond a shadow of a doubt.

"The Wise shall inherit glory but shame shall be the promotion of fools." Proverbs 3:35. ". . . With the lowly is wisdom." 11:2. "The Kings favor is toward a wise servant but His wrath is against them that causes shame." 14:35.

Our wonderful Savior said, of Himself, "I gave my back to the smiters and my cheeks to them that plucked off the hair, I hid not my face from shame and spitting Isa. 50:6, Ps. 22.

As for us? Messiah has this to say, "Fear not for you shall not be ashamed, neither be you confounded for you shall not be put to shame, for you shall forget the shame of your youth and shall not remember the reproach of your widowhood any more. For your Maker is your husband and the Lord of hosts is His name, and your Redeemer the Holy One of Israel, The God of the whole earth shall He be called. For the Lord has called you as a woman forsaken and grieved in spirit, and a wife of youth when you were refused, saith YOUR God." Isa. 54:4-6.

So saith *my* God. The One True God of Abraham, Isaac and Jacob. As for my enemies? "For their shame they shall have double and for confusion they shall rejoice in their portion . . ." (correct reading, "For your shame ye shall have double and for confusion they shall rejoice in their portion . . ."). Isa. 61:7.

Peter and other apostles were jailed at Jerusalem by the council. Taken out and beaten and warned never to preach in the name of Jesus again. Instead, they went to the temple and began all over again. The council took them once again and would have beaten them once more had it not been for a Pharisee named Gamailel who said, "You men of Israel, take heed to yourselves what you intend to do as touching these men. For before these days rose up Theudas boasting himself to be somebody . . . After this man rose up Judas of Galilee in the days of the taxing . . . And now I say to you, Refrain from these men and let them alone, for if this counsel or this work be of men it will come to nothing. But if it be of God you cannot overthrow it, lest haply you be found even to fight against God. They agreed. And when they had called the apostles and beat them, they commanded them they should not speak in the name of Jesus then let them go. They departed from the presence of the council rejoicing that they were counted worthy to suffer shame for His Name." Acts 5:33-41.

Jesus our blessed Savior, Paul said, "Looking to Jesus the author and finisher of our faith who, for the joy that was set before Him, endured the cross—despising the shame—and is set down at the right hand of the throne of God." Hebrew 12:2.

God our Father said, "To me belongs vengeance and recompense, their foot shall slide in due time, for the day of their calamity is at hand, and the things that shall come upon them made haste."
Deut. 32:35

"The righteous shall rejoice when he sees the vengeance: he shall wash His feet in the blood of the wicked. So that a man shall say, verily there is a reward for the righteous. Verily, He is a God that judges in the earth." Psalms 58:10, 11.

Paul knew, we are human, and humans hurt other humans, sometimes for no reason at all, other then, possibly, we don't look like they would have us look, we don't dress the way they would have us dress. We don't give them the answer to their question they wanted to hear. For this we are ostracized by them with unkind remarks, trying to change or rearrange our true character into one they wish we had, but don't. For instance, they attach debilitating names to us, such as liars, cowards and etc. etc. None of which are true. Thus we have Pauls admonishing; "Let love be without dissimulation. Abhor that which is evil. Stick to that which is good. Be kindly affectioned one to another with brotherly love, in honor preferring one another. Not slothful in business, fervent in spirit, serving the Lord, rejoicing in hope, patient in tribulation, continuing instant in prayer, distributing to the necessity of saints, given to hospitality. Bless them which persecute you, bless and curse not.

Rejoice with them that do rejoice and weep with them that weep. Be of the same mind one toward another.

Mind not high things, but condescend to men of low estate. Be not wise in your own conceits.

Recompense to no man evil for evil. Provide things honest in the sight of men.

If it be possible, as much as lieth within you, live peaceably with all men.

Dearly beloved, avenge not yourselves, but rather give place unto wrath, for it is written vengeance is mine, I will repay, saith the Lord. Therefore if your enemy is hungry, feed him. If he is thirsty, give him something to drink. For in so doing you shall heap coals of fire on their head.

Be not overcome with evil, but overcome evil with good."
Romans 12:9-21.

Little children, readers, we must; we just must be better overcomers. There are a lot of things I do know, and most definitely much more I don't know. One thing is for sure and certain, when asked, if I don't know I will say so, as should we all. In all my life I have never tried to be something I am not. I'm just plain old, and I do mean old, Belva. Nothing more.

Yeshua said in the book of Revelation
". . . To them that overcome I will give

1 – To eat of the tree of life which is in the midst of the PARADISE of God.

2 – Be faithful unto death and I will give you a crown of life.

3 – He that overcomes shall not be hurt by the second death. Rev. 20:6.

4 – To him that overcomes I will give to eat of the hidden manna

225

5 – And will give him a white stone

6 – And in the stone a New Name Written which no man knows except he that receives it.

7 – And he that overcomes and keeps My Works to the end, to him will I give power over the nations,

8 – And I will give him the morning star.

9 – And you shall walk with Me in white for they are worthy.

10 – He that overcomes the same will be clothed in white raiment,

11 – And I will not blot out his name out of the book of life, I will confess his name before My Father and before His angels.

12 – Because you have kept My patience, I also will keep you from the hour of temptation which shall come upon all the world, to try them that dwell upon the earth. Behold, I come quickly, hold that fast which you have that no man take's your crown.

13 – Him that overcomes will I make a pillar in the temple of My God. And he shall go no more out

14 – And I will write upon him the name of My God and the name of the city of My God which is New Jerusalem, which comes down from out of heaven from My God, and I will write upon him My New Name.

15 – To him that overcomes will I grant to sit with Me in My throne, even as I overcame and am sat down with My Father in His throne."

Rev. 2; 3;

Our Lord Savior Yeshua said, "I saw satan fall like lightening" from the sky (The four Gospels). He is our redemption Lamb "slain before the foundation of the world." There would have been no need for a redeeming Lamb if satan had not fallen, and all his demonic angels with him "Be—for the foundation of the world."

"And I heard a loud voice, saying in heaven, Now is come salvation . . ." Our Saviors life, torment, death resurrection. ". . . Salvation and strength and the kingdom of our God and the power of His Christ, for the accuser of our brethren is cast down . . ." He was with Adam and Eve in the garden of Eden. "Which accused them before God day and night. And they overcame him by the Blood of the Lamb, and by the word of their testimony . . ." Our testimony must consist of a happening in your life caused by satan. You will know it without doubt when it happens, And how you were able to overcome him by declaring the Blood of God that did flow in Jesus' veins. ". . . And they loved not their lives unto the death." Rev. 12:11.

CHAPTER 30

PRIESTHOOD

PRIEST in Hebrew is cohen, meaning to foretell? Or a mediator, a messenger, Job 33:23. The word Priest means one who presides over things relating to God or, as Paul says "Every High Priest taken from among men is constituted on the behalf of men, with respect to their concerns with God that He may present both gifts and sacrifices for sins, Hebrews 5:1. Adam is the first recorded priest; Noah was the first after the deluge. It is probable that the patriarchs were priests as in Job 5. The prophet differed from the priest in receiving supernatural communications of knowledge, of the past, present, and future.

In the patriarchal system, the firstborn male was the priest of the family and succeeded his father. The mosaic system substituted the tribe of Levi, instead of the first—born, Ex. 28. The Hebrews were promised that if they would keep the law of Moses, they should be, "A peculiar treasure," "A kingdom of priests," "A holy nation," Ex. 19:5, 6. The age of which they were permitted to serve was not definitely fixed, as in the case of the Levites but was, probably at maturity—20 yrs. old.

The support of the high priest was the tithe of 1-10th. of the tithes assigned to the Levites, Num. 18:28, Neh. 10:38. The candidate for orders must prove his descent from Aaron; be free from bodily defects, Lev. 21:16-23, must not mourn outwardly; must marry only a young woman. They were to keep the sanctuary and alter, Num. 18:5; to keep the fire always burning on the alter (the brazen—burnt—Alter), Lev. 1:7, 6:13, to to prepare the burnt offerings and kill the Passover 2 Chr. 29:34, Ezr. 6:20, to do the work of a certain part of the sacrifices, generally:

1 – Offerings
2 – Sacrifices
3 – Attend to services of "Day of Atonement
4 – To blow the trumpets for all occasions
5 – To prepare the ointment, or perfumed oil
6 – Prepare the water of separation
7 – Act as assessors in judical matters
8 – To assist in the work of organizing and encouraging the army.
9 – To keep the books of the law, Deut. 20:1-4, 21:5, 31:9.

The high priests' were permitted to eat, at the sanctuary the flesh of the various offerings—also to carry away (it) to be eaten in Jerusalem—certain parts of offerings. They had a right to the First-Fruits of oil, wine, and grain, and certain parts of sacrifices, Deut. 28; the price of redemption of a man and of unclean beasts; Restitutions, and all devoted things; the skins of the sacrificed animals—which was a rich-very rich-perquisite; donations, and might also own land 1 Kings 2:26, Jer. 32:7, 8.

The total income is supposed to have been about 1 5th of the entire national income, Gen. xlvii:24. The priesthood was a perpetual inheritance, transmitted from father to son.

After the captivity those who could not prove their descent from Aaron lost their privileges as priests. The corruption of the priesthood, by making their office a means of amassing wealth, intriguing, in politics, for political power, hastened the ruin of the Jewish nation.

Christ is described in the New Testament as the First-Born, the King, the anointed, a priest after the order of Melchizedek, Hebrews 7:8.

God rested on the 7th day. Adam created on the 8th day. In Hebrew there is no such word as coincidence. Therefore Hebrews 7:8, is NO coincidence.

The priesthood in the Christian Church is a spiritual matter deriving its powers and privileges from the Holy Spirit. Christ is our Priest forever!

TEMPLE

Temple in Hebrew is MISH'KAN meaning dwelling; an open inclosed place, which can be dwelt in, Ex. 35:9, Lev. 8:10, 17:13, Num. 1:50-53. It connects itself with the Jewish word SHECHINAH, as describing the dwelling-place of the Divine Glory—OHEL; the tent, as a whole, or perhaps, the covering, or roof only, Gen. 4:20, 9:21. This is used when applied to the Sacred tent, Ex. 26:9. KODESH = Holy. MIKDASH = Sanctuary, Ex. 25:8.

TABERNACLE of testimony: The Bragen Alter that held the testimony of Aaron's stick that budded. Some manna of the angels food, and the two stone tablets God gave Moses were-all-in the Ark.

The Tabernacle was a tent-like structure, adapted to the Nomadic (roving) life of the desert, and made more important than the ordinary tent, or even than the best tents of the wealthiest sheikhs which are lined with silk, or fine linen, or wood, and very showy in form and color.

Its form was twice the length of its width, 30 cubits (45 feet) long by 10 cubits (15 feet) wide, and the side-walls were 10 cubits high. It stood in an in closed place, 50 cubits (75 feet) wide, by 100 cubits (150 feet) long, 15 feet from the west end (see drawings elsewhere in this book).

The Holy of Holies where the brazen alter is, was at the West end, was a cube of 10 cubits each way, and in it was the MERCY-SEAT on the lid of the ark (alter), the cherubim, the ark, and the Book of the law.

The room in front of the Holy of Holies, separated by the Veil, was 20 cubits long by 10 cubits wide, and called the Holy Place. In it were the table of shew—bread and the seven—branched candlestick, The Menorah, and the alter of incense Ex. 25.

The tent had a ridge forming a right-angle over which the roof-coverings of cloth and skins were thrown. These extended 5 cubits beyond the walls all around the tent, like wide, projecting eaves. There were three coverings to the 4 sides. The inner of fine linen, the next, of badger-skins; the outer of rams-skins dyed RED; and besides these the roof had one of goats-hair. It was made under the direction of BEZALEEL and AHOLIAB. Its place was in the center of the camp, where it was set up on the first day of the second year of the mass Exodus from Egypt ex. 11:2. It was the place where man met with God, Numbers 11:24, 25. (Note) Adam met with God in the "Cool of the evening in the Garden of Eden. God loves PEOPLE and has always wanted to live among us but we've proved we're much to evil and in bad, bad need of a heavenly Savior. Man has proven MAN cannot save himself! A much higher and completely innocent celestial being was the ONLY way man could be redeemed from—WHO? From himself! And Celestial BLOOD, pure as the crystal river in heaven flowing from God's throne was *the* one—*the* only Blood that could be shed to deliver us from death and destruction of our body *BUT* our spirits and souls were designed to live forever. And live forever they shall! In heaven or in hell. Man, and man *alone* sends himself to either place. God gave each and every one of us *FREE-WILL* to CHOOSE for ourselves where we will live when we die. Good works. Lots of works or no works at all will help any of us on judgment day. Thats why our Savior—Redeemer Yeshua the Christ said "You *MUST* be born again. If you don't, no matter how much you want to see your loved ones gone before you, if they went to heaven and you never got around to doing what Jesus said you will never ever see them, and vice-versa.

TABERNACLE

This temple—tabernacle was moved from place to place (a moving Bethel). In the wilderness and in Canaan until the Temple was built, or rather, until it lost its glory, when the ark was captured by the Philistines, 1 Sam. 4:22, Ps. 128:60. The form and size of the tent were symbolical, and to the Hebrews who believed in the mystical and occult powers of numbers, it was peculiarly sacred because of its peculiar structure.

On its alter of incense no strange fire must ever be used.

VEIL

A VEIL was a covering; to keep people from seeing in someplace, or people out of someplace, keeping people either in or out from seeing in or out of someplace.
Genesis 24:65, Rebekak took a veil and covered herself so Isaac could not-as yet—see the face of his future wife.
Genesis 38:14, So did Tamar cover herself for a different reason.
Exodus 34:33, Moses' face shined like the sun and the Israelites begged him to cover his face with a veil. Ex. 36:35, another veil of blue, the same as in 2 Chr. 3:14, Ex. 26:31.

"After the death's of Aarons two sons, the Lord spoke to Moses and said, "Speak to Aaron your brother that he come not at all times into the Holy of Holies within (behind) the veil before the mercy seat which is upon the ark, so that he does not die: for I will appear in the cloud upon the mercy seat." Lev. 16:1, 2 (read all of chapter 16).

"And behold the veil of the temple was (hit by lightening) split into two pieces from top to bottom, and the earth quaked and the rocks split in to two, and many of the graves were opened and bodies of many saints which slept arose and came out of their graves *AFTER* His resurrection, went into the holy city Jerusalem and appeared to many." Matt. 27:51-53. This, *after* Jesus cried with a loud voice and died, verse 50. Mark 15:38, Luke 23:45.

2 Corinthians 3:11-14, The veil that separated the people from God who sat upon the mercy seat on the other side of the veil in the Holy of Holies, Paul called the veil and the Holy of Holies "glorious, Seeing then that we have such hope, we use great simple words in our explanations, and not as Moses which put a veil over his face that the Israelites could not steadfastly look to the end of that which is abolished: but their minds were blinded, for unto this day remains the same veil untaken away in the reading of the Torah: which veil *is* done away with in Christ's death and resurrection.

There is a hope set before us, "Which hope we have as an anchor of our soul, both sure and steadfast, and which entered into that within (behind) the veil; who (Jesus) is the forerunner for us, Jesus, who is now made a High Priest *for ever* after the order of Mel-chis-e-dec." Hebrews 6:18-20.
"Melchisedec, King of Salem . . ." Ancient name for Jerusalem.
". . . the High Priest of the Most High God, who met Abraham returning from the slaughter of the kings, and blessed him" Hebrews 7:1.

"Then the first covenant also had ordinances of divine service and a worldly sanctuary. For there was a tabernacle made; the first wherein was the candlestick and the table of showbread, which is called the sanctuary. And after the second veil, the tabernacle which is called the Holiest of all; the Holy of Holies, which had the golden censer, and the ark of the covenant overlaid all over with gold, wherein was the golden pot that held manna, and Aaron's rod that budded, and the tables of the covenant; and over it the cherubims of glory shadowing the mercy seat; of which we cannot now speak particularly."

"Now when these things were thus ordained, the priests went—always—into the first tabernacle accomplishing the service of God. But into the second went the High Priest alone! Once every year and not without blood which he offered for Himself(?) and for the sins of the people. The Holy Spirit thus signifying that the way into the Holiest of all was not yet made manifest, white as the first tabernacle was yet standing: which was a figure for the time then present in which were offered both gifts and sacrifices, that could not make him (priest) that did the service perfect, as pertaining to the conscience, which stood only in meats and drinks and diverse washings and carnal ordinances imposed on them until the time of reformation. "Reformation meaning the coming to earth a Savior from God Himself, to do away with the earthly.

"But Christ being come a High Priest of good things to come, by a greater and more perfect tabernacle NOT made by hands, that is to say, not of this (earthly) building; neither by the blood of goats and calves but by His own Blood He entered into—ONCE!—into the Holy of Holies (on high) place, having obtained eternal redemption for us."
"For if the blood of bulls and of goats, and the ashes of a heifer sprinkling the unclean sanctifies to the purifying of the flesh: Then how much more shall the Blood of Christ, who through the eternal Spirit offered Himself who is without spot to God purge your conscience from dead works to serve the living God."

"And for this cause He is the (our) mediator of the New Covenant, that by means of death, for the redemption of the transgressions that were under the first covenant, they which are called might receive the promise of eternal inheritance. Because where a testament (covenant) is, there must also, out of necessity, be the death of the testator. For a testament is of force after men are dead; otherwise it is of no strength at all while the testator lives."

"Whereupon neither the first testament was dedicated *without* blood. For when Moses had spoken every precept to all the people according to the law, he took the blood of calves and of goats, with water and scarlet wool, and hyssop, and sprinkled both the book and all the people saying, this is the blood of the testament which God had enjoined unto you. Moreover he sprinkled with blood both the tabernacle and all the vessels of the ministry, and almost all things are—by the law—purged with blood: and *without* the shedding of blood there is no remission of sin (ex. 29:20)."

"It was therefore necessary that the patterns of things in the heavens should be purified by these; but the heavenly things themselves with better sacrifices than these." For satan polluted heaven as well as earth when he rebelled and was cast out. High Priests go—often—into the Holy of Holies but, "For Christ *is not* entered into the holy places made with hands which are the figure's of the true; but in heaven itself now to appear in the presence of God for us."
Jesus is our middle wall of partition (veil) now. Its through His veil of Red Blood that we appear before the Father God and are able, because of Christ's Blood, to cry "Abba!" Father help me!
"Nor should He offer Himself often, as the high priest enters into the Holy Place every year with blood for sins of others."

"For then He must OFTEN have suffered since the foundation of the world . . ." This, right here, is proof satan fell before the foundation of the world.

". . . But now, ONCE, in the end of the world has He appeared to put away sin by the sacrifice of Himself. And as it is appointed to men ONCE to die and after this the judgment; so Christ was ONCE offered to bear the sins of many and to them that look for Him shall He appear the second time without sin unto salvation."

Hebrews 9

Hebrews 10:19-22, "Having therefore brethren, boldness to enter into the Holy of Holies by the Blood of Jesus, By a new and living way which He has consecrated for us through the veil, that is to say, His flesh, And having a High Priest over the house of God, let us draw near with a true heart in full assurance of faith, having our hearts sprinkled from an evil conscience, and our bodies washed with pure water."

High Priests were to be teachers, 2 Chr. 15:3.
High Priests teach for hire, Micah, 3:11.
Priests lips should keep knowledge, Malachi 2:7.
Priests were obedient to the faith, Act 6:7.
Jesus has made us unto our God kings and priests, Rev. 5:10.
Our High Priest: the Son of God Heb. 4:14, 7:3, 10:29,

THE living Son of THE living God, whose very own DNA in (again) His own Blood flowed in His ONE, His ONLY Son who fulfilled all the duties of the human, earthly priest and is now our very own High Priest of God in the heavenlies:

"For there is NONE good but one . . ," Mk. 10:18, Luke 18:19.
"I and my Father are ONE . . , John 10:30, 17:11, 21, 22.

Since the High Priest performed all these duties in the earthly temple, he was considered a king. We have a heavenly king, spiritual king for now, Acts 17:7. Eph. 4:5, "Faith in ONE Lord . . ."

John 3:16, 18, 10:36-38, 11:4, 10:30.
"For God loved the world so much that He gave His ONLY begotten Son . . ." They that believe on Him is not condemned. But he that believes NOT is condemned already because he has not believed in the NAME of the ONLY begotten Son of God."
"Jesus answered them "Is it not written in your law, I said, You are gods? If He called them gods, unto whom the Word of God came (from), and the Scripture cannot be broken, You say of Him, whom the Father has sanctified and sent into this world, You blaspheme because I said I Am the Son of God? If I don't do the works of My Father, well then, don't believe me! But If I do though you believe not in Me, (at least) believe the Works; that you may know and believe that the Father is in Me and I Am in Him."
"This sickness is not unto death but for the glory of the Lord God, that the Son of God might be glorified thereby." John :30, "I and my Father are ONE."

Since we have established our Lord Savior Jesus the Christ, is our High Priest Forever more, one of the duties of the High Priest is to be a lawyer as well. What does Websters have to say about the duties of a lawyer?
ATTORNEY: At law, an agent, an officer of the Court of Appeals, authorized to appear before it as a representative of a party (you or I) to a legal controversy.

ATTORNEY GENERAL: Appeals to the highest court in the land of the United States of America. The Chief law-officer of a country or state and head of its legal department. A member of the President's cabinet."

All this I learned in 7th grade's Civics classes. But for your sake we have went to Mr. Webster to confirm.

We have now learned our Messiah Jesus the Christ is:—our king. 2 – our High-Priest. 3 – and now He is also our mediator; our

237

Attorney General to appeal to the Grand-Highest-Court in all the Universe whose ONE ONLY Judge is YHWH.

"For unto us a child is born, unto us a Son is given, and the Government shall be upon His shoulder: and His Name shall be called: Wonderful, Counselor (Lawyer?), THE Mighty God, The Everlasting Father, The Prince of Peace. And of the increase of His Government and Peace there shall be NO end, upon the Throne of David and upon his kingdom to order it, and to establish it with judgment and with justice from henceforth (hereafter) even for ever. The Zeal of the Lord of hosts will perform this." WOW! And wow, wow, wow! Isaiah 9:6, 7.

Here are all the different Titles of Christ:
1 – Adam the second, 1 Cor. 15:45.
2 – Advocate (lawyer) 1 John 2:1.
3 – Alpha & Omega, Rev. 1:8, 22:13.
4 – The Amen, Rev. 3:14.
5 – Apostle of our Profession (gospel of life-death-resurrection), Heb. 3:1.
6 – Author and Finisher of our faith, Heb. 12:2.
7 – Beginning of the Creation of God, Rev. 3:14.
8 – Blessed and only Potentate, 1 Tim. 6:15.
9 – Captain of Salvation, Heb. 2:10.
10 – Chief Cornerstone, Eph. 2:20, 1 Pet. 2:6.
11 – Chief Shepherd, 1 Pet. 5:4.
12 – Dayspring, Luke 1:78.
13 – Desire of all nations, Haggai 2:7.
14 – Emmanuel, Isa. 7:14, 8:8, Matt. 1:23.
15 – Everlasting Father, Isa. 9:6.
16 – Faithful Witness, Rev. 1:5, 3:14.
17 – First and Last, Rev. 1:17, 2:8.
18 – Good Shepherd, John 10:14, Ps. 23.
19 – Governor, Matt. 2:6.
20 – Great High Priest, Heb. 3:1, 4:14.
21 – Head of the Church, Eph. 5:23, Col. 1:18.
22 – Heir of *all* things, Heb. 1:2.

23 – Holy One, Mark 1:24, Acts 2:27.

24 – Horn of Salvation, Luke 1:69.

25 – I AM, John 8:58, Ex. 3:14.

26 – The Just One, Acts 7:52.

27 – Lamb of God, Jn. 1:29, 36, Rev. 5:6, 12, 13:8, 21:22, 22:3.

28 – Lion of Tribe of Judah, Rev. 5:5.

29 – Lord God Almighty, Rev. 15:3, 22:6.

30 – Lord of Righteousness, Jer. 23:6.

31 – Messenger of the Covenant, Mal. 3:1.

32 – Messiah, Dan. 9:25, Jn. 1:41.

33 – Morning Star, Rev. 22:16.

34 – Prince of Life, Acts 3:15.

35 – Prince of Peace, Isa. 9:6.

36 – Prince of the kings of the earth, Rev. 1:5.

37 – Resurrection and Life, Jn. 11:25.

38 – Root of David, Rev. 22:16.

39 – Savior, 2 Peter 2:20, 3:18.

40 – Shepherd and Bishop of souls, 1 Pet. 2:25.

41 – Son of the Blessed, Mk. 14:61.

42 – Son of the Highest, Lk. 1:32.

43 – Son of Righteousness, Mal. 4:2.

44 – Wonderful, Counselor, Mighty God, Isa. 9:6.

45 – Word of God, Rev. 19:13.

46 – Word of Life, 1 Jn. 1:1.

47 – The Head of the Church:

48 – Declared by Himself to be Head of the corner, Matt. 21:42.

49 – Declared by Apostle (Saul) Paul, Eph. 4:12, 15, 5:23.

50 – As such has pre-eminence in all things, 1 Cor. 11:3, Eph. 1:22, Col. 1:18.

51 – Saints complete in, Col. 2:10.

"There is ONE Mediator, the Man Christ Jesus," 1 Tim. 2:5, Heb. 2:7.

Anyone with the spirit of anti-Christ deny's all these things of our Savior, even denying Him to be CHRIST, the ONE, the ONLY Begotten Son of YHWH, 1 John 4:3, 2 John 7.

Even denying His Omnipresence, Omnipotence, and His Omniscience, Matt. 18:20, 28:20, John 3:13, 16:30, 21:17, Phil. 3:21, Col. 1:17, Heb. 1:8-10.
This antiChrist spirit denys that Christ Jesus is the ONE, the ONLY, object of Divine Worship, Acts 7:59, Heb. 1:6, Rev. 5:12.
Sorry! But Yeshua the Christ *is* the Lord from heaven, 1 Cor. 15:47, and I rejoice in that piece of knowledge.

CHAPTER 31

THE BACKBONE OF THE WORD OF GOD

Mark 12:30, 31, Rom. 7:25, Respectively. "You shall love the Lord your God with all your heart, soul and mind, and with all your strength, this is the 1st. Commandment and the second is parallel to it . . . I thank God through Jesus Christ our Lord. With my mind I myself serve the law of God, but with my flesh (body) the law of sin." Rom. 7:24, "Oh wretched (wicked) man that I am *who* shall deliver me from this body of death?"

Also Matthew 22:37-39

Even a lawyer of the Pharisees' said to Jesus, "You shall love the Lord your God with all your heart, soul and all your strength and mind." Luke 10:26, 27. Jesus answered the lawyer saying, "You have answered right. Do this and you shall live." V-28.

If people can't bring their body into subjection to this law then their body shall surely die. This is the "sin unto death." Many many people just cannot bring this earthly clay (dirt!) body in line with all their heart, soul, mind and strength. And therein is our problem, "all our strength." Paul wrote the Words of our Savior when he said "My flesh is weak but my Mind is strong." Our flesh allows for food. Our spirit is parallel to the flesh; We must feed both! If there is no balance with both, one of us is going to die, Gen. 9:3, Rom. 7:5, 8:1, Gal. 3:3, 5:17, 6:8. We simply must control the "lusts of our flesh" 2 Cor. 7:1, Gal. 5:16, 6:8, Col. 2:11, 1 Pet. 4:2, 1 Jn. 2:16.

Lev. 17:14, "The life of all flesh is in our blood."

19:28, "We are not supposed to make cuttings of any sort in our flesh." Tatoo's anyone?

Moses prayed to God who was angry at some for their sinning and would have destroyed all the Israelites in the desert because of it but, "God spoke to Moses and Aaron 'get away from this congregation for I Am about to consume them all!' Everyone fell on their knees, faces to the ground and prayed 'Oh God! The God of the spirit's of all flesh, because of one mans sin will You be angry with all the congregation?" Num. 16:20-22.

Job prayed to God inquiring about Jobs illness; "Remember I beg of You, that You have made me of the earths clay, and will You again bring me back to it? Haven't You already poured me out as milk then curdled me as cheese? You have clothed me with skin and flesh, then fenced me in with bone and muscles? You have granted me life with Your favor, and Your visiting me has preserved my spirit. All these things You've hid in Your heart but I know that You remember these things. If I sin, You then mark me and You won't stop me from my iniquity. If I'm wicked You gently bring me back to You. If I'm righteous I—without shame—lift my head up to You. I am completely confused! Please see my affliction because it is increasing. You pursued me like a fierce lion showing me how marvelous You are . . . Why then, have You brought me from the womb, alive? I wish I had given up the spirit and no one had looked upon me! I should have been born dead! I should have been brought from the womb straight to my grave. Haven't You numbered my days? Take them all away so I may have a little comfort, before I go—to where I can't return back to this earth—even to (death) the land of darkness where is the shadow of death. A land of darkness which is darker even then its own self where there is no order, even where light? Is as darkness."

Job 10:8-22

Scott, I am of a firm belief that yours and my beloved loved one—your dad and my best friend and brother, Larry, continually, was—like Job—praying Jobs prayer. Not a day here, a day there, but continually. Our Father in heaven and His Son Jesus put an end to his continual suffering.

A few days before I spent Larry's last nine days on earth, our Father gave me a vision about our blessed loved one:

"A very lush mountain side. On the lower slope of that mountain was a well worn foot path, very narrow, so narrow no two people could pass one another on it.

Larry was on this path that led upward and he continually stumbled and fell. Always Jesus was there picking him up and letting Larry continue on up the path. The path became steep and Larry fell again. Jesus came back to lift him up again. Always Larry was following behind our Savior Jesus. When Jesus picked him up this time, He gathered Larry in His arm as a mother would her little child just learning to walk. Together they went on the path, faster, up the hill and out of my sight." END

Timbers

Pillars in Hebrew is AMMUD, and in Greek—STULOS. Pillars were an important feature in Oriental architecture—1 – for monuments, Gen. 28:18. 2 – in building, Judges 16:25. 3 – As objects of idolatrous worship, Deut. 12:3. 4 – Figuratively of symbolically, Ex. 33:9, 10.

Lots Wife became a pillar of salt, Gen. 19:26.

Jacob's helix ladder stretched from earth to heaven. The stone he had used as a pillow the night before was in the shape of a pillar, "Jacob awoke from his sleep and said 'surely' the Lord is in this place (Mt. Moriah) and I did not know it,' then he became afraid and said further, 'How dreadful is this place! This is none other than the House of God and this also is the gate of heaven.' Then he took the stone he had used as his pillow, set it up like a pillar and poured oil on the top of it calling the place Beth-el, but the name of it at that time was called Luz. 'This stone that I have set for a pillar shall be God's house and of all that You give me I will surely give You the 10th of it.'" Genesis 28.

"And God Himself said 'I Am THE God of Beth-el where you anointed the pillar, where you vowed a vow to me. Now, arise get yourself out of this land and return again to the land of your relatives." Gen. 31:13.

"Jacob buried his most beloved wife, Rachel, and set a stone pillar upon it." Gen. 35:20.

"It came to pass when Moses entered into the tabernacle the cloudy pillar descended and stood at the door of the tabernacle while the Lord talked to Moses. And all the people saw the cloudy pillar standing at the door of the tabernacle. They all, then, arose, went into their own tents and worshipped the Lord too." Genesis 33:9, 10.

"Moses wrote all the Words of the Lord rising up early in the morning, went out and built an alter under the hill, and 12 pillars according to the 12 tribes of Israel. Gen. 24:4.

"The Lord spoke saying, you shall make a vail (veil) of blue and purple and scarlet . . ." All colors of royalty even in this day and age! ". . . Fine twined linen of excellent work . . . then you shall hang it upon four pillars of shittim (shy-tim) wood overlaid with gold: their hooks pure gold, upon the four sockets of silver." Ex. 26:31, 32.

"Twenty pillars and twenty sockets of brass the hooks of the pillars, their fillets shall be of silver.

. . . And four pillars at the gate of the court." Ex. 27:10, 11, 16.

On the south side of the court—20 pillars: Ex. 38:10, 11, 12, 17:

North side	20 pillars
West side	10 pillars
East side	3 pillars

1 Samuel 2:8, ". . . The pillars of the earth are the Lord's and He sat the world upon them."

King Solomon sent one of his aides to go to Tyre, inquire of King Hiram if he would come to Jerusalem and help him with the fine "jewelry" of the temple, "And he made the pillars . . . on top of the pillars he made works of lilies, pomegranates. Then he set up the pillars of the porch of the temple. He sat up the right pillar calling it Ja'chin. Then he sat up the left pillar calling it Bo'az. Upon the top of the pillars was lily works, so was the work of the pillars finished." 1 Kings 7:13-22. 1 Ki. 7:21, 2 Chr. 3:17, Jachin: "He strengthens."

Bk. of Ruth, Matt. 1:5, Boaz: "Cheerfulness," Ancestor of David

Boaz and Ruths first child, a boy, was named OBED.

Obed is the father of Jesse.

Jesse is the father of King David.

Eliud begat Eleazar,

Eleazar begat Matthan,

Matthan begat David,

Jacob begat Joseph, the husband of Mary of whom was born Jesus who is called Christ. From Abraham to David was 14 generations. From David to the carrying away into Babylon—14 generations. From Babylon to Christ—14 generations. Matt. Chapter one.

Our Lord—Savior—Jesus—the Christ came from a clean earthly generation, and an absolute One Only generation of the heavenly Blessed and Only Potentiate 1 Tim. 6:15, Heb. 2:10, 12:2, Rev. 3:14, Eph. 2:20, 1 Pet. 2:6.

Since our Lord Savior Jesus is the First and Last generation of THE One and Only Living God our Father, and children are *always* born with their fathers BLOOD and not the Mothers it is just plain old common sense along with Scripture throughout, that our Savior had the pure unadulterated clean throughout BLOOD of YHWH God! Blessed reader(s), myself—you—or any other human on earth ever born, here and now, or ever will be born cannot dispute that great and wonderful fact—not theory—continued throughout all Scripture, read Isaiah 9:6, for further proof. "And I will set My tabernacle among you: and My Soul (Jesus) shall not hate you. I will walk among you and will be your God and you shall be my people." Lev. 26:11, 12.

Lets read what Webster's has to say about Pillars and Pillars of Smoke:

245

PILLAR: "An upright* shaft or structure of proportions to its heights and of *any* shape in section by selection, made of *Stone*, brick, or other material. Used as a building support, or stand alone as for a monument. A natural formation resembling such a construction; a pillar of basaltic rock, a pillar of Smoke,* pillars for holding the bearings of a watch or a clock . . ." Someone has to be a pillar of time, because? Of beginning of TIME of the one thousand year reign of our King Jesus, to let us know when that reign ends. Why? We will be too happy and elated to be bothered with time, thank you very much.

". . . Watch or clock movement."

Here is the part that thrills me no end:

". . . A mass of mineral in a subterranean cavern, mine . . ." stalactites (coming down from the ceiling)—statamites (coming up from the floor), and there is no end to their length. In Carlsbad Caverns they've found these mineral deposits boring thru the ceiling or the floor from whence they've dripped and solidified for millions of years.

". . . A person who is a chief supporter of a town, state or country, or an institution of some sort, ie "count on me sir (mam) I support your beliefs; (slang) "Hey man! I'm wit-ya."

SMOKE PILLAR: "The visible vapor and gases given off by a burning or smoldering substance especially the gray, brown or blackish mixture of gases and suspended carbon particles resulting from the combustion of wood—peat—coal—or other organic fossil matter.

"Something resembling the above ie, "their hopes/dreams went up in smoke," or, "When the smoke of controversy has cleared you will recognize them as the great persons they really are."

"Physics, a system of solid particles suspended in a gaseous medium. To ride or travel with great speed. To cure meat, fish, etc., by exposure to smoke. To force into public view or knowledge to reveal, ie "the agent swore he would smoke out the leaders.""

SMOKE TREE: "Also called venetion sumac. A tree-like shrub that climbs and clings to whatever it is near. If nothing is near it clings to the grass and vegetation that is around. A tree of Europe and Asia Minor. Its flowers are small in large panicles that have a light, feathery appearance resembling smoke."

To the astric's:
*UPRIGHT: "Erect or vertical as the position or posture, adhering to righteous, honest, just, ie "An upright person in accordance to what is right." Something standing erect or vertical as a piece of timber (columns), an upright piano, goal-posts on a football field. Plumb; perpendicular implies that something, someone, is in the posture of being straight-upward ie "A decaying tree (column) no longer standing upright."

ERECT: "Emphasizes the straightness of posture or position*, ie proud and erect, a flagpole, vertical suggests upward direction along the shortest line from the earth to a level above it. Used in Math, ie the perpendicular side of a right triangle, a pier, a pile, a column."

"The trees went forth at a times appointed to anoint a king over them, and they said to the olive tree, reign over us. But the olive tree said to them "Should I leave my fatness?" Loaded down with ripe olives that needed to be pressed. ". . . Wherewith by me they honor God and man and go to be promoted over the (other) trees? And the trees said again Come you and reign over us." Judges 9:8-11. There is a good deal more verses of this same chapter referring to the olive tree never giving in to rule over the common (Gentile) trees that the olive tree (Israel) thought of all Gentiles as dogs. Soon the trees found a bramble, "And the trees said to the bramble Come you and reign over us. The bramble said to the trees, if in truth you anoint me King over you then come, put your trust in my shadow; and if not, then let fire come out of the bramble and devour the trees of Lebanon." 14, 15.

The book of Job explains Jesus as a tree, "For there is hope of a tree if it is cut down, that it will sprout again, and that the tender will not cease. Though the root of it grows old in the ground and the stock therefore dies in the earth, Yet, through the scent of water underground it will bud and bring forth boughs like a plant." 11 7-10.

This tree began in the garden of Eden, was sold out and cast out of the garden to the land that God cursed full of briers, brambles and thorns. God taught Adam and Eve how to do sin sacrifices for Him and make this husband and wife clothing out of the hides He would also teach them how to tan those hides. Adam and Eve taught this to their children and because Cain was of the devil, 1 John 3:12, "Not as Cain who was of that wicked one . . ."

These blood sacrifices continued on a regular bases even through the flood, "And Noah built an alter to the Lord . . ." After he and his family stepped off the ark. Gen. 9:20. Continuing on with blood sacrifices even unto the Jewish Sanhedrin laid the "AXE to the tree (Jesus) through the crucifixion. By the way they arrested Jesus outside the garden Gethsemane which in Hebrew means: oil-press garden—winepress (Gath, wine) "A small farm." 800 feet from the sealed Eastern Gate of the temple John 18:1, Matt. 26:36, Mk. 14:32. These are all in parallel to Isa. 53. "Though the root (Christs earth part of His body Heb. 10:5) was there 3 days/3 nights "the root of it grows." Jesus came and began a fledgling church, was put in the ground, arose, but the seeds of a New Covenant grew and grew and grew, "grows old in the ground." *We* are made of the ground. We believe on our Lord Savior Jesus and all He stood for, that He was of God on earth (ground) but His wonderful ideas live on, now and forever.

". . . Through the scent of water underground . . ." We are of the ground and Jesus said "Out of your bellies shall flow *rivers of living water.*"

". . . It will bud and bring forth boughs like a plant." Jesus said "Any tree that brings forth fruit My Father will tend it and cultivate it so it may bring forth more fruit."

"I Am the vine (trunk of *the* tree) you are the branches, they that abide in Me and I in them the same shall bring forth much fruit: for without Me . . ." living—abiding? In your heart! ". . . you can do nothing. If people do not abide in Me they are cast forth as a branch and it withers, then others gather them and cast them into the fire and are burned." John 15:1-6. Deut. 20:19, "The trees of the field are peoples lives."

"Who is this that comes out of the wilderness like *pillars* of *smoke*, perfumed with myrrh and frankincense with all powders of the merchants?"

Sol. 3:9

This is the basic (base) all column's are built upon.

1 – The round center column is given a name.
2 – The capital and base are unnamed.
3 – This plain un-ornate column is what the builder will work from.

Someone has to be the capital of this—as is—beautiful column. Likewise the same for the base, Zech. 4:10, "For who has despised the day of small things? For they shall rejoice and shall see the plummet (plum line) in the hand of Zerubbabel with these seven . . ." V-2, ". . . I have looked and saw a candlestick (a Menorah) all of gold with a bowl upon the top of it and His seven lamps on it, seven pipes leading to the seven lamps which are on top of it." Continuing the verse above, now; ". . . for they are the Eyes of the Lord which run to and fro through the whole earth."

"And they shall be mine (v-16), saith the Lord in THAT DAY when I make up (pick & choose) my jewels." Malachi 3:17.

So, the builder of the basic column can now work His magic on the decoration of His beginner column.

If a person builds a house there has to be a basic plan. In his mind he saw it through to completion. This—mind thought—was a seed. His seed had (very crude now) sex with his soul, then his fingers, then a large blueprint was made. This, is called "A Master Plan." Sound familiar? *THE* Master Planner before the earth was formed was none other than the Almighty Living God of Abraham, Isaac and Jacob. His master plan included "a place-land-to put it—hence—the earth. His Master plan included a "pure, unadulterated, spotless, carved* Cornerstone," Isaiah 53.

Jesus shall say—in that day—when Jerusalem has become, "A burdensome stone (Stone?) for all people, all that burden themselves with it shall be cut to pieces (carved by the One, the Only Cornerstone!) even though all the people of the earth be gathered against her." Zech. 12:3. ". . . And in that day the Lord shall defend the inhabitants of Jerusalem . . ."

Zech. 12:8

Then people ask Jesus, "But He shall say, I Am no prophet! I Am a husbandman, for man taught me to keep cattle from my youth (notice He said MAN taught me. Not our/His Father in heaven). Then one shall say to Him; "What are these wounds (scars) in your hands?" Then He will say, "These are they which I was wounded in the house of My friends." Zech. 13:5, 6, 1 Kings 6:18.

A house has to have a plan. The land to put it on has to have a plan. So too a column also has to have a plan, and a basis of where the basic's will be.

Think of it as a meal. A meal has to have a plan. Lets say we are going to make a roast beef for dinner. Someone had to kill the cow the "cut of beef" comes from to prepare for our roast. Someone else had to plant seeds in a planned plot of land to grow all the vegetables that will be added to our roast. Someone somewhere had to have a plan of his design for a roasting-pan we bought to put our roast in.

A plan for the electricity or gas.
A plan for the cooking stove to put our roast in.
A plan for the house in which the stove sits, and so on, etc., etc. Wisdom. In all this dates back to YHWH.

A plan was made for a body for us to live in, "Before I formed you in the womb I KNEW you. And before you were birthed from the womb I sanctified and ordained you . . ." Jer. 1:5.

Isaiah 49:16, "Look! Saith the Lord, I have CARVE you (us!) in the palm of my Hands', your walls are continually before Me."

King Hiram of the City of Tyre sent sculptors, jewelers, builders of wood, makers of cut (carved) stone, brick layers etc. to King Solomon in Jerusalem to build—carve—and so forth, all of King Solomon's temple working from Solomon's plans.

"Now the God of peace that raised from the dead (back to us again) our Lord Messiah that great Shepherd (Ps. 23) through the BLOOD of the everlasting Covenant (1st. sin offering Gen. 3:21,) Make YOU perfect in every good work to do Messiah's will working in YOU that which is well pleasing in (YHWH's) His sight through our Lord Messiah to whom be glory for ever and ever Amen . . . Salute all of them that have rule over you and all the saints as well." Hebrews 13:20, 24.

"All those who have rule over you . . ." meaning State and civil authorities including policemen, Government officials and our President. Paul wrote in another place "Pray for *all* those who have rule over you." That takes care of all our moral—carnal obligations. Paul also meant in all these statements of his "that have rule over you . . ." spiritually as well. An *Elder* in the church does not mean all "those in the church *older*" than you. No. It means "all those more learned in Scripture" than you. That could mean someone a hundred or over. A person your own age, or even a child as soon as it learns to read, "Suffer the little children to come to me," Messiah said. He also said "and a little child shall lead them." Isn't this wonderful when we can understand the "short-hand cryptic" letters our Lord and Savior wrote to us. As for me, every time I learn something new even though I've read it or heard it hundreds' of times over and over again. If we don't understand, all we're doing is reading words. We may as well be reading another language book we know not what the very first word even means.

Short-hand and Cryptic's are all like a giant scavenger hunt. You know, where our teacher takes us on a giant field trip where she has numbered each scrap of paper leaving a clue on each numbered piece of paper. When all had been gathered she calls the class together asking whom ever had found number 1 thru—10-20 how ever many scrapes she'd numbered. Each child began "No. 1 read your note," number 2 etc. etc., until all notes had been read. The teacher had only one goal in mind, that of a subject the kids could never understand. Not even the brightest of children in her class, who by the way always—but always—sat on the first row, the dumbest on the last row. There is—truly—a message to the madness of everyone much smarter than I who sends me cryptics although not numbered, that I—we—must interpret. The whole world is this way. By the way I was a back row student.

Now you have the KEY to knowledge of Scripture. Also to the knowledge of the carnal world who is ignorant, even the most learned of the carnal world—does not have a clue they even have the key. That's why Paul and Jesus wrote "They are ever learning and never come to the truth." Truth being; who among us—even Einstein the most learned of all, could write such a large book (Bible) of which every page is cryptic? No one, now—or who were ever born, or will be born. Period.

One more reason why we must always pray to our Father for wisdom to understand what we read and knowledge of how to use that wonderful knowledgeable wisdom He has just opened our spiritual eyes to see, "eyes to see and ears to hear but they see not and hear not what the Holy Spirit is trying to reveal to them." Jesus said this to the apostles about—who else?—Church members! Matt. 13:13-15.

You appear to me to be such a wise person for your age, dear. Therefore our Savior says to you, "To the pure of heart all things are pure, but to they that are defiled and unbelieving there is nothing pure. Even their mind and conscience is defiled. They profess (with they're mouths) they know YHWH but in their works they deny Him, being abominable and disobedient themselves and to good works they are reprobate." Titus 3:11. The verse after this explains because they are that way, they send themselves to hell. Actually it says to damnation.

Paul wrote in Hebrews 16:25, "Now to Him that has the Power to establish you according to my gospel . . ." Pauls gospel was that of Jesus Christ, Him crucified for sins of all mankind, the curd persecution Roman stake, death of it and His resurrection. The only really true gospel of our Father in heaven. Shed blood for sins—daily—until Jesus who shed the BLOOD that existed way before the world ever began—that DNA BLOOD of the Father in heaven thru the veins of His One/Only Son Jesus, "since the world began . . ." Genesis 3:21.

". . . Of my gospel and the preaching of Jesus our Messiah (love of one another who love and believe in the exact DEITY of Christ our Savior) . . . "According to the revealed mystery which was kept SECRET since the world began."

All the races were created on the 6th day, YHWH rested on the 7th day, on the 8th day Adam was created, to be put in the Garden of Eden the 9th day for some rest & relaxation of all who believe in The Almighty.

On the 10th day Eve was created from the (DNA) curve—the helix curve-ing-bent circle-not "a RIB." Well ouh!!! That revelation blew all the worlds Catholic belief that God took a rib from Adam. Adam himself had the DNA Blood of our Father, which gave him the mind of Christ, which is why "and the man became a living soul." Where is our "soul" anyway? I have not studied for countless years on our mind's not to know the answer to this; after having two husbands whom I love and both lost their minds—one in Viet Nam—the other to that dreaded disease Alzheimers.

Our soul and spirit are in the brain of everyone. Our bodies—that Paul calls our—"clothes," our "house even our "body," which will be changed from mortal to immortal, "that

253

which is corruptible to incorruptible just carry us around where ever *we* want to go." Not our brain and face! Our corruptible bodies that go "back to the earth" (Eccl.) and our spirits back to God who gave it" to us in the first place. So it was Adam's Mind—the Mind of Christ—which puts us BACK FACE to Face with God as was Adam who talked face to face with God in the garden, "in the cool of the day." Genesis 2. Morning and evening is "the cool of the day," even in our lifetime. Moses was also face to face talking with God.

God our Father made Adams SPIRIT and SOUL to die when he and Eve ate the forbidden fruit. His body—clothing—house-as Paul calls it, never died for many many years later.

When Jesus our Savior came, Scripture says "By one mans—Adam—sin, sin came into the world." whereby all men are dead! ". . . And by One Man—Jesus—atonement came" that all may come face to face with The Almighty Living YHWH once again, "And by Him, Jesus, we may all have eternal life." How? And why?

Because God wanted something He created to have a MIND!?? To choose for themselves who they would serve; God or satan. These are the only two ways every human being can go in this journey to the end we call "life." Jesus said all who come to Him and obey His Words would have eternal life, "And lo, I Am with you even to the end," of this earthly life.

So sorry, to all those reading this; but there is only ONE way to paradise. Only One Way to The Door. Only ONE truth of that Way, "the door, the truth and the light. No one comes to the Father of Paradise (Eden—New Earth—Heaven) and that is through and by ME," John 14.

By Him for Deity can only come to Deity THROUGH ONE sinless—spotless—without guile—sin offering, Jesus. Jesus *is* Deity because Jesus had His Father's DNA in His Blood. The very Blood of the Great I AM, God—the Living and Only God . . . "for there are many gods," Scripture says. Not Shirley McLain's religious god, not Tom Cruise's god, not Oprah's god, not David Karrish's god or even Sun-Yun Moon's god. These are just a few false gods (not Ali either) and is the Very reason Paul wrote "For the preaching of the cross is to all who perish—foolishness. But to all (born-again believers) who are saved—it is the Power of God . . ." Another reason is this ". . . For it is written—I Will destroy the wisdom of those who think themselves wise (in their interpretation of Scripture) and will bring to nothing the understanding of the prudent . . . ." All those who thought and acted to others—you can't touch me in my (carnal) wisdom, the Scripture says ". . . For after we've learned the (real) Wisdom of God, the world by its (carnal) wisdom did not know God at all, therefore it pleased God by the foolishness of preaching, that those who do believe (silliness of preaching) would believe (be saved)."

1 Cor. 1:18, 19, 21

Paul said please! Stop your rejoicing of the wisdom and salvation of Jesus Christ in me ". . . for I die daily," in the knowledge I do have in Him, to keep my own self humble and saved.

1 Cor. 15:31

If any person on earth, now—before—or ever shall be on earth, "Loves Not the Lord Jesus Christ, let them be ANATHEMA MARANATHA." 16:21.
ANATHEMA: Divine punishment. Curse. Consign a thing or a person to damnation or destruction. Detested. Loathed.
MARANATHA: "O Lord Come." Used as an invocation in or after Anathema in 1 Cor. 16:22. Greeks, Aramenians, Syria, Mesopotamia and Palestine, all spoke this Hebrew word.

In the Old Torah (Testament Covenant) "the burning of flesh and the oil in the flesh . . ." Who doesn't like the smell of a good steak cooking on the ba bb i (B.B.Q.?) outside!?! ". . . On the Altar of The Almighty in the Holy of Holies, God Himself called "A sweet savor" to His nostrils." That is why, Rabbi's I've heard speak, that the "Walls that separated the Holy of Holies from the rest of the Temple "Breathed in and out, then God spoke to the

255

High Priest concerning His children making that sacrifice. Their sins were covered for the next coming year." This does not—did not—or ever will—give anyone a "license to sin" all they want to. NO! Genesis 8:22, Exodus 29:18.

Paul, in the New Covenant informs us—who believe—our prayers now are the "sweet savor to the nostrils of God" in Jesus' Name who lets us be face to face with our ABBA Father, our only person we may call "daddy." That is what ABBA means.

This is in answer to avenging of one's enemies. Paul wrote "Alexander the metalsmith did me a great deal of harm and the Lord will render to him according to his works." 2 Tim. 4:14, "And you also should be on guard against him." This metalsmith made idol gods for everyone. Making a good living at it too. When Paul came preaching the gospel of Jesus Christ Biblical history recalls this smithy was going to burn Paul to death after he attacked and captured him. A lot of people ran away, but still more stayed and rescued Paul. Then Paul said, "The Lord stood by me and gave me power to proclaim the full message for all the Goyim (priests. In this case false idol god priests) and I was rescued from the lions mouth.* The Lord will rescue me (us!) from every evil attack and bring me safely into His Heavenly (Paradise) Kingdom."

Gal. 1:10, 2 Tim. 4:17, 18

*Paul was using the old Torah "Daniel in the lion's den." The heat of the Smithies work reminiscent of the three Hebrew children in "the firey furnace."

Galatians 2:20, "Christ lives *in* us."

Question:

Then, heres the other unanswered question you had "how can a person as good as your dad, my only and best friend and brother, Larry, die so early? After all he was a Christian. He'd given his heart to the Lord?

Answer:

"Don't delude yourself: No one makes a fool of God! A person reaps what they sow. Those-who keep sowing in the field of their old nature . . ." There is Spiritual nature. There is carnal nature. When we become born again we have a spiritual nature, but we are still in our old carnal nature body. Only at our resurrection will our bodies be redeemed or be spiritual nature. There are an awfully lot of people who are redeemed in their/our mind, where our spirit and soul live, but just cannot seen to have, or find it within themselves to overcome the carnal old nature, so they continue to sin against their/our bodies. This is why Scripture explains, "There is none good but God. Jesus' Words." "All have sinned and come short of the glory of God." This is why our MIND is so precious to Abba Father. When the devil comes after us, or torments us, its our MIND he's after. He could care less about our bodies. He *knows* they will be redeemed at 1 Thess. 4:15-18. Its our mind that houses our spirit and soul. This is why God Himself said when you become spiritually born again, "You will have the Mind of Christ," not the body. Christs body was redeemed and glorified at His resurrection. Job said His skin, "became that of a new-born baby."

To continue on with the Scripture now: ". . . In the old nature, in order to meet its (our bodys of earth. satan owns the earth Gen. 2:3:) demands, will eventually reap ruin. Those who begin and keep sowing in the field of the spirit (Mind of Christ) will reap from the Spirit everlasting life. So let's not grow weary of doing what is good, for if we don't give up (if we overcome Rev. 12:11, 12), in due time, we will reap a harvest while we live, and especially to the family of those who are trusting and faithful." Galatians 6:7-10.

You, Scott, are of; "the family of those who are trusting and faithful household."

People "sow" bad seeds everywhere and all the time. But because they sin against their own bodies does not mean their spirit and soul sins too. People sin by—as in your dads' case—against his body by smoking. satan does not care he owns this clay body of earth anyway. People sin by any kind of a habit, another one can be overeating. How well do we all know that! Again satan does not care. Its his in the first place. satan wants what lives in our brain, our spirit and soul. When we become born again spiritually, its our mind. How do I know? Because Christ His very own Self will not live in an unredeemed mind. We cannot redeem ourselves, as every church here in Colorado Springs believes. Or so it seems to me, at times. It was written in the Co. Sprs. Gazette that it is, "the *cult* capital of the world." Not just the good old U.S.A.

When people—such as you and I—We must try and think—there's that *mind* again!? Like the Boss of the company we work for, wants our little area to conform to what is best for his company. After all he's been the CEO of the company since he conceived and birthed it. He alone knows how it works and what will make it work even better so as to bring in more money.

Our Father in heaven has a company, only He has turned His Kingship over to His blessed and only Son, Jesus. Jesus has been instructed in all aspects of His Father's company. That is why and where Spirituality comes from and it is imparted to our minds when we become born-again of our spirit. So, with the Mind of Christ, He imparts in our mind, the positions His Father wants us to have, in His Kingdom, through His Holy Spirit that Christ Himself said was the Comforter the Father sent to live inside our redeemed brain John 14. satan *cannot* read our minds. Only God can.

VOTE: "Scott, I love you and yours dearly and I do pray all I've written puts new understanding in your *MIND* about your dad (my blessed Brother). Love you, Aunt Sissy.

Joseph "Oh little town of Bethlehem . . ." is a fruitful bough by a well (Jacob's well) whose branches run over the wall: The archers have vexed and grieved him, shot at him and hated him: But his bow abides in strength and his arms and hands were made strong by the Hands of the Mighty God of Jacob from whence is the Shepherd, THE STONE of Israel even by God the Father . . ."

Genesis 49:22-25

Joshua, chapter 15 explains where the earthly cornerstone for Judah is laid.

"Then Joshua wrote all these dimensions of the tribes of Jacob's land—in words—in the book of the law of God. Then he took a great stone and set it up there under an oak that was by the sanctuary of the Lord. Then Joshua said unto all the people—Behold this stone shall be a witness to us because it has heard all the words of the Lord which He spoke to us, it shall therefore be a witness to you lest you deny your God." 24:26, 27.

". . . The Palestinians brought the Ark of the Lord—for they had stolen it—unto the Great Stone of Abel and sat the Ark on it. And to this day—Joshua's day—Abels Stone remains in the field of Joshua the Beth-she-mite." 1 Sam. 6:18.

Solomon's temple for the Lord was well on the way of being finished (Hiram King of Tyre chapter 5) and the stone masons, "And the house when it was being built, was built of stone—all made ready before—it was brought forth to be laid so that there was not the sound of the hammer or axe, nor any tool made of iron heard in it; while it was being built." 1 Kings 6:7.

Verse 18, "And the house—that is—the temple before it was 40 cubits long. The ceder(s) of Lebanon) of the house within was carved with knops and open flowers all of cedar covering the stone, and there was no stone exposed."

"Behold now I have sent a cunning man, skilled with understanding, of Huram my father's, the son of a woman of the daughters of Dan and his father was a Man of Tyre skilled to work in gold, silver, brass, iron, stone, timber, in purple, blue, and fine linen, in crimson, also to engrave any manner of engraving, and to find out every device that shall be put into his hands . . ." 2 Chr. 2:13, 14.

"Iron is taken (dug) out of the earth, brass is melted out of stone." Job 28:2.

"The Stone which the builders refused is now become the Head Corner Stone of the corner."

Psalm 118:2

Our own precious Lord Jesus said, one day when He was teaching in the temple. The Pharisees came and said "By what authority do You teach these things? Jesus answered, I will answer you if you tell me by what authority did John baptize? Was it from heaven? Or of man? They said "We cannot tell." Jesus said "Neither will I tell you by what authority I speak these things" . . . Did you never read in the Scriptures, "The Stone which the builders rejected (them!!) the same has become the Head of the corner? THIS is the Lords doing and isn't it marvelous, right before our eyes?" Matt. 21:23-42.
Verses 43, 44, "Therefore I say to you (who run the temple) The Kingdom of God shall be taken from you (NOT all Jews) and given to a Nation bringing forth fruit." And something else you should know," Whosoever shall fall on this Stone shall be broken (hearted): but on whosoever this Stone shall fall on, it will grind them to powder." Mark 12:10.

King Nebuchadnezzar had a dream that Daniel interpreted for him. A giant figure of a man made of all sorts of material, silver, gold, brass, stone, clay and so on; "And in the days of these kings shall the God of heaven set up a kingdom which shall never be destroyed, and the kingdom shall not be left to other people . . ." Meaning the Pharisees and Sadducees as was just explained to you before this Scripture in Daniel 2:44, 45,
". . . But it shall break in pieces and consume all these Kingdoms and it shall stand forever. For as much as you saw that the Stone was cut out of the mountain without hands, and that it broke in pieces the iron, brass, clay, silver, Gold, the Great God has made known to the king what shall come to pass here after, and the dream is certain and the interpretation of it is sure."
The Stone laid before Joshua (24:26, 27) for the corners of Judah which is Israel, the angel of the Lord now says, ". . . If you will walk in my ways, and if you will keep my charge, then you shall also judge my house and you shall also keep my courts and I will give you places to walk among all these that stand by. Hear now O Joshua the high priest, you and your fellows that sit before

you for they are men wondered at: for behold (look) I will bring forth my Servant the Branch. Look, the Stone I've laid before Joshua. Upon one of the Stones there shall be seven eyes. And look, I have engraved the graving that is on it." Zechariah 3:7-9.

There was a mountain before Ze rub ba believe, "Who are you O Great Mountain? You shall become a plain and Zerubbabel shall bring forth THE HEADSTONE of it with shoutings, crying, Grace, grace unto it . . . The hands of Zerubbabel have laid the foundation of this house; his hands shall also finish it, then you shall know that the Lord of hosts has sent me to you. For who has despised the day of small things? For they shall rejoice and shall see the plummet in the hand of Zerubbabel with those seven eyes; they are the eyes of the Lord that go back and forth throughout the whole earth." Zech. 4:6-10. The word Zerubbabel means; "Sown in Babylon and scattered, EZRA 2:2, 3:1, Neh. 12:47, Hag. 1:1, 14, 2:1, Matt. 1:12, 13.

We—ourselves—are the temple of the Lord now. When He lives in our hearts, soul and spirit, then it is He in us that go back and forth in the earth seeking who we may explain the love of our lives—Jesus—to. Praying, hoping we say the right words so they too will have a desire to know Him. John wrote, "And I wept much for there was no man found worthy to open the book and to read the book, neither to even look at the book. Then one of the elders said to me, don't weep for look, the Lion of Judah, the Root of David has prevailed to open the book and to untie the seven seals upon it. I looked and in the midst of the throne and of the four beasts, in the midst of the elders, stood a Lamb as it had been slain, having seven horns and seven eyes which are the seven Spirits of God sent forth into all the earth." Rev. 5:4-6.

Rev. 1:11-18, "I Am Alpha and Omega, the first and the last: What you see (John) write in a book and send it to the seven churches which are in Asia: Ephesus, Smyrna, Pergamos, Thyatira, Sardis, Philadelphia and Laodicea. I turned to see the voice that spoke to me. Being turned I saw the seven golden candlesticks. In the midst of these seven candlesticks, one like to the Son of Man, clothed with a garment down to His feet, a golden belt around His upper waist. His Head and His hair were white like wool, as white as snow; His eyes were as a flame of fire, His feet likened to fine brass as if they burned in a furnace, and His voice as the sound of many waters.

"He had in His right hand seven stars, and out of His mouth went a sharp double edged sword and His countenance was as the sun shinning in all his strength. And when I saw Him I fell at His feet as though I were dead. Laying His right Hand upon me He said, Fear not, I AM the first and the last: I AM He that did live and was dead and now look, I AM alive for evermore, Amen; and have the keys of hell and of death."

Perhaps we should check in with Peter and John who were blind-sided about this Stone. Just like a horse that spooks easily and has need of blinders, ". . . The priests and captain of the temple and the Sadducees came upon Peter and John, being grieved . . ." Is "grieved?" A better disguise than "lived with anger?" For that is exactly what they were, angry to their core. ". . . That they taught the people, and preached through Jesus, the resurrection from the dead. So they seized hold on them and put them in hold until the next day, because it was evening near sundown. However many of them that heard these two preach the Word.—believed, and the number of them that heard were about 5,000.

"The next day they released them. Then, their rulers, elders and scribes, Annas the high priest and Cajaphas, and John, Alexander and many others of the relation of the high priest were gathered together at Jerusalem. When they had set these two men free, in the midst of them they asked "by what power, or by what Name have you brought this upon yourselves?"

"Then Peter—filled with the Holy Spirit—said "You rulers of the people and elders of Israel, If we—this day—be examined by the good deed done to this impotent man, by what means he is made completely well, let it be known to you all, and to all the people of Israel that by the NAME of Yeshua the Christ of Nazareth whom you crucified and whom YHWH raised from the dead, even He—by Him—this once sick man stands before you—whole—THIS is the Stone which you set aside—*you*—the builders—has now become the very Head Corner Stone. Well, there is NO salvation in any other (name): For there is NO other Name Name under heaven—given among men—Whereby we all must be saved." Acts chapter four.

As before said, these people were lived with anger. Not at Peter and John per sa, but at the One—Only—Name under heaven given among men—that will either save them or grind them to powder. They chose the latter of course as the rest of chapter four explains.

"Wherefore it is contained in Scripture—look!—I place in Zion—A Chief CornersStone, elect, precious, and all they that believe on Him . . ." not just His precious Name but HIM! A personal relationship with and of Him. After all salvation for each of us is personal and up front with Him only. He is the only way "the door-the truth-the life (light) whereby *ALL* must be saved."

". . . That believe on Him shall not be confused. Ever! Unto all you who do believe, He is precious. But to all you who do not believe—which are disobedient—the Stone which the builders refused to be allowed to be used—the same is made the Head Corner Stone. A Stone of stumbling. A ROCK of offence. Even to those who stumble at His Word (Jesus), even to them which stumble whereas they too were appointed" this opportunity. Acts 17:24-30, 1 Peter chapter two

One Peter two and four explain, this Stone is "A living Stone . . . Chosen by YHWH and precious . . ."

In the wilderness YHWH instructed Moses to take his staff and strike the ROCK once so the children of Israel could have water to drink. Moses was so angry at these people and their constant complaining that he—as you and I would say—lost it and struck the Rock twice! Because Moses did this he was denied entrance into the land God had promised them. Our Rock Jesus suffered *once* and for all mankind. Then the Father from heaven said, "You shall not add to My Word which I command you, neither shall you diminish anything from it, that you keep My Commandments which I have commanded you."

Num. 20:7-13, Deut. 4:2, Rev. 22

Our Father in heaven is—and provided for us—THE ROCK "HE is the Rock, His work is perfect . . ." Deut. 32:4, Ex. 17:6, 33:22, Deut. 8:15, 32:15, 31, 1 Sam. 2:2, 2 Sam. 22:2, Psalms 18:2, 31, 92:15.

Yeshua (Jesus) creates "The One New Man" from Jews and Gentiles. Jesus came to break down the wall of separation between Jew and Gentile. The Messiah was a Jew, and the first believers were Jews. But how did something that started so Jewish become the opposite of Jewishness? God's answer for restoration is the creation of the "One New Man" as stated in Ephesians 2:14-16. He wants to reconcile His "family" which has grown apart for centuries. When this happens, the stage is set for worldwide revival.

For He Himself is our peace, who has made both [Jews and Gentiles] one, and has broken down the middle wall of division . . . so as to create in Himself one new man from the two . . . .

EPHESIANS 2:14-15 NKJV

CEREMONY: "The formalities observed on some solemn or important public or state occasion; the coronation ceremonies continued for weeks. A formal religious or sacred observance. Strict adherence to conventional forms: formality. *Stand on Ceremony.* A formal dignified acts on religious."

FOUNDATION: "That on which something is founded. The basis of groundwork of anything. The natural or prepared ground or base foundation on which a structure rests. The lowest division of a building, wall, usually of masonry and (partly) or completely below the surface of the ground, setting up, establishing a legacy.

*Christ said to Peter "Upon this ROCK I will build my church (Truly You are the Son of God) and the gates of hell shall Not prevail against it."

Adam was the first created to husband YHWH's own garden, the garden of Eden. Foundations from the beginning of the world were laid in "the Name of the First born" 1 Kings 16:34, Ezra 3:10, 11. A ceremony for the foundations Cornerstone was enacted, "Where were you Job, when I laid the foundations of the earth . . ? Who has laid the measures of it or who has stretched out the line upon it . . ? Where are the foundations fastened . . ? When the Morning stars sang together and all the sons of God shouted for joy?" Job 38:1-7. All these for the foundation and Corner Stone of the World.

Then we have this about the foundation and Corner Stone of the smaller version of YHWH's temple in heaven. The year was the sacred year of ZIF, our middle of the month April, to the middle of May; "The King commanded and they brought very large stones, costly stones that had been hewn from other larger stones to lay the foundation of the temple house . . . in the fourth year of the foundation of the house being laid for the Lord in the Month of Zif." 1 Kings 5:17, 6:37.

David wrote, "His foundation is in the Holy Mountain (Moriah). The Lord loves the gates of Zion more than all the houses in Jacob."

Psalms 87:1, 2

In Scripture when our Lord speaks of "Jacob," He is speaking of secular Israel so the foundation spoken of here is the earthly temple in Jerusalem. If His word speaks of Israel in Jerusalem, it is those born-again whether Jew or Gentile.

"Of old You have laid the foundation of the earth and the heavens are the Work of Your Hands . . . You are the same and Your years never shall end." Psalms 102:25, 27.

"Who laid the foundation of the earth that it never should end, for ever." Ps. 104:5.

"The Lord by Wisdom has founded the earth and by Understanding He has established the heavens . . . When the Father appointed the foundations of the earth." Proverbs 3:19, 8:29, respectively. All this of the foundation of the earth and earthly temple. This too lest I forget, "In the beginning was the Word . . ." In Scripture the "Word" is Jesus. Yes, the word "Word" is a person.

". . . And the Word was with God and the Word was God. The same was in the beginning with God." John 1:1. When remembering Genesis chapter one, we read there where; everytime our Father opened His mouth and thing sprang into existence, is it any wonder that in the New Testament our Savior had written "A *body* have You prepared for Me" Your Word. Heb. 10:5. Not the earthly body of the dear sweet Virgin Mary mother of Jesus. No. It was the baby body that needed to be conceived, birthed and grow up as Isaiah said, "Full of knowledge." "For to us a child is born, to us a Son (First born) is given, and the government shall be upon His shoulders (A Born Leader!), and His Name shall be Called—Wonderful—Counselor—THE Mighty God—THE Everlasting Father—THE Prince of Peace."

Isaiah 9:6

"The same was in the beginning with God. *All* things were made by Him (Jesus—THE WORD) . . ." Well, yes! Because if we recall in the first book of the Torah-Genesis, everytime our Father in heaven spoke, whatever He said came into existence, so yes, other than "utter one more Word" He would create an earthly vessel to tone down His Omnipotent powerful voice. If no one on earth could stand our voices and shut their ears some way, we would think of ways to tone down our thundering—hurt your ears when we speak—voices. Stick your own head in a 55 gallon-empty-drum, give a shout, then count how many minutes your ears "ring those golden bells" for you.

". . . And without Him there was not anything made that was made. In Him was Life and the Life was the Light of men". John 1:2-4.

". . . The righteous is an everlasting foundation. The righteous shall never be removed. The lips of the righteous know what is acceptable." Prov. 10:25, 30, 32.

"Out of Judah came forth the Corner (Stone), Out of him came the nail, out of him the Archers bow for battle, out of him every oppressor . . ."

Zech. 10:4

Moses and Aaron's temple in the wilderness was supposed to be the "church" that would bring the Savior and it did. Just not in the way it was expected to. The Pharisees, Sadducees and the Sanhedrin had so—slyly—undercover of "Church" corrupted the temple and its sacrifices so badly, Moses and Aaron both would have found it unbelievable, as Jesus did when He turned the "stockholders" tables upside down, with His righteous anger. Still, Christ did as YHWH did to Cain, "You can still do right with your sacrifice." Talk about patience, WOW!

The Stone which the builders refused has now become the head Stone of the Corner." Ps. 118:22. In our Savior Jesus' day and time on earth, it was Herods temple and not Solomons. Solomons temple-as was Herods—"garnished with every precious stone." 1 Chr. 29:2, 8, 2 Chr. 3:6, 32:27, Ezek. 27:22. 26:10.

In speaking of the Church and Christ the precious Corner Stone laid for it, Paul wrote in 1 Cor. 3:10-13, about this very thing: "According to the Grace of God given to me, as a—wise Master-builder—I have laid the foundation, while another builds on it. Not to be fooled though, let every man be very careful how he builds upon this foundation for another foundation no man can lay that is already laid, and that is the foundation Jesus Christ.

"Now if any man build on this foundation—gold—silver— precious stones—wood—hay—stubble—every man's work shall be made manifest (recognized) for the day shall declare because it shall be revealed by fire and the fire shall try every mans work of what sort it is."

Just as any employer would do, asking you of which job he had an opening for? What are your qualifications for this job? Or any other job I have to offer you. Remember now, this personal manager works for a *KING*. Did you catch that? A *KING* not some factory or corporation no matter how large or small they may be. You or I can work no higher than under a king. After all We ourselves can't be king. A prince or princess maybe, but no king or Queen. So get your qualifications in order and lets get to work people!

If we're good for the job we've applied for Paul writes, "If any mans work stands the test (whether written test or physical test) of which he has tried to build upon (Jesus Christ and Him only) then he shall receive a reward. But if any mans work doesn't stand the test of coming through a fiery hot flaming blaze you shall suffer loss but you yourself will be saved.

"Don't you know *YOU* yourselves are the temple of God and that His Spirit lives in you? If any man defile's this temple of God him shall God destroy; for the temple of God is holy which-as said before—you are the temple of." V-15-17.

"... We are fellow citizens with the saints and of the household of God, and are built upon the foundation of the apostles and prophets, Jesus Christ Himself being the Chief Corner Stone, in who alone all the building is fitly framed together growing into a holy temple in the Lord Jesus Christ."

1 Peter 2:3, 7, "... If you have tasted that the Lord is gracious, who came as a living Stone whom men disallowed, *but* chosen of God and precious. You also are as lively stones are building up a spiritual house (temple), a holy priesthood to offer up spiritual sacrifices, (of praise) acceptable to God by (and through) Jesus Christ. That is why it is also contained in the Scriptures—look—I lay in Zion a Chief Corner Stone—elect-precious and he that believes on Him shall not be confused. To all you that believe—though—He *is* precious! But to them which are disobedient this Stone which the builders disallowed? Well, this same Stone is made the Head of the Corner and a stumbling Stone, a ROCK of offence, even to them that stumble at the *WORD*,

being disobedient, where unto they were appointed . . ." to be disobedient in the first place.

"But *YOU* are a chosen generation—a royal priesthood—a holy nation—a peculiar people, that you should show forth praises of Him who has called you out of darkness into His marvelous light."

In closing we have this, "Burdens are like wings and wings have weight. When wings lift us the weight of the burden is lifted. Wings lift us up easing our burden."

Author Unknown
Shalom in Yeshua

CHAPTER 32

EMOTIONS EXPRESSED WITH A GLANCE

Passions. Everyone has them; fear, joy grief, love, hate, pride, shame. Emotions, we all have and we recognize emotions in others, but, do we really understand what emotions are, and what they signify? We deceive ourselves about their meaning, and it is truly remarkable how often we are wrong about our own emotions and misread the emotions of others. This makes us puzzle over the very nature of our emotions. The deeper this mystery becomes, the more we know that we know nothing, as yet, like we would like to know about emotions. A mystery? You bet and is by no means solved. It is one that requires careful, philosophical analysis.

Having read somewhat about the "religion" of Scientology, of which, it appears, more than half of Hollywood, especially actors, belong to this New Age Movement. Believe "Our emotions are really the key to the meaning of life." One thing we do know and that is Sigmund Freud, the great psychiatrist believed this.

Emotions are building blocks for the range of emotions yet to come. Or, is jealousy—a genetic trait—shared by all humans? Or is it something learned. Are emotions in our conscious or subconscious mind? (Maybe they're under "conscious" control?)

Our Father God gave each of us five senses, some of us are blessed with six:

1 – Seeing
2 – Hearing

3 – Sense of smell

4 – Sense of touch

5 – Sense of taste.

6 – Some people are expert at knowing when a person they've just met are good or bad, and worth the effort—on their part—whether it would be in their best interest to continue this newly born friendship.

satan came into God's Garden of Eden when Eve was alone one day and seduced her with all five of her God given senses; "Now the serpent was more subtle (like a fox!!) than any beast of the field which the Lord God had made—he said to the woman, 'hasn't God said to the both of you; not to eat of every tree of the garden? . . . "Twisting our Father's Word from the very beginning!" . . . Eve said to the serpent, 'we may eat of the fruit of the trees in the garden, but of the tree which is in the middle of the garden God said we should not eat of it or touch it because we will die if we do. satan said to Eve you will not surely die for God knows the day that you do eat of it your eyes will be opened and you too will be as Gods knowing good and evil." Genesis 3:1-6.

The Lord God said of all the trees (Gen. 1:29) "I have given you . . ." the races of people created on the 6th day (Gen. 1:26-28). ". . . every herb and tree bearing *SEED* . . . Which is the fruit of the tree yielding *seed.* If all the other "fruit bearing trees whose seed is within itself, the tree of the knowledge of good and evil fruit also had *seed* within itself, and Eve ate, as well as Adam the evil fruit. satan would have had a volcanic eruption if Eve had picked the good fruit. For this very reason 1 John 3:12, was written, "Not as Cain who was of that wicked one . . ." If Cain was not *son of satan* I pray My very own Father in heaven strike me dead!! Here and now or in the near future at the very least!

Our Father invented the sexual act, an act of love, the greatest gift married couples can give one another. How else can "one give of themselves" to their

271

What have we learned here? If anything:

1 – Seeing = Eve saw the fruit
2 – Hearing = listened to satan
3 – Smelled = the odor of the fruit
4 – Touch = Eve touched and picked the evil fruit "Whose seed is within itself" guided by the urging of satan.
5 – Taste = Eve tasted, found it to be delicious and gave to Adam to taste of it as well.

satan used all five God given senses on Eve, against our Father God. All these senses are used in the sexual act as well.

Cain was born first, "then Adam knew his wife and Cain was born then Abel."

An award winning neuroscientist, Professor Jeannette Norden of Vanderbilt University explains, "Considering everything our brain does, how can this relatively small mass of tissue possibly be the source of our personalities, dreams, thoughts, sensations, utterances, and movements? "An astonishingly complex organ.

Our Father, The Lord God created our brains to last for ever.

Our Lord Jesus said "There is nothing outside the body that entering into him (food—drink) can defile him, but the things that come out of a man ('s mouth!?!) those are the things that defile a person." Mark 7:15, 16.

"For from within, out of the *heart* of men proceeds evil thoughts, adulteries, fornication, murders, thieves, covetousness, wickedness, deceit, lasciviousness, an evil-eye, blasphemy, pride, foolishness. All these evil things come from *within* and defile men."

Mk. 7:20-23

"A good man out of the good treasure of his heart brings forth (through our mouths) only that which is good, but an evil man out of the evil treasure of his heart brings forth that which is evil for of the abundance of their heart their *MOUTH SPEAKS.*" Luke 6:45.

"And thus are the secrets of his heart made manifest . . ." Spoken aloud. Confessed aloud, etc. ". . . so falling on his knees down on his face he will worship God and report that God is truly in you." Luke 14:25.

"Out of the same mouth proceeds blessings and cursings. Brethren! These things ought not to be." James 3:10.

"Their throat is an open pit, with their tongues they have used deceit, the poison of Asp's is under their tongues, whose mouth is full of cursing and bitterness, their feet are swift to shed innocent blood, destruction and misery are in their attitudes . . . that every mouth may be stopped and all the world may become guilty before God." Romans 3:13-19.

". . . The Word of the Lord is near you even in your mouth and in your heart, that is the Word of faith which we preach. If you shall confess with your mouth the Lord Jesus and will believe in your heart that God has raised His Son Jesus from the dead you shall be saved. Because with the heart man believes unto righteousness, and with the Mouth Confession is made to salvation."

Romans 10:8-10

". . . Speaks the truth in his heart." Ps. 15:2.

We HEAR with our ears and it settles in our heart's. Our minds ponder on it. Why? Because our hearts have no ability to think or speak.

1 – Hear with our ears.
2 – Settles in our hearts.
3 – Our minds ponder on it.
4 – Our mouths speak it.

What, more than this, do we need to know about our Minds that our Father created and put in it our spirits and our souls.

Nothing breaks the heart of God like our rejection of Jesus Christ!

Jealousy has long been termed "the guardian of love," but more often its the very down—fall of love. Typically blaming our partner's for paying too much attention to another. The real issue here though, may be what jealousy teaches us about ourselves.

Here's one for you; A beautiful dark haired girl with a stunning disposition that a gentleman, making a delivery at her work place, took a fast liking to her. Within days of their meeting, bouquets began arriving at the office for her. As if it were the NASDAQ index of her appeal flashed across Times Square, she relished the surprise deliveries—and the admiring notice of officemates.

He himself made less of an impression; he was ordinary looking and wiry, with a slight nervous edge. His retro style of dressing did stand out: Plaid jacket and saddle shoes made him look as if he were always sneaking a quick break from a low-budget comedy act.

Over weeks, then months, he showed up regularly to take her to dinner or out with friends. He called frequently to make sure she got the flowers, to find out who ogled them, or just to hear her voice. If she wasn't at her desk the calls oftened bounced to her increasingly annoyed colleagues.

She said he had a goofy side that appealed to her at first. She just kinda thought he was love-struck. She was charmed and amused. Gradually she realized the flowers were a kind of camouflage, since he seemed to have a need to know where she was every minute, and if he didn't "hear what he liked" his voice would crack with rage, which really kind of scared her. One day she awoke to the thought: Why does this romance feel like it's becoming a prison? It was then she knew she had to get out. True story.

The flowers notwithstanding, he exhibited many of the classic signs of jealousy—fear of losing his lover, lack of trust, anger at real or imagined attention to others, the need to control a loved one. Even the flowers were a time—honored mate—retention strategy of the kind kicked-off by jealousy although, we, as a whole, are more inclined to associate jealousy with negative tactics, from vigilance to violence.

Jealousy, more often than not, feelings flare with such intensity that they burn a hole in the brain, obliterating rational thought and setting off behaviors that create a self-fulfilling prophecy by pushing away the very person one desires, or needs, the most. Case in point—think of astronaut-in-training Lisa Nowak, who, in 2007, at age 44, drove a thousand miles nonstop from Houston, Texas to Orlando, Florida, with a diaper on, the quicker to kidnap the new girlfriend of a fellow astronaut with whom she had—had an affair. Isn't it ironic that an impulse that arises from love can so easily destroy it.

Experts say, a certain amount of jealousy is a survival mechanism, although what is most at stake is a matter of debate. The most destructive of passions—its a leading cause of homicides—and the least studied.

It is, like all emotions, born of necessity, with roots deep in our past's. Its purpose was to help maintain intimate relationships. I'm not sure what it is now.

Jealousy is not envy although the words are often used interchangeably, "jealousy arises when a relationship is infringed on by a rival who threatens to take away something that is in a sense rightfully theirs, explains Richard Smith, professor of psychology at the University of Kentucky. The rival may or may not have features that would incite envy. To feel jealousy one need not have any sense of what the third party is like. Envy on the other hand, derives from the basic fact that so much of the spoils of life come from how we compare ourselves to others. It arises when another person possesses some trait or object that you want and includes a mix of discontent, a sense of inferiority, and a frustration that may be tinged with resentment.

Here's the shocker: Jealousy may be losing its utility in contemporary life, useful to our ancestors more so than us, given our penchant for changing partners. As our high divorce rate attests, sometimes, we're just not all that interested in saving our closest relationships. Jealousy says more about the insecurity of the bearer than about the deeds or misdeeds of a mate.

In attempts to define exactly what jealousy is, experts have come up with—after much study—that it is a complex emotion and involves at a minimum such distressing feelings as: fear, abandonment, loss, sorrow, anger, betrayal, envy and humiliation, and it recruits a host of cognitive processes gone awry, from doubt to preoccupation with a partners faithlessness. There's a part of everyone's brain called a primal area, that seems activated when jealousy is shown.

Jealousy—according to the University of Texas psychologist David Buss—is a necessary emotion, a potential to a deterrent to infidelity that arises in both men and women when a threat materializes to intimate relationships. Boyfriend talks to a beautiful girl at a party and smiles admiringly at her; to girlfriend? A rival is born, a flesh and blood warning that what she thought was hers might now be endangered. Or, wife suddenly embarks on series of brief out-of-town trips with co-head of her team. What is at stake is survival of our most valued relationships and thus the future of our children—born—or unborn. Which is to say—the species. For instance "men explode violently," but jealousy is not the main motivation for spouse battering. Sexual jealousy is the leading cause of spousal murder worldwide. Even then its' not really jealousy that's to blame. Professor Buss contends; "its the delusion that a loved one has committed an infidelity when none has occurred." "This double-edged defense mechanism would not exist if long term love hadn't emerged among our primals. Neuroticism."

"Agreeableness is negatively correlated, and low-agreeable people tend to use cost-inflicting mate-retention tactics," he says. "Tactics like yelling at a partner for talking to someone else, cutting partners off from friends, family, derogating the partner, undermining a mates self-esteem, or threatening violence against a partner or perceived rivals. "The jealous person sees them as abhorrent—the mate that is. The jealous person is hyper-jealous and full of neuroticism, revealing themselves only through time."

Professor Buss explains "Jealousy is accompanied by a sense of inadequacy in an insecure person times an insecure relationship. Its these insecure people who tend to destabilize relationships and make them insecure. An insecure person is not just sexually jealous but jealous of any kind of friendship a spouse might have, even with a child. Anything that takes attention away from them. Inadequacy in its greatest form."

He speaks further, "Its inadequacy is hard to bear and most people convert the discomfort into anger, which they regulate by trying to control a spouse or partner—distrusting them, going through their belongings, cell-phones, call logs, making accusations, behaviors more likely to drive a partner away. It's a mistake to assume jealousy involves love. A man who despises his wife becomes jealous when someone else looks covetously, or just looks at her. This jealousy activates the amygdala and hypothalamus regions rich in testosterone receptors involved in sexual and aggressive behavior."

END

To all those who buy our book, write me. I will send you—FREE—a short glossary of visuals as well as written explanations of all you might be unfamiliar with in this God Given Book. Title given by our Savior as Well.

The title I was going to use was "Burn After Reading," for I knew from the start of this book we would end up with more enemies, then friends.

CPSIA information can be obtained at www.ICGtesting.com
Printed in the USA
BVOW042232020713

324830BV00001B/1/P